Sabre Jets Over Korea:
A Firsthand Account

Sabre Jets Over Korea:
A Firsthand Account

by Douglas K. Evans

FIRST EDITION

FIRST PRINTING

Printed in the United States of America

Library of Congress Cataloging in Publication Data
Evans, Douglas K.
    Sabre jets over Korea.

    Includes bibliographical references and index.
    1. Korean War, 1950-1953—Personal narratives, American.
2. Evans, Douglas K.   3. Korean War, 1950-1953—Aerial
operations.   I. Title.
DS921.6.E94   1984   951.9'042   83-24145
ISBN 0-8306-2352-3 (pbk.)

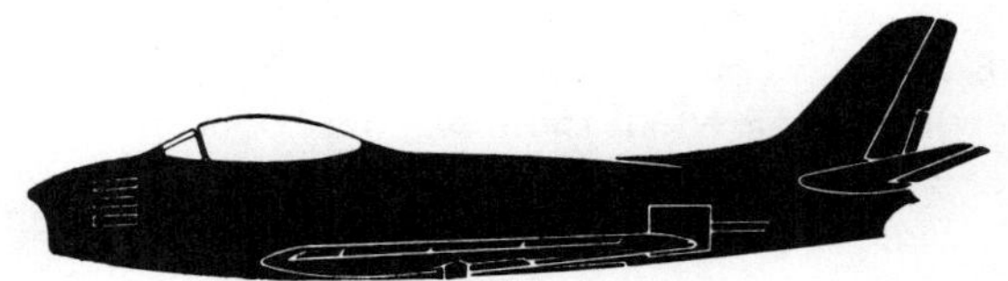

Contents

Dedicated to
my brother
Tom
Francis T. Evans, Jr. 1921–1953
Captain, U.S.A.F., 100 missions, P-47, E.T.O.
With whom I shared all those soaring boyhood dreams of
flight and followed in the great fortune of seeing those early
dreams come true in the fascinating life of the fighter pilot.
And
in appreciation
To all those pioneer pilots of my father's time whose
annals of absorbing experiences and generous wisdom
have so inspired us all.
To all those men of the wars, challenges, and wings of
my time whose shared adventures and comradeship are the
priceless privilege of a lifetime.

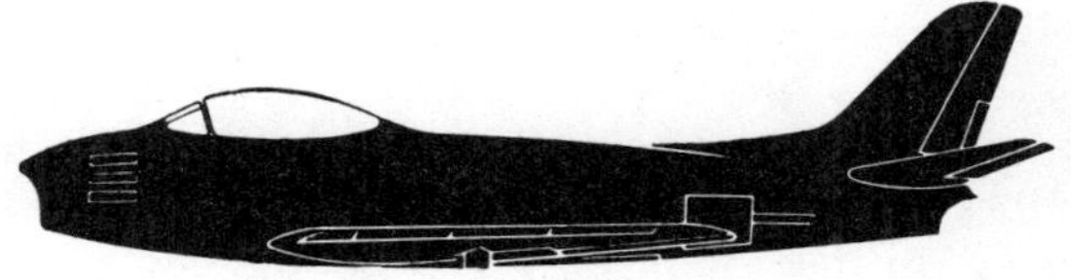

Preface

During my combat tour in the Korean War I carried on a sort of arm's-length, continuous conversation in my letters home, and for use in ideas for expansion in those letters I jotted notes of personal thoughts and kept a brief log of reminders of the highlights of activities. Numerous personal thoughts remained separate until they were merged into the narration of this book, most of which came from those regular lengthy letters. For me, aerial combat was such a fascinating experience that I couldn't resist attempting to capture and confide at least its essence on paper.

Recounting experiences (as fighter pilots always do when together) kept alive rather vivid memories shared with my friends over the years. When comparing action with pilots of other outfits and other theaters of war, I often dug back into these writings to better illustrate events, and I still have at hand the map I carried on every mission. I felt sure that other veterans of exciting times regret the fading of details with the dimming of memory. Here was a chance to revive particular moments of hazard and humor, and each review brought back additional recollections stirred up by familiar episodes. As time went by, the feeling grew that this available story of those who flew in a great fighter outfit deserved a better fate than fading and fraying in a battered briefcase.

The task of linking the various sources of the full story naturally required some pruning and blending of the clipped jargon of certain hasty passages scribbled down at irregular moments. There was also the need to clarify incidents, places, or individuals, as well as rephrase some narration for address to the general reader. Overall, though, the story is just as I retained it by pencil and pen long ago as the days and months rolled on. Just as the language of sailors of the high seas enthused in their familiar ways of full-rigged sail may be somewhat mysterious to the layman, so may that of the youthful exuberant fighter pilot absorbed in his special calling. To have attempted to completely clarify or interpret an environment so fundamental to fighter pilots would have given the story a diluted quality obvious to those who have "been the route." I learned long ago when setting these events down that the joy of flying fighters mixed with the jumble of action, impressions of which you are attempting to retain and convey, can be difficult to relate to others. And now when I begin again with the first letters, I am reminded how inadequate was my imagination for the adventure that was to come.

I mention in a number of passages how highly I valued the experience, and today, years of flying later, I believe it to be beyond measure. No substitute could equal the living of it, the remembering, and the retelling.

This way I won't lose it.

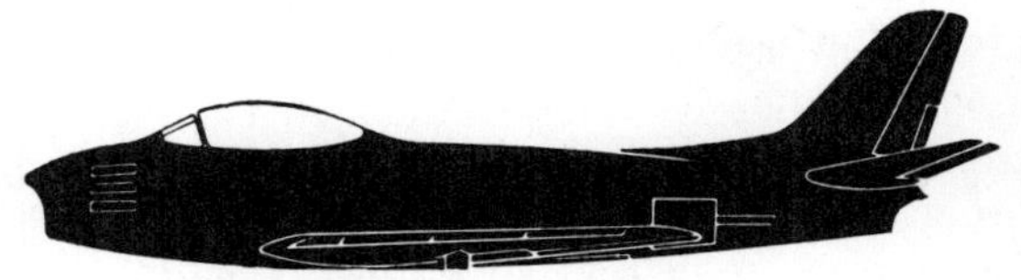

Historical Note

I have always considered myself very lucky to have been able to not only be a member of the great outfit of this story, but to fly, *in combat*, with the 4th Fighter Group. A brief look at its record should explain my reasons.

The 4th began its long history in World War I, when it was first formed in France as the 4th Pursuit Group in October 1918 for duty on the Western Front. The four squadrons of the group were called Aero Squadrons and were the 17th, 25th, 141st, and 148th. The 17th and 148th Squadrons had seen combat service in Sopwith Camels, and along with the 141st Squadron were re-equipping with SPAD XIIIs, while the 25th Squadron had SE5s, the only American squadron so equipped. Many pilots in all four of the squadrons had previous combat flying with British squadrons. The war ended before the 4th Pursuit Group could conduct operations as a unit.

When World War II began, American pilots, remembering tales of the Lafayette Escadrille of WWI, and seeking exciting action, began to join the British Royal Air Force. Eventually they were assembled into an American-manned regular RAF squadron. This was No. 71 Fighter Squadron formed in September 1940, with the name "Eagle" Squadron denoting its American cast. Two more squadrons were formed, No. 121 in May 1941 and 133 in August 1941, making three in all. They began operations in Hurricanes and converted to Spitfires. During their time of RAF service the pilots of the three squadrons were credited with 73 enemy aircraft destroyed.

In September of 1942 the three Eagle Squadrons were transferred to the US Army Air Forces and designated the 4th Fighter Group, with the original squadrons being redesignated the 334th, 335th and 336th Fighter Squadrons.

Because of its combat experience, the 4th became a sort of nucleus of tactical know-how for the growing American fighter forces in the European Theater of Operations (ETO). Flying in continuous combat until the end of World War II, the 4th changed cockpits from Spitfires to P-47 Thunderbolts to the hottest of them all, the P-51 Mustang. The group became the premier fighter unit, closing the war score with 1,016 enemy aircraft destroyed, leading all groups in WWII in Europe *and* the Pacific.

In Korea this illustrious group initiated the first jet-versus-jet air battles, and with 506 enemy aircraft of various types destroyed, topped the score of MiG kills in that war in the tradition of its motto: "Fourth but First."

To be technically correct, by the time of the Korean War, the 4th had been designated 4th Fighter Interceptor Group, to indicate its primary air-to-air mission. But, just as in our general conversations, in this story I've left out the *Interceptor* part of the title. To the pilots, 4th *Fighter* said it all, and *Interceptor* was superfluous.

There are references in this book to 4th Wing and 4th Group. The Wing (4th Fighter Interceptor Wing) was the actual top of the command structure; under it were the Fighter Group, Air Base Group, and Maintenance and Supply Group. Today there are no active duty Fighter Groups; the squadrons operate directly under Wing command. The 4th is now designated the 4th Tactical Fighter Wing and presently based at Seymour Johnson AFB, Goldsboro, NC.

At the time the events of this book occurred, carrying on the habit of WWII and the 1940s, fighter pilots generally referred to their top unit as "Group" rather than Wing.

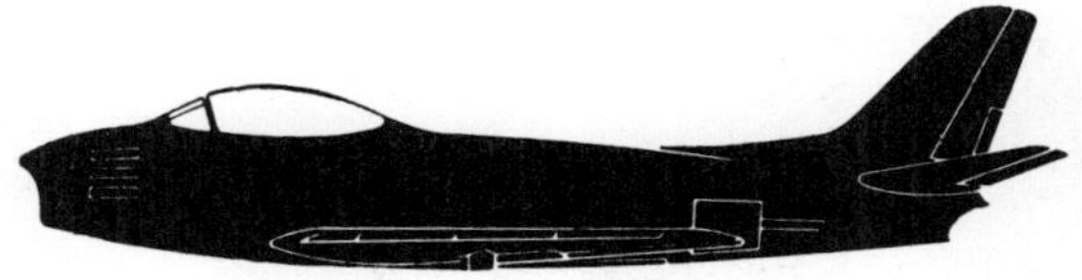

Introduction

The shipment of the group of replacement pilots with which this story commences occurred at a time of a notable increase in activities and strength of the Communist air forces committed to Korea. In their anticipation of action the pilots had not grasped the full implications of this threat, overshadowed as it was by other headline events. There had been great surges to and fro of the ground forces in Korea, the Inchon landing, and intervention of massive Chinese armies. We pilots had followed all these activities with avid and growing interest as our personal involvement in the war became more evident.

While awaiting departure in the San Francisco area we had encountered a few returning fighter pilots, even some old friends of past years who had filled us in on the sort of war stories and details in which we were keenly interested: typical missions, airfield conditions, weather problems, enemy air and flak capabilites, and our own aircraft situation. We gathered that though our facilities and aircraft were at a bare minimum, the relentless interdiction attacks by our fighters were having a most obvious influence on enemy fighting capabilities. The target opportunities of the congested invasion of South Korea had really intensified the "tiger" attitude so essential in fighter operations.

The United States was being awakened from the lethargy of World War II victory and the success in combat of our forces, and those of our United Nations Allies, had taken such a toll of material and lives to the Communists—nearly a million battle casualties in the first year—that they were expressing a desire to "talk things

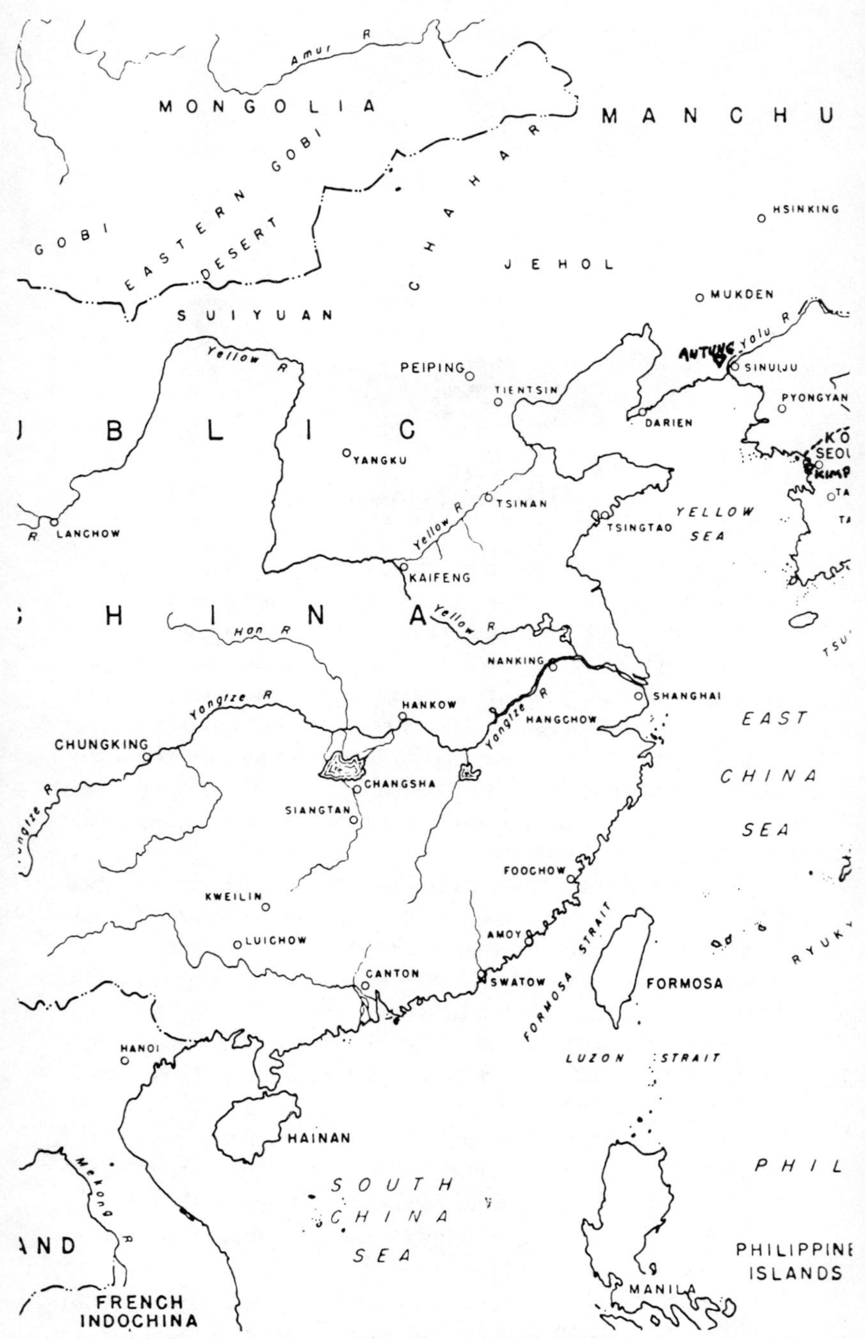

Far East general map. Front Line indicates general defense line during

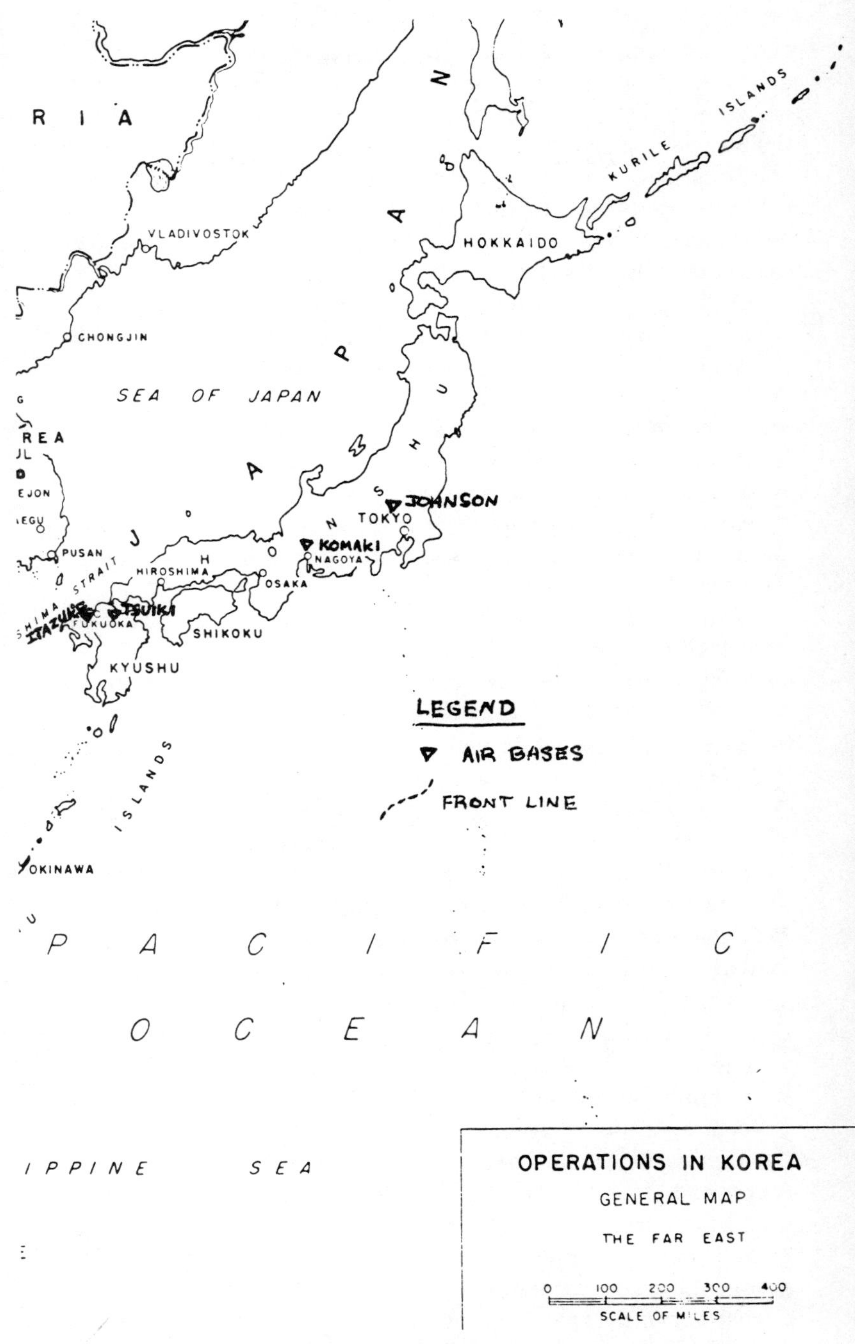

the period of the Armistice talks, November 1951–July 1953.

over." The impact of US airpower had in particular been a disastrous experience for the invaders. In the meantime (though we were not filled in on the big picture), they set about employing their version of this decisive force in their favor, first expanding and projecting supposedly overwhelming odds to control the sky and thus reattempt to force their designs on the unfortunate peninsula. Without realizing it, the pilots of this story were to be confronted with this trial.

As the year of 1951 progressed, the monthly counts of MiG-15 sightings and engagements were to increase by hundreds, then thousands. The F-86s on any one mission were usually between 24 and 36, yet even with those humiliating resources, the trial was sustained. While the truce talks dragged on in frustration, the front line settled into a stalemate fractured by localized convulsions. But above and beyond the front lines there was no barbed wire in the sky, no trenches or bunkers for cover. Thus, over top of all persisted a roving, exposed battle for a heavily-contested airspace, that space to go to the most determined.

The air battles of the autumn of 1951 should stand out historically as one of the significant and influential tests of opposing airpower and the introduction of the impact of the Jet Age. Attention to this period is not meant to obscure the air fighting which took place before and after—rather, to manifest that such a massive, clear, and serious challenge for access to the sky was not again attempted. Without such knowledge or intent when written on the spot, the compiling of this book plus a lifelong interest in the history of aviation drew my attention to this aspect. This was not meant to be a history (that work was competently done years ago); this was to relive a high-water mark of aerial combat in which the reader may join as a spectator.

Few people, if any, outside of the US Air Force were aware of the significance at the time. Who even *remembers*, much less weighs its value today? Memories also tend to fade of the responsibility heaped on the aircrews. There is perhaps an ironic reward for the achievement: If those men had failed in their test, the free world would have been only too painfully aware with regret and alarm far beyond Korea. The consequences of failure would have been rapid and surely worldwide: the loss of United Nations bargaining power in the truce talks, the exposure of UN ground forces to a renewed, well-supplied Communist ground offensive, and the specter of their victorious airpower confronting Japan, and in turn, Western Europe. The Korean War was anything but a sideshow. I, for one, am proud to have had some small part in it.

The unknown outcome of this period was a source of tension for the crews of all types of our committed aircraft. We who flew the F-86s often debated about the views and discussions that must have occurred among the pilots of the MiG-15s. The extent to which their aerial failure shattered the confidence and subdued the plans of the Communist hierarchy must be left to the reader's imagination.

This period of fighting was not, of course, considered by the pilots in any historical context, but of the strain and seriousness we were well aware, as we were of the blue chip fortune of flying a very capable day fighter. The reader will find gripes and certain discontent intruding about the F-86: the A and early E models committed at the time. There were certain deficiencies compared to the MiG-15: acceleration, rate of climb, and extreme altitude performance—minor perhaps, but discernible in the tense balance of advantage or disadvantage experienced in aerial contests. Since World War I this discernment has been a trait among fighter pilots who are uncomplimentary about any shortcomings in their planes. We were happy and proud to fly the Sabre, one of history's great fighters, but that same pride in both airplane and country gave a sensitivity to any inferior points in our favorite plane or deficient support or attention from our country.

The actual play of the contest itself is unusual. The countering of odds of hundreds of MiGs (for the most part during this story), the responsibility of one F-86 Wing to block interference with our vital interdiction forces, indicate the charge undertaken, but the unique aspect is that the decision was won by the minority deep in the area most favorable to the majority. The stretching of the mission radius of the F-86 200 miles to seek decisive action was a capability that only two years before would have been considered impractical, if not impossible. That this gamble was taken successfully by the Sabre pilots and not by the MiG pilots is in itself a signal mark of air superiority.

The occasional comments on tactics that appear here are really only a small indication of the countless hours of endless discussion fighter pilots devote to flying and fighting techniques. Operations as always had to be judged and juried in that court of ultimate trial: *combat*. During the period of this story, except on rare occasions, we were committed to squadron formations on standard patrols with all their unwieldy and attention-demanding

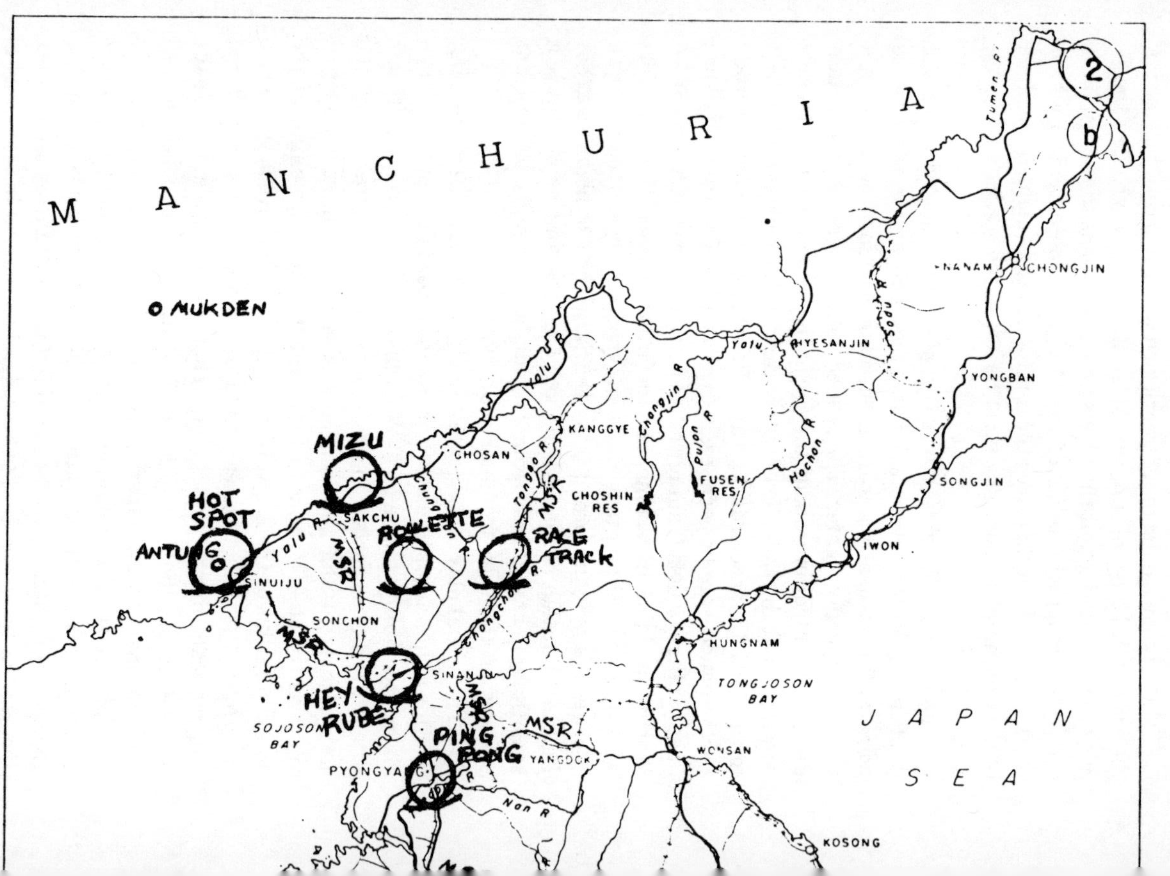

MANCHURIA
O MUKDEN
JAPAN SEA
Tumen R
CHONGJIN
HANAM
YONGBAN
HYESANJIN
Yalu
SONGJIN
KANGGYE
CHOSAN
CHOSHIN RES
FUSEN RES
IWON
HUNGNAM
TONGJOSON BAY
WONSAN
KOSONG
MIZU
SAKCHU
HOT SPOT
ANTUNG
SINUIJU
Yalu R
MSR
ROULETTE
RACE TRACK
SONCHON
MSR
HEY RUBE
SINANJU
SOJOSON BAY
MSR
PING PONG
PYONGYANG
YANGDOK
Non R
KANGGYE
Chongjin R
Pujon R
Hochon R
Chungga
Tongbo R
MSR

North and South Korea. Front Line indicates general defense line during the period of the Armistice talks, November 1951–July 1953.

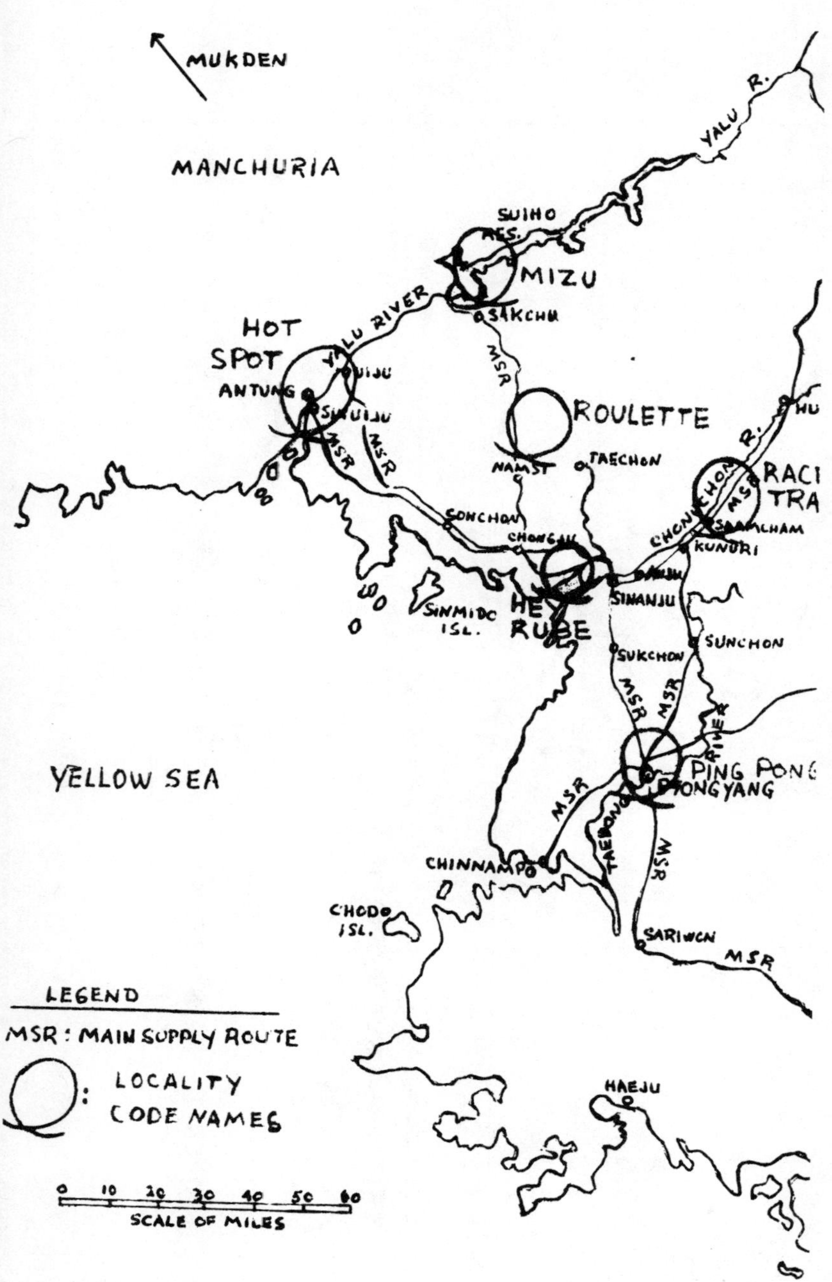

MiG Alley, showing points of reference mentioned in this book. Front Line indicates general defense line during the period of the Armistice talks, November 1951–July 1953.

KANGGYE
CHANGJIN R.
MSR
CHOSHIN RES.
HAGARU
CHON
C K
NORTH
SEA OF JAPAN
MSR
WONSAN
KOREA
KOSONG
MSR
PYONGGANG
IRON TRIANGLE
KANSONG
FRONT LINE
CHORWON
KUMHWA
FRONT LINE
INJE
KAESONG
IMJIN R.
HAN
CHUNGPYONG RES.
SEOUL
KIMPO
INCHON
HOME PLATE
SUWON

features. While this did give us a concentration of limited resources, our opportunities for innovation were restrained. As it was, the smaller formations had to be resorted to in order to accomplish the job after the shock of engagement rather than before, and frequently with the enemy initiating the clash from a position of attack advantage. These hard-won lessons resulted in revised formations as the war proceeded.

Each fighter war seems to generate its own renaissance of the art of tactics out of sheer necessity. The men of this story applied themselves to that need in such a way as to prove again that it is the potency in the cockpit that really decides the issues. While in the main they went at the fight without spectacular heroics or particular medals or recognition, their achievements at a crucial time should not be dismissed as mere idle war stories. It so happens that this was the story as I witnessed it, but it could have been expressed by any of those around me—the sights, the sounds, the feelings, and the thoughts. This is a story focused to the view of those who flew—some fighter pilots who lived and shared the great adventure.

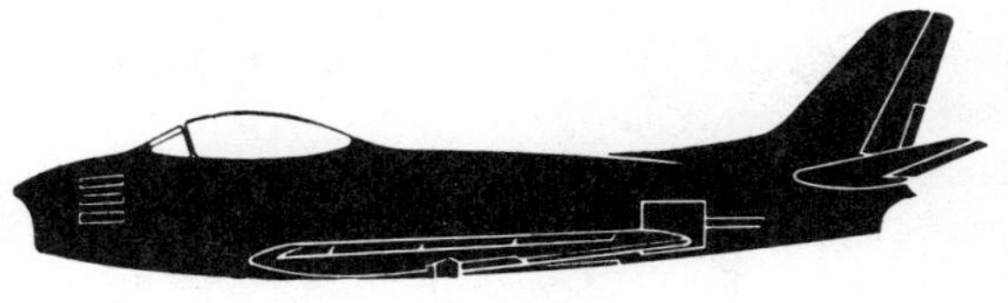

I

On The Way

Although this replacement center is not the halfway point as far as mileage is concerned, it is a turning point of personal adjustment. At least, that's the way it strikes me. The end of farewells and the familiar, and the beginnings of . . . anticipation? Curiosity? With such a long way to go, at this particular stage I'm now impatient to feel movement that indicates we're at least getting closer to finding answers.

During the long grind of the airline flights from Washington, DC, to San Francisco, the weather was clear most of the time so the view was excellent. I filled the hours in the only sensible way while airborne—observing the changing scenery, like old times after flying and driving a car over most of that route in the past. The old C-46 airliner droned along, particularly low over the desert, and we made one fuel stop at Prescott, Arizona, instead of Albuquerque, as I had hoped. As soon as we hopped through the pass I looked for Kirtland Field and could see it as we skirted to the north of Albuquerque. Now that I'm in the mood to travel, even the final bus ride was enjoyable, from Frisco to camp through these rolling hills, the pines, palms and lakes north of Oakland.

All the Air National Guard pilots on the shipment from Newcastle and our Andrews gang are now here except for one Newcastle jock left behind with a broken ankle. Combs and Counts are around while Shellum and Thawley are across the hall in our BOQ. I knew none of the 142nd Squadron fellows before our arrival, but we're already swapping flying stories and getting acquainted.

Some of us took a stroll around the camp today after processing activities. There were scenes of marching formations and troops falling in in front of barracks that reminded me of camp life in the last war. One of the boys sort of expressed our thoughts: "Say, didn't this already happen?"

My answer was, "Yeah, but at least we don't have to start out at the beginning again."

While looking over a bookstand a title caught my eye—*Galactic Patrol* by "Doc" Smith, and I bought it on the spot. Years ago my brother and I both read that fascinating science fiction story. I'm looking forward to enjoying it again and will save it for the trip over.

I am surrounded by bulging baggage—I refer to my own as my condensed personal world. To get away from the clutter I moved a chair over by the window of my room to do some writing and from here I can see men ambling up and down the street. After awhile I'll hike on over to the O-Club and watch the milling of the mixed crowd that gathers there. They wander around dropping coins in pinball machines, standing, then sitting, staring at the walls, puffing cigarettes and burping up 3.2 beer. Nobody knows anybody else very well so it's all real jolly.

The collections of different uniforms are something to see. A few of the fellows are in the new blues, some in gabardines or khakis, with others in greens or ODs. Most of us are just wearing out our old uniforms and not really accustomed yet to the new blues.

MAY 20th

We finally got our orders nailed down—we're "lucky," we're going on a boat; throw in a little oil and we'll be sardines by the time we get to the Far East. Crossing the Atlantic in one of the Queen Liners for military use is one thing, but the Pacific, crammed in a troopship—ouch!

With that prospect in mind and personnel processing almost settled, everybody has been hot to trot in the big town. The St. Francis is the usual first fueling stop for the revolving door action. All the fellows are living it up while we still have time and we run into each other throughout the race pattern from Union Square to Nob Hill, on foot or while clutching onto cable cars. We took in the view from the Top of the Mark by day and by night—it's a must,

If you think *you* started out young in the flying game, beat *this*! Author on right, and brother Tom, on left. Seated on their new tricycle gear "airplanes" right after Christmas 1928, in Port-au-Prince, Haiti.

and handy for pit stop progress reports. It was generally too quiet for our mood so we'd change the scene with a hop over to the Fairmount—by elevator, that is. The Boom Room, as I call it, is some bar: booming thunder, lightning flashes, a blackout with more lightning followed by a surprise rain shower. The dancing girls that faded with lights-out then appear as sarongs suspended in the dark, wriggling in flourescent illumination—a temptation for closer inspection. There are various *lingua flya* names for these favored spots.

I ran into pilots I hadn't seen in months and years who are also here for shipment, and others have run into familiar faces. We've gotten some good up-to-date poop on the war from celebrating pilots who are just returning from the war. None of us follow all the news too avidly, but we do keep up with the leading events that concern us—the shooting events. One bit of info passed on by a grinning pilot returnee was: "I don't mean to ruin your trip, you guys, but the flak over there is improving every day. We caught a small column one morning, trucks and a few troops. The old fifties did a good job as usual, like a hand reaching out in front slapping things around, when suddenly I thought I was in the middle of a swarm of fireflies—large-sized tracers everywhere."

The infantry officers I talk to aren't exactly in the dark as to what to expect in their line of work. Some of them got battlefield commissions the hard way in the last war and after these years as civilians, inactive in the Reserves, are being sent in again. They kind of laugh at the so-called "conditioning" they passed through before coming here. One lean-looking guy, sort of old for a First Lieutenant, told me: "I've seen enough newsreels about those hills in Korea. Damned if I like the idea of climbing around like a goat."

We're well aware of our own hazards because most of us pilots have kept at it by jamming fighters around for years. Crashing and burning is our fare for keeping our hand in; combat just provides more causes. And from the latest dope, the fighter boys in Korea have a lot more to contend with than the home front hears about. We were told by one returnee, "Boy, we worked out of some beat-up airstrips. They're tearing up airplanes about as bad as combat. It's bad enough for the prop stuff, but in jets we're staggering into the air . . . or crunching off the short end. I'm glad I was flying F-80s; that's the sweetest bird over there for hunting targets of opportunity."

Another pilot warned: "Watch that low fuel state and stinko weather. We had people running into rocks in the clouds letting down, groping for home. And several flamed out to belly in in a

Author getting into Stearman PT-17 while an Aviation Cadet in Primary at Chickasha, OK, in WWII. Author's pilot class had the unusual opportunity to be able to fly *both* the PT-19 and PT-17 in Primary training in 1944.

nearby river bottom trying to locate the field. A hell of a deal after getting shot at and missed."

Since I'm supposed to go to F-86s and the 4th Fighter Group, I had to ask about the air-to-air situation: "Did you get to tangle with any fighters?"

"Naw," came the reply, "a few guys lucked out getting at some Yaks. We did see MiGs high up occasionally, but never tangled with them."

The hotter the stories, the faster the bar action. With everybody further primed up, we'd move in a happy bunch to try another of Frisco's finest.

The thought just came to me: Tom must be going to McGuire Field today to fly air defense alert for a week. He'll be the flight wheel on this trip. I wish we could have gone on that TDY together before I shipped out, but after all these years it was great finally being with my ol' brother in the same squadron for a few months. That was something I had always hoped for, and we finally made it.

We've sure had a whoopee marathon in Frisco and now our fun money, which we won't need in the middle of the ocean, has run out to the point where the coming hibernation is a necessity and very timely for a rest cure. We're consoled by our patriotic efforts in pumping up the economy and round-the-clock stamina for winning the war. For iron rations I'm taking a little joy juice along and so are the rest of the boys. It will come in handy once in awhile on "A Slow Boat to China," as the song goes.

WEDNESDAY MORNING, MAY 23rd

The officer's "lounge" seems to be a pretty good place to get on with some last letter writing—and waiting. I hope we'll get the hell on our way today; this business of being the advance detachment yesterday means we've got a day shot on board already. At the moment we're waiting for the infantry to board so we can haul anchor this afternoon. While nosing about the ship I almost choked when I witnessed the loading of private automobiles which I guess are for United Nations officials or other civilians who are reported to be aboard. Perhaps we would be more appreciative of these "absolute necessities" if we had a better grasp of the big picture. From our knowledge of priorities, we'll settle with the possibility of roller skates.

At present there is just enough room in our lounge, but I think the number of officers will be doubled at least, and then we'll be as crowded as in our cabins—cabin or *cell*? Well, it's deep enough to be two bunk-lengths long, triple deckers on each side with body passage the whole length and a washbasin by the hatch. Each guy has two good-sized bags and these are stacked at the far end of the passage or under the bottom bunks—quite a cage for twelve animals.

A harbor boat, the *San Leandro*, brought us from Camp Stoneman, down the Sacramento River and across the bay to the main docks. Just before reaching the docks we went right by Alcatraz which attracted everybody to one side of the boat for a good look. Boy, did that tub ever list over! The thought of being stuck on The Rock for life should be enough to keep anybody on the straight and narrow.

From the bow of this trooper we can look right into Frisco, and I guess that's our last view of importance of the USA for awhile— the final split. I'm interested to find out how this ship takes the

Author in cockpit of BT-13 Vibrator while an Aviation Cadet at Perrin Field, Sherman, TX in WWII.

storms at sea; we'll probably hit several on such a long voyage. Yahoo—hang on and ride! With time to ponder, it begins to sink in about how far it will be to the end of the way. A look at a map after the hours and miles of country already covered conveys a sense of the distance across the entire Pacific to the rim of Asia. For our final gesture, as we pass under the Golden Gate, it is customary to toss a penny overboard for good luck. With so much ahead of us, I am asking for my letters to be kept. They will probably get more . . . interesting?

AT SEA

At the end of this voyage the officers have to pay for all their meals whether they miss them, are seasick, or whatever. Everyday the three big events are meals and I never miss 'em. I'm glad I've been at sea before; I'm as hungry as a bear and can put away all the chow that's available. Some of these unfortunate jokers can't put away much of anything, and on all the decks there is regular disquieting evidence of meals that people couldn't keep down. In addition to acquiring our sea legs, we have to be choosy where we step.

There are unexpected amusements, like a little act several of the gang have gone through, in different company:

"Did you know there are four nurses on board?"

"You saw fourteen nurses?"

"You mean they're trying to hide forty nurses?"

"How many? Four hundred nurses on board? Where?"

Some fresh fish could occasionally be caught with this sneaky cast.

The ship's store is doing a booming business in pocket book sales; as we read them, we swap these literary gems around. When the reading wears out my eyeballs I join with other fellows to explore around the ship, lean on the rails, talk a little, and stare at the sea. Sometimes I go alone so I can just think and set my own path; the rise and fall and roll of the ship has a hypnotic effect that induces a prolonged absent study of the sparkling water and contrasts of blue and green when touched by the cloud shadows that appear as giant footprints pacing the waves.

Occasionally we've seen porpoise and flying fish which prove that there is life in all this remoteness. Not far outside the Golden Gate several whales were sighted in the distance. That was a passage; all those on board who were free at the moment watched the Golden Gate slowly sink into the horizon until there was only the sea and the sky. They were all pretty quiet with their thoughts. For me, the back trail fades as I focus now on what is ahead. A persistent question intrudes my private thoughts: What will it be like?

As much as anything, I enjoy dropping around for visits in the different cabins of the officers' quarters to swap experiences with the interesting mixture of men. In that way we get visitors to our cabin. Confined as we are, we have gotten close and friendly in a short time. As the majority of officers are infantry, I was wondering how our relationship was going to be, recollecting some of the unpleasant attitudes of the last war. Feelings couldn't be better; I've gotten to know several infantry fellows very well and we've enjoyed exchanging a swell variety of yarns. I guess it's because we're all going into combat, the unknown gamble our conversations reveal, and which we all share in common.

It seems as if everybody had the same idea and brought a little hooch aboard in anticipation of this endless ocean. We have a few snorts together and this got me acquainted with Al Harris, my infantry chum, whose company I particularly like. We enjoy talking more about airplanes and fun flying than the war. Some of the cabins, staterooms, or whatever they are called that the infantry occupy are bigger with more men than those for the fighter pilots. In these larger cabins we've had some real laugh and noise sessions singing group songs. It's great how a little joy juice gets everybody in the mood. This Captain Anzini (infantry) is in charge of some of these officers and he reminds me of one of those tough but friendly characters out of Mauldin's book, *Up Front*. Am I glad he's on our side.

When we get one of our whoopee sessions going, all the quiet "dead" guys lock the doors to their rooms. Most of these infantry fellows are Reserve call-ups too, with the care-less philosophy; as they say, "What the hell are they going to do about it, *send us to Korea?*" And everybody roars with laughter. We sing our songs at the top of our lungs; Tom Shellum can give piercing whistles, George Dunn and I do the rebel or cowboy yell, while Al Harris puts out the muleskinner's holler. At least that's what we say the noises are supposed to be. That one big jam session must have sounded like The Last Roundup or The Mutiny on the Bounty— Yahoo!

Harris is mighty keen on doing a good job over there and so are all the real tigers in our mixed group. I hope these infantry fellows make out okay; we've all gained a lot of respect for each others' jobs.

Author on left and brother, Tom, in January 1951, just before recall to active duty for the Korean War. Tom was actually a Captain in the AF Reserve and had taken a temporary reduction to 1st Lt. to get into the DCANG Fighter Squadron, so we could fly together.

While it lasts, two weeks in such crowded conditions feels like forever, and somehow so do friendships. It seems impossible that we'll probably never see each other again. We never talk about that . . . I wonder how many think about it?

WEDNESDAY, JUNE 6, 1951

Here we is—in the land of Nippon. We got off the "Slow Boat," the longest step on the way, on the morning of the 4th, and after a five-hour trip by train from the port of Yokohama, through the outskirts of Tokyo and intervening farmland, we arrived at Johnson Field—a distance of 30 or 40 miles. How slow can you go? We thought we were never going to get our feet on solid ground.

I still have to chuckle over the amusing incidents on the train trip. The outlying suburban areas of both cities were packed and spread out for miles, and every foot of the rural areas was used in intensive farming. Our situation as a troop train meant continuous changing of tracks, stopping in stations, and waiting on other trains. We were so tired of staring at water for two weeks that we gaped at everything. At each stop all the fellows stared at the Japanese milling about the stations—they stood there looking at us and we sat there looking at them. I was wondering which side was the zoo.

At one point, while at a slow pace through farm fields tended by women, two particularly well-formed gals, either to straighten their backs or view the train, stood up at close range . . . *topless*. There was a crunching rush to that side of the train with all hands poised for a swan dive out the windows. Somehow the cars didn't topple right off the tracks.

Completely bushed by the time we hauled our junk into the BOQs, everybody piled onto their assigned sacks for a much-appreciated siesta. Then off to the Officer's Club for chow, after which we leaped gleefully into the pattern at the bar. This bar has

The front entrance of the Johnson Field Officers Club, or the Johnny O-Club, scene of considerable whoopee by members of the 4th Fighter Group.

just got to be the longest and curviest in the Air Force. What a Number One club; people talk about overseas occupation duty . . . oh, is it rough! All the war is in Korea, no doubt about that! After two weeks packed aboard that troopship everybody was so ready for a party we all immediately started pulling streamers off the walls. I had good intentions of writing a letter with my shipboard notes, but that one was too good to miss. In the midst of all the hullabaloo and elbowing for priority at the bar, I made an unnecessary statement: "What a place to live it up!"

Big Bob Draney said, "Just don't get in my way," and waded into his favorite—boilermakers. He likes to demonstrate how to finish off an empty beer by holding the can at arm's length between thumb and fingers, and crushing it.

The people stationed here at Johnson Field with their families have really got it made, but time and distance have separated us from all that; from the standpoint of being fighter pilots, we've got the best deal in the whole Air Force.

JUNE 7th

We have had a thoroughly busy day with many lectures, briefings, and processing. The morning was spent listening to some well-organized lectures by Lt. Cdr. Paul Pugh, one of the Navy exchange pilots with the 4th Fighter Group. He got himself a MiG-15 awhile ago and gave us some darn good scoop about combat with the MiGs. The very latest word was passed on by the other Navy pilot with the 4th, "Swabby" Evans, fresh out of Korea where he just got a MiG. From the sound of things so far, there are shades of Buck Rogers in this aerial war between the F-86s and MiG-15s with their speed and altitude possibilities.

Two Air Force pilots who recently escaped from enemy territory passed on the benefit of their experiences in some *very* interesting talks. One was an F-51 jock who had been shot down by flak and had a wild helicopter rescue. He told us: "I was in a pile of rocks pinned down by enemy rifle fire. When the helicopter set down, I jumped out of hiding and ran like hell toward it with my head down. As the rescue boys hadn't seen me at first, their medic ran for my spot, head down too, bullets ricocheting all over, and we must have passed each other in our foot races." Then he said they had to wait in a sweat till the medic raced back before they could take off through all the shooting.

The other pilot had spent 16 days with some ground troops fighting his way out through the lines and darn near starved while he was at it. He had been a Forward Air Controller and the Army outfit he was attached to had been overrun and bypassed by Communist ground attacks. Mighty hairy stories with fortunate endings.

Bob Draney got a letter yesterday from his mother with a newspaper article and pictures of McClellan's takeoff crash in an F-84 of our 121st Fighter Squadron back at Andrews. Bob and I were both surprised by that bit of bad news; one of our boys in this outfit got killed on takeoff in Korea yesterday. You just don't stand a chance in these hot ships if the rubber band pops at that critical time. All we can do is our best and I'm going to put everything into it.

I share a room in the Q with Bob Draney, the monster, George Dunn, and Dave Freeland who came from the 81st Group at Moses Lake. Charlie Hogue, Charles C. Charles with swagger stick, from Newcastle, is in the next room and just got here by air. He arrived at Stoneman the evening before we left by ship and so missed out on our two week Pacific "cruise."

As I have that bit of F-86 time from the past I'm slated to fly the bird ahead of those with no 86 time; that should mean an early trip to Korea. I'm itching to get at it, and also getting very rusty on this aviating. We gather that the flying weather has been marginal so far this summer and could put a serious kink in our transition schedule in Japan. I hope we don't get too hung up, as we are not making any tracks sitting here at Johnson Field.

I understand we can mark *FREE* on our mail from Korea, just as we did in the last war. If it's true, that will be a break from stamp-hunting. In attempting to make up for the shipboard interval and pass on a little philosophy in a letter home, I wrote: *I feel sorry in a way for gals who marry fighter pilots, and yet there are no better men and you gals should aspire to nothing but the best.* Whatta line!

JUNE 8th

We're really getting in the mood with more lectures and especially discussions in which we yak about combat situations. The MiG sounds like a hell of a good aircraft. I've got to get cracking on the 86 before I can sensibly relate with all this and my hopes are up for a first flight tomorrow. I'll have to be on the ball as I'm "slightly" uncurrent in the bird—a year and a half has elapsed since that first checkout—and in addition, we've now had five weeks of ocean and ground pounding.

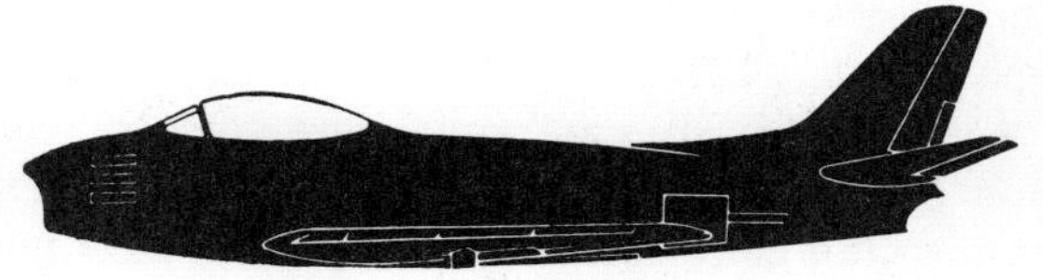

II

Practice For Real

TUESDAY, JUNE 12th

As we feared, accomplishing our transition program is going to be a challenge to our patience. Each day we view the dismal sky and wonder when, but yesterday morning—happy day—I made off in the F-86—great sport again and first light in what has become a long tunnel to combat. The pilots with no 86 time have had to fill out the questionnaire, get supervised starts, practice taxing around the ramp, and (for some) a ride in the T-33 for a check of the local area. The rest of our shipment of pilots, with lots of 86 time, were flying the plane until they left for this assignment and I've been put in with them although I'm sort of an odd case with those few hours 18 months ago. My old questionnaire was acceptable as these are all A-models, and I discussed procedures with the pilot in charge of my section, plus other pilots, so they just assigned me an airplane and I went out, hopped in, and leaped off. Quite a checkout, but my memory is good and evidently they had confidence in me.

When I got the gear up, I just pointed that li'l ol' beauty into the blue in search of a piece of private sky where I'd have room to begin that very personal relationship each fighter pilot must establish alone with a single-seater—the wonderful secret bonds unknown to other fliers who operate in a straight-and-level fashion. It always pays to begin the affair with careful respect and then step up the pace of maneuver as your sense of feel and confidence in the exploration picks up—the great thrill and satisfaction of probing the limits that separates fighter flying from all the rest.

After a good fling at my own particular sequence of experiments in the limited time available, still cautious and rusty, I was feeling my oats enough to make some playful passes at the other boys getting checked out. Some of them said they felt kind of awkward after six weeks or so out of the 86. *Six weeks?* Ha, ha. I didn't admit the strangeness I felt, but what a pleasure it was to be up once more in the Sabre.

I've been determined to get some more personal equipment and paraphernalia before we leap off for Korea. Our supply just doesn't have certain necessities such as flying boots or gloves. As the weather was impossible today with no hope of flying, Dunn, Freeland, and I acquired a jeep and driver for a trip to Camp Drake. The camp held a certain interest for us as that is where all the infantrymen went who were aboard our troopship.

After the ride on that back-country safari I feel as if my backbone had been sprung and kidneys displaced—what roads! The trusty old jeep proved again that it is often more rugged that its occupants. We drove for miles through village after village on winding roads consisting of muddy holes, ruts, rocks and wash-outs. None of us were certain of the route to Camp Drake, but we finally made it just before the QM Sales closed. I bought a pair of Army combat boots, thin leather dress gloves for flying, sets of fatigues, and more underwear. While we were gathering up our purchases, a real tropical deluge set in and continued for the entire sloshing, jouncing trip back to Johnson.

A topic of discussion on the trip was the recent news report of a flight of F-84s that cracked up back in the States. As Dunn and I have been flying 84s, we had a few anecdotes to compare. Another news item of interest to us has been the return to the States of Captain Jabara from our 4th Fighter Group. Apparently he got a terrific reception as the first jet ace of this war.

MONDAY, JUNE 18th

The weather has been disgustingly stinko for days now with such high humidity that everything is saturated. Even the walls are sweating. Our towels stay damp; clothes and socks are soggy in the morning with the sweat of the day before and have a ripe odor; shoes, boots, and leather jackets are showing persistent mold and appear to grow things overnight. And with the night comes a damp chill that seems to soak right into you and cause the sweat to freeze. This has really fixed me up with a cold the last couple of days.

With these conditions it wasn't until Friday that I got up for my second hop in the 86. This bird is a lot more sensitive in formation than was the F-84C with its variable boost, so I was supposed to get another solo exercise sortie before team work, but

14

the schedule set me up for combat flight formation and tactics, plus leading the element. Boy, I could tell I need some more private sessions to properly manage the plane. I was really working hard, but felt rather clumsy in some scraps with other flights. You just can't compress the time required to get a handle on the critical feel and control for sharp clean reaction so necessary in violent maneuvers.

Sunday morning the low weather aced out the flying so when the schedule was scratched I joined a couple of fellows and a locally stationed Major who were setting out on a drive in search of fishing tackle. The Major was planning a fishing trip in the mountains and had heard there were some bargains in trout flies in the town of Ome. I was glad for any reason to escape sweating out the weather frustration.

It seems as though country road navigation here is a common puzzle so we rambled on another Cook's tour that suited my curiosity about Japan, where some of the up-country scenery reminds me of New England. On the way we drove alongside a river set in a deep interesting gorge, and the view from one of several bridges attracted a halt for picture taking. In passing through some very neat pine forests and pretty bamboo groves, I

Jim Jabara, on the right, the first jet ace of the Korean War, tells some of his pals, in fighter pilot sign language (originating in WWI), how he got his score. On left, Holley, Kemp, and Nelson. (Air Force photo)

15

F-84Cs in formation. Author's wingman very close, wing tip tanks indicating line abreast formation.

noticed the thatched roofs on many of the homes were over a foot thick. The village streets and roads of most of the hill country were very narrow with steep banks above and below held in place with very precise walls of rock. Some of the localities were obviously ages old, worn down by generations of these people. I got a strange sensation of a vast span of time in a remote world that was living its own way when there was only wilderness on our continent.

The way these great trucks and three-wheeled vehicles bellow down the roads and through villages, it's a miracle that we saw no accidents or people getting run over. The procedure seems to be to ignore the brakes and forget about slowing down; just blare the horn, close the eyes, and charge through. In spite of the war

Author on wing of F-84C ready to fly at Andrews Field, MD. This was while in the 121st Fighter Squadron of the DCANG before combat tour in Korea. The 84C model required seat pack parachutes.

Author on wing of his F-51D Mustang ready to fly. The insignia is the 95th Fighter Squadron, 82nd Fighter Group, home base Grenier Field, Manchester, NH. This is between WWII and Korean War.

casualties the countryside was swarming with children, so evidently production in that line is booming.

This morning the weather was relatively good and although I was not, with this cold, I figured I'd better fly anyway because of the uncertainty of our schedule. We went up in elements of two and practiced high-speed attacks on each other with evasive tactics, trying to keep one another in our gunsights. That's the stuff I need to polish up to get back in the saddle of the 86. They really mean high-speed here—maximum plus.

The Group over in Korea got into a big scrap with the MiGs today. One of the fellows I met in Stoneman, who shipped early by air to the 4th, got himself shot down right off the bat. He had the most flying time I ever heard of for a pilot of his age, mostly a mass of civilian flying while he was out of the service. That's good flying, but doesn't mean a thing in the dogfighting business. His fighter time had been crammed in since recall to active duty, and when he got here he rushed through his 86 transition. In this line of work you must get exposed to a lot of wild situations and flight attitudes to understand and judge when you are ready. Today's combat in Korea emphasized that! Most of the guys have more hours in the 86 than I have total jet time since Mustang days, and they are still

The author's crew chief in the 95th Fighter Squadron cleaning up their F-51D while on war game maneuvers at Pope Field, NC, during period between WWII and the Korean War.

working on their proficiency. Shortcuts don't impress the enemy or any hot fighter pilot who knows the score.

WEDNESDAY, JUNE 27th

All these blasted rumors about peace talks are very unsettling to everybody. That's the sort of stuff that ruined the end of the last war and caused us to demobilize and give it all away. Anyway, our flying is picking up. Saturday, after a dandy morning hop, the whole 334th Squadron had an afternoon picnic frolic by the dam and lakes south of Johnson Field. As I was in a good mood from flying, I considered it another interesting trip into new country rolling along in the open 2-1/2 ton GI trucks through some pleasant scenery. There was plenty of cold beer, baseball and volleyball, and clowning around with lots of pictures taken by the many cameras that were carried along. The O-Club Japanese Hill Billy Band supplied the music—my gosh but they're good, and really made me sit up and take notice. The inevitable rains came and chased everybody to the hotel by the top of the dam where we got into a regular jam session. Although there was plenty of private booze available and consumed, none of the troops broke their necks fooling around and nobody drowned in the lake—amazing.

Yesterday I flew twice with more all-out combat tactics and more chances for element lead. While our fuel was heavy on our second flight we practiced instrument let-downs to Johnson, then with dry drop tanks we jumped on some of the other boys to start a ripping good dogfight that attracted everybody who was up. At one point when the hassle worked down low, two others dove into the scrap. We whipped back in a reverse, catching them in a trap where-upon they flicked over to escape in a split-S. I think we all yelled at once, "No, no . . . your altimeter . . . the mountains!" They both did violent half-roll recoveries and pulled out to the side. When we landed they were still ashen-faced at the thought of almost going straight in in that high country—a close call. Such incidents are always good for bar business at the end of the day. I feel real good now—ready! I'm concentrating hard and it's bringing good results.

We've lost two more pilots in the Group in Korea and I guess things are getting rougher now in "MiG Alley." I keep this in mind when we tangle with each other in this "Clobber College."

JUNE 28th

Last night while the club was having a dance, our gang collected to observe all these occupation folks enjoying their social life. We got our entertainment out of the floor show that provided Japanese acrobatics—and dancing girls—at first several of the tall, exotic oriental type. Some piercing whistles rent the air over their performance. The part that gave me mixed feelings was a line of Japanese gals doing the hula in tune to "Aloha Oe." I couldn't

The famous Baka Bomb, a piloted missle dropped from Japanese bombers and flown by the Kamikaze forces. The nose *was* the bomb. On display at Johnson Field, Japan.

help but think back to Pearl Harbor, nearly ten years ago. These days we use a joking expression here: "So solly, we flends now."

What continually amazes me in Japan is the terrific show this country put out during the last war. From looking around in what travels I've had, I wonder where all that war effort came from. This Korean War is sure different from the last in one respect: So many servicemen are camera bugs. There was a small fortune in photographic equipment aboard the *USNS Pope* coming over, and I notice the same sorts of gear on this base.

In the latest squadron rotation, the 334th departed for Korea yesterday morning and the fellows from the 336th got in last night in time for the club show. Some of the boys who shipped over with me and have already been to Korea were with them. It was something to see the hands zooming around the bar in the fighter pilots' universal sign language that illustrates all dogfight stories. There has evidently been more real dogfighting in the last month than all the time before for the 4th Group. The damned MiG pilots must be learning too much and everybody here says the MiG is really *it*. Some of it sounds pretty hair-raising. Those guys carry rather big cannons, one 37mm and two 20mm jobs. The anticipation generates a lot of thoughts and conversation among those of us who haven't been over. I know it's going to be *some* experience.

MONDAY, JULY 2nd

On Saturday I had two more bang-up flights; I'm getting to feel at home again in the 86 and hacking that trim better all the time. During the first flight I was frisking about at low altitude with one of the other Guard boys in trail. I always like to know the minimum maneuver room of which my plane is capable, so with previous practice, I thought I'd check this guy's tiger blood in a quick test. I wrapped over into a snappy split-S and honked back on the stick. Over the radio I heard a very distinct squawk of shock and on pullout, skimming the treetops, saw my tracker making an abrupt recovery in the opposite direction. From the rocking of his wings I knew he'd lost me and had other things on his mind, so while laughing I dodged over some nearby hills and then zoomed back up to gain a good bounce position for myself.

On the second sortie Captain Lane was leading the flight of four when Hitt had to abort I moved up to element lead as we taxied out for takeoff. The weather was worsening all around so we stayed low under most of the thick stuff and worked on our high-speed tactics in real solid air. For a change I tried using the amber lenses in my goggles to cut the thick haze, but I feel the effect is a little too weird.

Everything on this flight was maximum. We were spread out blasting along on top of one cloud layer and beneath another when Lane signalled to close up—*now*. We layed into him, he popped speed brakes, ducked his nose, and we were down a tight hole. Out the bottom in a sharp pullout, everybody tucked in tight and rigid, then a quick yank to tactical spread again and balls to the wall. That kind of work puts snap in your flying and sure makes you feel great. When we got enough maneuvering room among the clouds

Baka Bomb rear view showing three rocket motors used after launch by the pilot to propel the craft to impact target. Displayed at Johnson Field.

we went into a tight interval rat race and worked up a good old sweat. To top off the day's work, I greased both final landings on the spot. Now that's the kind of flying that really does things for you. As I've found before, it pays to be particular.

JULY 5th

We've been playing a lot of ping-pong lately; some of the games get fast and furious. Everybody lets off excess steam by going all out; taunts, challenges, growls and cheers are supplied by both players and onlookers. At least this keeps our reflexes sharp while sweating out the weather. The sorry weather gave Tom Shellum and Larry Miller a chance to visit our operation while waiting to ferry more F-84s from Yokota back down to their base at Itazuke. They are with the 49th Fighter-Bomber Group now and, like us, are still in training and not doing much flying either. They said Glen Stalker and Bill Hall are also in the Group and they have about 85 missions in now! If we could only get going.

On top of all this waiting, we understand now the cease-fire conference will take place Sunday, July 8th. What the hell will happen then? Will that end the war and leave us stranded here on occupation duty? We *will* go nuts then, but I suppose I'm getting ahead of myself, the war isn't over yet. The Reds may be pulling a fast one for all we know.

Yesterday, the 4th of July, we had a big outdoor fireworks display in the evening followed by a great big ol' party. It sounded like a war in the club with everybody well-loaded and throwing firecrackers and torpedos all around the bar. I thought they were going to blow the place up—what sport. Somebody threw a firecracker that slid under some Captain's shoe and went off. He panicked and scrambled to our table to ask me if I'd thrown it. I told him no, but couldn't help laughing at the same time. Later, he explained that he didn't mean to be sore about it, but he was somewhat shook-up and on an R&R from Korea. I figured he was some hard-working fighter-bomber pilot and didn't worry about it. We later discovered that he was a Public Information Officer and those terrible Bedcheck Charlie's were clanking him up—did the boys get a laugh out of that one!

We're all feeling a little burned-out with this monotony and getting so we are even losing our taste for the partying. The permanent base personnel here tell us there are two ways to go crazy in this routine of theirs—one is from drinking and the other is from *not* drinking. Not much choice there.

Saturday morning I had a generally fouled-up flight. I discovered at altitude that I was much lower on fuel than I should have been (I found out later my drop tanks didn't feed right and I had a fuel leak), so I left Prindle and headed for Johnny Field, but a bunch of weather had moved in and covered everything. Don Griffith called an emergency with a boost failure and was somewhere in the vicinity trying to get on the ground as soon as possible.

I let down and got oriented by my ADF and caught a glimpse of the field back under a shelf of clouds. When I ducked under this stuff the visibility went to zilch and I found myself in a terrible mess of traffic. The ceiling was about 700 feet and I had to get down to 500 feet to see much of the field. Griff was having trouble setting up a pattern in this tangle and I was trying to keep out of his way so he could land first.

The way the weather was deteriorating, everybody wanted to get down and there were planes circling in the murk in both directions with a number of close dodges. I was becoming concerned about my fuel as it was getting critical. Every time I'd try to set up a pattern to land, planes would appear and the maneuvering would put me out of position or I'd momentarily lose the field.

Right at this wonderful time, Chandler, who had been out on

F-86A on final approach. One of the 4th boys coming in from an alert scramble at Johnson Field, Japan. Sept. 1951.

an intercept scramble, came in with his element escorting a Navy TBF (buzzing Mt. Fujiyama)—more confusion. Everybody was complaining at once and there were calls of low fuel although none were as low as me. I finally called out that I had 40 gallons and came banking in, but saw just in time a plane go right underneath me which forced me to pull up and make a tight 360. As I did so, I met two others head-on. My position was bad but I essed and side-slipped down to the runway close behind this other character, wondering if I might not be able to land short enough to keep from overrunning him. I came over the fence in a near vertical bank and just said to myself, "You'd better make it; you won't go far around the pattern on 30 gallons!"

So—plunk! On the ground. That affair up there in the pattern must have looked like a madhouse from the ground with planes whistling around in the murk over the field while the radio chatter contributed to the effect. It was really a relief and a big laugh when we were all on the ground—chalk up some more experience. I guess I'll have to get used to marginal fuel or less and be prepared to make the right move.

The weather remained poor so flying was scrubbed for the day. Anyway, most of the planes were out of commission. Later in the afternoon I went to see this movie we've been hearing about, *The Thing*. Wow, it's the greatest suspense and horror story that I recall ever seeing, with some real hairy ideas about visitors from outer space.

TUESDAY, JULY 17th

The radio news says the peace talks are still up in the air—*hot* air, we call it. There is some new proposal for a discussion site, apparently a snag factor. Either the talks get down to business or they are a Communist sham, and all hell will break loose—especially in the air. We get word that there are about 400 MiGs all getting jazzed up now in the Antung area while we have *two* F-86 squadrons in Korea—a neat situation to contemplate.

For us, that's just more incentive to get on the ball, and while we're at it I'm acquiring that wonderful feeling again of really belonging in an outfit. I am particularly glad to be in the 336th Squadron as they seem to be the best bunch in the 4th. Dick Panter came over here with the 4th and he and I, both restless and on the wild side, are hitting it off great. They've made up some good songs here and in the evenings together we really give 'em the business. I think the best one is "When it's Springtime on the Yalu," a real fighter pilot's song. Dick tells me the words were written by his best buddy who was shot down not long ago. Sunday afternoon Dick and I joined some of the boys who were having a get-together in the indoor dance room. We had the place practically to ourselves and relaxed with some cool beer and the ever-ready flying stories. Off to one side were four Australian fellows who had been around for a couple of days with a tennis tournament. I noticed they were bored by themselves so I went over and invited them to join our gang. I knew how they felt as I've been milling around here for weeks. The Aussies were appreciative of the company and we all enjoyed the opportunity of having some different experiences to talk about.

While I was mailing some stuff home the other day I ran into Soltus from the old Grenier Field gang. He just returned from flying 100 missions in F-51s and is flying them here at Johnson in this outfit they are forming up. He's stuck with some more overseas time as he flew his 100 in 90 days! Soltus said one day he flew six missions and 15 hours of combat time and he still feels pooped out. That sure is one way of getting rid of all the retread reserve pilots. He told me how C.B., my old next door chum of 82nd Fighter Group days, bought the farm. It seems C.B. was on his 100th and last mission when he got shot down and bailed out of his 51 right into a bunch of Commie troops. As he landed in his parachute they burp-gunned him at close range. The guy flying with him saw the whole thing and dumped his napalm all over those Commies and then strafed the crowd with his .50s. No question about an end like that, and that's the word that went home, too.

I wrote a long reply to Dad's letter to compare some things with his many years of Marine Corps flying service. I mentioned the frustrations I wrote about in World War II while stuck in that pilot pool at Brooks Field, Texas, and how I was getting similar feelings. Last night while discussing these reminders I saw a familiar face I couldn't place . . . doggoned if it wasn't my former Squadron Commander at Brooks! A real prince of a guy and admired by all my buddies of those days. Major Larson was the only officer with rank who treated us junior birdmen like pilots and men. He and I immediately bellied up to the bar, calling for reunion drinks while laughing about those "career" Training Command clowns at Brooks.

Straight from combat with a hot record, this great guy had taken over us shiny winged kids. We hung on his every word and when I say hot, that inverted show in a P-40 on the weeds convinced us. And what's he doing now? Still a Major (wonderful promotion system), and a *supply* officer at some distant base in Japan! My God, what a waste of a fighter pilot. Bob Draney joined us and I brought up some comments from Dad's letter. Dad had reminded me that the only way to get ahead in aviation was to become a "waffle butt" (a staff type planted in the cane bottom chairs of his day), and drive the pilots crazy by ruining the joy of flying. After all the laughs, my old C.O. said, "Stick with the flyboys, Doug. This flying a desk is crap for the damned birds." He was pleased to hear I was flying F-86s and I sure agreed with him that I'm mighty lucky to have this assignment.

Author's father, far left, with part of the first organized class of naval aviators at Pensacola, FL. The aircraft is a Curtiss F-Boat. Author's father was the only Marine, the rest Navy. Left to right: Evans Naval Aviator #26 and Marine Aviator #4, Scofield NA #28, Paunack NA #27, Norfleet, Read NA #24, Saufley NA #14, Johnson NA #25, Corry NA #23, Edwards, Haas. This photo had never been seen anywhere before by the author, in histories or museums, until discovered in the author's father's collection. Apparently an extremely rare historical photo record.

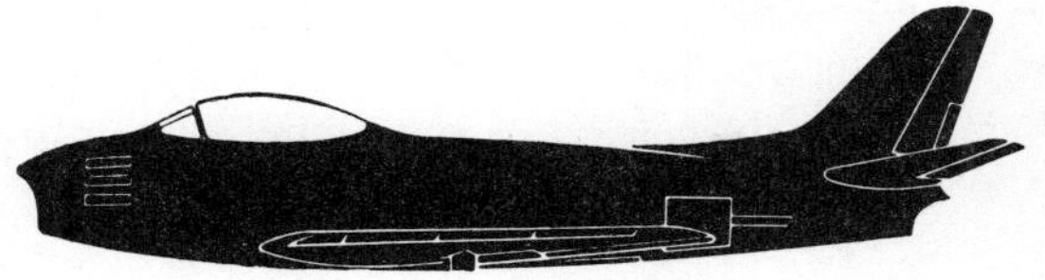

III

A Taste of Action

K-13 SUWON, KOREA
JULY 31st

While we are settling in, I'd better cover some events to get up to date. Those of us remaining in the Cobbler College flew like mad just about every day of the last week before leaving for Korea. On the 26th I flew three times and got four hours. What a happy improvement in routine. On one flight by myself, I couldn't resist a mood of celebration and went hog-wild, attacking and fighting everybody who was up.

That night in the wee hours someone woke me up; after prying my eyelids open I recognized Tom Shellum. Then Glen Stalker walked into the room and we talked until 4 a.m. He and Tom were up to ferry more 84s back to their outfit. Glen pooped me up on their news; he is an instructor on 84Es, a flight commander, and may get spot Captain. He told me about Braswell buying the farm—there had been low weather and mountains in the target area where Bras went in.

The next day, the 27th, Glen watched four of us fire up for a special flight and then went on his way. This special job was a fly-by for a newly arrived aircraft carrier in Tokyo Bay that was loaded with a shipment of F-84s. In our passes we were right down on the water, tucked together in four-ship fingertip formation and looking up at the carrier deck as we whipped by the bow. We started one pass across the rooftops of the Naval Base on a point that juts into the bay (Yokosuka?). It must have really blasted them. When we were skimming over the waves, about ten feet at .8 to .85 Mach, sheets of shock vapor were popping off the canopies and wings, and the air was as rough as a cob. From our view it looked like we put on a real sharp show.

That was about the hottest temperature in the cockpit that I've ever experienced in flying (we've had readings of 130°); I felt like I'd been boiled alive and my brains had turned to oatmeal. All of us were soaked through and the sweat was pouring right off our flight suits. Prindle just about fell on his can when he climbed out of his cockpit, he was so pooped. All of us must have looked in pretty sad shape and my face was as red as a beet. It's too bad we can't take up ground-bound critics who believe pilots loll about the skies in the lap of luxury. Operations said we could knock off for the day, but as there was a chance to fly again, I took it and went up after lunch. There were some clouds in the area piling up like stacks of pillows inviting somersaults, so I obliged by zooming up the sides for a lazy roll over the tops to go togogganing down the opposite slope. Porpoising over the clouds in that way is a sport I have enjoyed since the first fling at them as a Cadet in the open cockpit PT-19, bare-headed and laughing into the slipstream. Only other fliers can guess the secrets behind the happy smile of a pilot who has just returned to earth.

Yesterday several replacement pilots and I made the long-awaited and often-postponed move to Korea. We came over on the "cow" (as we refer to the courier); the whole route was under clouds which prevented my hoped-for study of the new scenery, so we gave up and slept most of the way. After we unloaded our junk, Major "Bones" Marshall, C.O. of the 335th, took us on a skoshi tour of K-13. I noticed a few knocked-out, bogged-down Russian tanks scattered around that remained from past fighting, and there seemed to be a fair amount of new construction and tents going up. We stopped for a visit in Combat Operations and had a chance to meet some of the wheels. After the tour we moved into our tent, the one for the people flying with the 335th as Dunn, Todd and I are; eventually I'll rejoin the 336th Squadron. This is the end of the long tunnel. From now on, when I strap in I'll be learning the inside story.

Today who do I see in our circus tent mess hall but Ken Jackson, who is in the 51st Fighter Group across the field and flying F-80s. He left Andrews Field the month before me and is now getting his start with five missions after spending two months in Okinawa similar to my stay in Japan. After chow I went with Ken to his area across the runway and he told me that though they were doing quite well for the present, his outfit had experienced some heavy losses.

Ken showed me a very interesting airplane, a shot up F-80 set on blocks, that makes quite a story. Two days ago, Ken's outfit was jumped by MiGs after pounding an interdiction target and this 80 had survived a nose-to-nose encounter. It had been hit in each wing by 20mm shells and one evidently solid slug had gouged a trench across the top curve of a wing. But the biggest mess was just outside of the right intake from what must have been a square hit by a 37mm which blew out a great section of wing back into the main spar.

At K-13, Suwon. Ken Jackson, author's friend from previous squadron in the Air National Guard, sitting in cockpit of F-86. Jackson was flying F-80s in 51st Fighter Group across the field. Standing beside F-86 is Walt Raby, author's C-47 pilot friend in the 4th Air Base Group.

Fragments had torn open part of the fuselage while plowing into the engine area and yet this bird had made it home—good news for jet jockeys.

I had to meet the pilot of that duel and shortly Ken introduced us. His name is Bill McAllister, and right off he impressed me as the real charging type—so intense and enthusiastic about this combat flying that I sort of expected to see smoke coming out of his ears. He said that when the MiGs attacked they seemed to want to force the 80s off their path and one of them apparently picked him. Mac said *nobody* was going to make him change course and he went head-on at this MiG with all six .50s going. The MiG opened up with his three cannons and they proceeded to shoot the hell out of each other. Mac heard and felt the crashes of the shells hitting him and he could see his .50s striking and flashing up the MiG's *intake*. Then *swish*; somehow they missed each other by inches and Mac kept right on going. He was too busy handling his beat-up plane to see what happened to the MiG and flew that tough little 80 back here and landed okay—what a tiger![1]

While I was visiting Ken's boys I ran into "Ollie" Arquilla, whom I hadn't seen since Grenier days with the 82nd Fighter Group. He, too, is in the 51st Group here.[2]

AUGUST 4th

To get the feel of things I have attended some mission briefings while waiting my turn to get on the schedule with the rest of the FNGs, as new guys are known. Yesterday I made a local hop with a flight of four that stayed in close show formation most of the time so I didn't get to see much of the area. There were also a lot of clouds obscuring the view. Toward the end of the flight we split up in two-ship elements and I went off with Larry Layton for a little simulated gunnery. I set up a course as target, but Larry lost me as he peeled away to climb into position. After I found my way back to K-13 we joined up again and I got in some close formation work while Larry racked it around. As I've been working on slow spot landings at Johnny, I make out fine on the combat strip here. It had been a week since my last flight in Japan so I didn't exactly mind keeping myself proficient, but now that I'm finally here in Korea, I can't generate enthusiasm for routine local flying.

Lately the missions have been scrubbed for one reason or another, so until the outfit starts completing some of the schedule, I'll probably keep on twiddling my thumbs on standby in the tent. Now the rain has started to pour down, which ought to cool the place off a bit and lay this infernal dust for awhile. It's so noisy beating on the tent it drowns out the talking so we sit here staring at the canvas walls—rain outside, sweat inside.

Jackson had supper with me again and I went over to his outfit to watch them bomb up. Some of the 80s had napalm and rockets for different targets. When they were ready, Ken and I stood by the runway to watch the JATO launch. What a smoke screen and stink—whew! After the leaders get off and obscure the runway, I don't see how the following elements find their way down the strip to take off. We could barely see them going right by our position off to the side.

AUGUST 7th

Sunday morning I got off the ground again, this time for my first look-see up north. I was to go with Cliff Thompson on a weather reccy, which I guess is the simplest way to get that first-time-over-the-lines business out of the way and at the same time allow a little more looking around than would be the case in a large formation with other details to consider.

The weather was solid over the field so I tucked it in on wing and we went through on the gauges. More and more breaks in the undercast appeared as we tooled up to Sinanju. I was getting a pretty fair view of the west coast the farther up we went. North of us, all above Sinanju to the Yalu River was very clear. Inland and to the south and southeast the terrain was pretty well blotted out by broken stuff. Thompson asked me if I could make out the bare area on the north side of the Yalu River near its mouth. He said that was Hot Spot and I strained my eyes looking for details while we swung around in a 180-degree turn over the Chongchon River, but due to the distance I couldn't make out any airfield, or even identify the city of Antung.

I returned my attention to the map in my lap for a comparison of terrain features, noting all the coastal bulges and peninsulas, islands, and rivers which I traced back into the cloud interference. All this map-reading made my formation a little ragged, and as the clouds closed on the way south I put my map away and settled into wing flying. There were cloud breaks when we got over the field, so we dropped through a hole and that was that.

When the late afternoon mission was ready to go, I went over to Jackson's side of the field and watched our two F-86 squadrons off, followed by the two F-80 squadrons. As soon as all the planes had climbed out of sight, we dashed into the 4th Group Combat Ops to listen in on the radio transmissions. We heard the 80s calling out bandits and then the 86s commented on them also. The RAAF Australian boys were very distinct with their accent. Evidently there were only sightings of enemy aircraft as no bounces were made by either side. When the mission was on the way home we hopped up on the sandbag barricade around ops to watch the gang come in. There were remarks that this was just like the stage for some Hollywood movie.

The sun had set and it was darn near night by the time the squadrons of 80s and 86s arrived one on top of the other, and the traffic pattern got overloaded and out of hand. The aggravation of the pilots was sure evident in their short-tempered remarks while trying to find a place in the mix-up. The planes that circled to the west appeared as darting shadows in the fading skylight; those to the east were bunches of lights floating about. A number of guys were calling low on fuel and it looked for a few minutes like some accidents about to happen. I can say now that that low-fuel, low-weather episode at Johnny Field was good experience for me after watching this lash-up. The crowd broke up, and Ken and I went to a movie preceded by some 4th Group combat gun camera film that was pretty interesting but of poor clarity due either to the camera setting or film development.

Full of anticipation of big doings, I made the team for my second mission at noon yesterday. We were to cover F-80s that started things off with a JATO launch that put us all in a dense fog. We could barely see enough to taxi and groped along while this PSP on which we operate kept rolling up in waves as our wheels pressed forward. Whenever a stop is necessary, a good blast of power is required to begin rolling again which just adds to the stink, smoke, dust, and flying debris.

F-80s of the 51st Fighter Group leaping off with a bomb load for North Korea from K-13, Suwon.

We made a weather penetration going out, while by the time we returned there were enough breaks in the overcast to get down through the holes. The same cloud coverage was quite extensive over the combat area where we set up a patrol and could hear other people up there occasionally calling out our 86s. A few bandits were reported by ground station broadcast but none were seen during our mission. In my eager condition I was trying to absorb all that went on, and while paying close attention to our patrol business, I monitored the F-80 boys getting some action during their attacks on ground targets. What was probably the only alarm of the mission occurred as we crossed the bomb line on our climb north. While sitting calmly in formation, all of a sudden I saw flame and smoke burst from the lead aircraft along with a loud explosive noise. It really startled me. Then came the light—test firing of the guns. I felt like a sap for being so surprised and quickly punched the circuit breaker, flipped the switch on, and pressed the trigger. All of my own guns going off gave me another jolt—a lot of smoke and a hell of a racket, deafening almost. Up to that moment I had never fired the guns at all in the F-86 and six of them at once was quite an initiation.

During the briefing for my third mission, the job of cover for F-80s was changed to escort for B-29s, and I was looking forward to some excitement with these new possibilities. Again, there were a lot of low clouds so I've yet to see all of North Korea at any one time, but I have seen enough to realize the ruggedness of the country. If anything happens to my flying machine I'm sure going to use the 'chute rather than ride the bird down like one of the boys did. He went into the mud flats where his seat fired on impact and he was lucky to come out with minor injuries such as missing teeth.

At about Pyongyang I was ordered home because one other plane had aborted and the squadron wanted to even out. I felt like I'd lost a roll of the dice and it griped the hell out of me as I peeled off and watched the formation sail away toward the action I was going to miss. As I cruised south, scanning the sky and what ground surface was visible, I could hear the rendezvous with the B-29s. My need of terrain study drew my attention to my map, which I used to locate K-14 and right afterwards K-13. So at least I got to do some navigating and map-reading above the lines by myself.

K-13, ah-so; knowing I had loads of fuel, the horns sprouted and I went into a steaming dive to the deck south of here for a bit of low level "exploration" of the back country. I got credit for a mission— gag—but it was still a good flight, I made sure of that.

I'm wearing the complete escape and survival vest with all the other junk and a pistol—or cannon, which is a better name for the .45. I suppose it's better, in this country, to have more than you need instead of less, but we look like walking hardware stores and are dripping with sweat as if we'd stepped out of a shower when climbing out of our planes. That's because we turn all heat full on to prevent any chance of frost on the canopy at the altitudes we have to fly. Our defrost system just isn't good enough to remove frost once it starts, so with the heaters on plus the sun blazing through the bubble canopy we really get cooked.

Bob Draney came over here yesterday and he and I spent part of this afternoon in Combat Ops looking at a few reels of interesting combat film. Some of those MiGs were really gyrating. I'd like to get cracking on my own film; listening to these fighter-bomber boys' war stories sure makes me want to shoot up something. Fighter pilots may sound like a crazy crew, but what the hell, shooting is what we're here for! A lot of the pilots who came over as the original 4th are leaving, so maybe the rest of us can move up a notch or so on the shooters list.

Meanwhile, the setup we have here isn't bad at all for a tent city. My tent is the one set aside for extra or visiting pilots with three other staff, non-combat officers. This isn't as good as some of the other tents or base areas, but when I have to I can live anywhere. I'm used to shaving with cold water again plus washing as necessary out of a steel helmet or basin—no different than a camp bucket, and as there is no abundance of water fit to drink, I use my canteen supply to brush my teeth. We have a pretty good field shower set up in tents

Author just returned from a mission at K-13, Suwon. The armament crews are already at work reloading the guns of nearby aircraft.

34

Big Bob Draney and author at rear entrance to author's tent. Author has on survival vest which was bulky but full of useful stuff. Life vests (Mae West) go over that and a parachute over all. Author has map in left hand after just finishing a briefing for a mission; he still has that map today. K-13, Suwon.

on the other side of a creek crossed by a board footwalk; officers can shower each day from 3 p.m. to 5 p.m. except Sunday (if there is water) and I certainly do because of this infernal heat, clouds of dust, and continual sweating. From all the talk about this place I expected a lot worse than what I've found. Evidently, a lot of fellows didn't rough it outdoors hunting or fishing or camping out in the woods when they were kids.

SUNDAY, AUGUST 12th

Another mission today in which the big thrill was getting surprised again by the test firing of guns, doggone it. We went below several cloud decks to take low cover for F-80s beating up main supply routes starting up near Antung and working down the coast. At the Yalu the sky was fairly clear and gave me a fine opportunity for a look look at the Antung MiG base. The low sun of the late afternoon reflected with a bright sparkle off the water—a very pretty sight, especially the glint of the Yalu estuary, the sort of view of the sea I've always liked. It seemed strange to think that there was a war on and I had to admit I'm lucky to be getting this unexpected, gradual break-in instead of a wild confusing intiation like some unfortunates.

There must have been four or five layers of clouds through which we went on the way to the target area. In that sort of weird

The back entrance to author's tent at K-13. No wood or screen side wall on this; just raise or lower the side canvas for ventilation. A bit dusty at times, but not a bad home, all in all.

weather you wonder who or what might be lurking to pull off a nasty surprise. Just as we were finished with our patrol and leaving the area, MiGs were reported somewhere about and I strained my eyes without success in sighting any. The illustrious leader said I look around "too much." This formation we're using is entirely too rigid for combat—really nothing but show formation slightly loosened up. It makes me feel cramped, and what good can you accomplish staring at your leader? I've flown in better damn tactical formation than this and, by God, I like to look around—it's my butt up there too! I was watching the leader enough to notice it was damned seldom that he ever looked in my direction.

The sky and view was refreshingly clear as we neared home and a great help in increasing my familiarity with Korea. I kept a no-comment watch on my fuel gauge and landed with 25 gallons.

Early this morning I had another turn at strip alert—on the ball at 5 a.m., but it's so blasted hot at night you can't get much sleep anyway. The sweat just rolls off of me so I toss and turn and continually wake myself up. When I write a letter I put paper under each arm so I won't smear the ink with sweat, then a gust of wind blows a cloud of dust that settles over everything, turning the sweat to mud.

While I was sitting in on a briefing today, Col. Gabreski got up

Thoroughfare through pilot's tent area at K-13. Author's tent on far left. The creek and laundry (open-air) is to right, off the end of walkway. Bricks improved looks and ditches ran off rain. Between tents can be seen sandbagged foxholes for air-raid shelters. Author used hole at left edge of photo. K-13, Suwon.

and told us we were moving to K-14, Kimpo. I guess he thought we were going to shout for glee, but there was only silence, so he said, "Come on boys, where's your spirit? That's a good deal."

I imagine that what first came to everyone's mind was the misery of another big move so soon after getting this base fixed up—the relocation problems and the discarding of all the personal touches accomplished in each tent. Beyond those considerations, of course, he was right—operating out of Kimpo will slightly shorten our range problems and give us a little more time in the patrol areas for hunting. He also passed the word that the 336th Squadron will get the new F-86Es that are being shipped in.

AUGUST 13th

What a crazy climate-one day clouds of dust and next the deluge. Along with the latest liquid cycle, the cloud conditions are screwing up the missions. The rains have caused a small flood in the living areas and some of the boardwalk washed away so we have to waste half a shower to wade the creek. A couple of days ago I thought the whole works was going to be flooded away for sure. To compound the downpour there was a teriffic wind. The tent seemed on the verge of a flying lesson, and early the following morning I was awakened by a shower in my face. The tent roof leaked, I was wet, my sack was soaked, and—uh-oh, my two handbags. I came roaring out from underneath my mosquito netting and started moving things around to locate a spot not under a leak, but my sleep was finished. This tent canvas can only take these hard driving rains for so long, and after I got the family pictures under cover the only recourse was to find a place to squat and sweat out the storm and sunrise. Speaking of storms. . . . I hear F-80s taking off on a mission; their JATO overrides the jet noise with a sound like a broken steam pipe and my nose tells me the usual cloud is next: We are about to be enveloped in another of those foul-smelling fogs. There is no escape in an open tent, so I'll just continue writing.

The latest news about my old outfit was given to me by one of our new GI replacements that just arrived from Andrews Field. He said the 121st Fighter Squadron would begin changing to F-94s by the 15th of this month. I'll bet the boys like that! I wonder what Tom has to say about it?

Changes are coming here too. Besides the pilots finishing combat tours and some GIs rotating home from the 4th, I understand there are nearly 20 new pilots in Japan for our group. Soon, the members of the original 4th will be rapidly dwindling. For the present there are flocks of wheels scheduled on every mission, probably trying to log as many as they can before their pending reassignments. Who knows, I may command a flight eventually when I get back to my own squadron. I would like to get in the position where I can practice some of my own ideas in this business.

Because I want to learn more about what our outfit does in this interesting war, I observe a lot of briefings and in the process I've been keeping track of the amount of rank on some of the missions. The two squadrons generally go out with three flights each and in

The laundry at K-13, the Korean houseboys washing our clothes with water from canvas tank at right with the creek running by. Our showers were in a tent just to the right (off photo) of the boardwalk foot bridge. The creek turned into a river after every heavy rain. The town of Suwon is beyond the hills in the background.

Author in cockpit of F-86A at completion of tenth mission, K-13, Suwon. A convenient temporary place to hang the crash helmet is on the windshield bow. Gun ports for three of the six .50-caliber guns are visible in the nose of aircraft.

one series of eight flights I noticed that two flights were led by Colonels and two by Majors, with a Lt. Col. leading an element. In another series of eight flights from several missions, four were led by Colonels and two by Majors. The biggest lineup of rank I noticed was six flights led by Colonels and Lt. Cols., and three by Majors. In that sort of brass brigade, the low-ranking tigers are pretty well restrained.

Author in cockpit of F-84C at Andrews Field, MD. Although the bubble canopy on the F-84 may look the same as that of the F-86, the Sabre's visibility was far superior. That visibility advantage was a definite factor in the Sabre superiority over the MiG-15.

The parking area is covered with pierced steel planking (PSP). The fighters were just about to start up for a mission. Author snapped this picture just before getting in the cockpit at K-13, Suwon, Korea, August 1951.

AUGUST 14th

Yesterday evening we had quite a gaggle of 86s on another cover mission for F-80s. Again, the target area was generally blanketed by clouds, especially close to the Yalu, which bothered the geography lessons that I'm hot on. To the west, part of Long Point and the islands beyond were visible. We set up a patrol and capped while the 80s went in and beat up the coastal roads from Sonchon southeast toward Chongju and Sinanju. The 80 boys called out some flak down low but they went in okay in train, dive bombed, and pulled out.

Some unidentified aircraft were seen flashing high in front of us; we never got near them and I couldn't tell if they were MiGs. Australian Meteors were patrolling with us and whenever we met we called each other out. Our continuous beat got boring, and from different radio conversations I thought there might be a possibility of a fight, but no such luck. From the way the formation was going I guess it's a good thing there was no fight. I think the Major who was leading my flight needs to brush up on his formation techniques; he would lose out in a turn and then jam on full power to catch up, which strung *us* all out behind with full throttle and no way to catch up until he got back into position, and then the entire flight had to go to idle. The tail guy on the other end of our six-ship flight was having the same problem I noticed. The way my throttle hand was going back and forth you'd have thought I was sawing wood. I hate to be the end man on a straggling formation, especially with the sun right in back of me as it was yesterday; that ball of fire was low, painfully

40

A squadron of F-86As of the 4th Fighter Group pouring out their tornado of exhaust on the runup for takeoff on a combat mission at K-13, Suwon, Korea, August 1951. Each aircraft carries a pair of external fuel tanks that were jettisoned in aerial combat. Each drop tank had a capacity of 120 gallons of fuel. The runway is surfaced with PSP—very hard on tires.

bright, and slightly above my left shoulder on all our easterly runs. I could almost feel MIGs sneaking out of the sun and crawling down my spine while hanging onto the end of this seesaw formation. The thumb in the sun method helped reduce the glare and I sort of unscrewed my head swiveling it around in those turns—always the awkward moments for a surprise.

About three o'clock this morning the warble sounded for Blue Alert and everybody went crashing around in the dark getting into some clothes. After that preparation we all fell sleepily back on our cots, only to have the siren wail and some of our heavy guns fire off a few rounds. They weren't shooting at anything; I think they just wanted to hear their guns go off and make the troops jump—and sure enough, everybody was excitedly ordered into the various foxholes in the tent area. One of the staff ground-pounders was in such a hurry jumping into our foxhole he evidently twisted his ankle. I felt someone bump me, then heard a thud, and looking around in the dark I could make out a crumpled body with a couple of guys checking him. It turned out that his ankle hurt so bad he had passed out. Gad, what a war.

There were comments passed around about a hint of the sound of an aircraft engine, but it was probably more of an overactive imagination than an intruder. Though the situation was sort of ridiculous, because of my attached status I remained standing with the crowd in our hole for about an hour, and it was such a clear black night we were able to witness a real display of meteors flashing through the heavens. We managed to salvage what sleep remained before dawn and heard later that someplace near here did get bombed.

We have a new houseboy for our tent as the other kid started back to school in Suwon. This other kid lost both his parents in the war. Many of these youngsters have lost their homes and families and friends. I wonder what they will do. The end of the war won't solve all their problems, yet these kids laugh and play, keep busy, and really enjoy simple things. We have it so good in America that we're never satisfied except when criticizing our own system.

When I went for the late mission, I saw by the briefing board that a hell of a big strike was planned and was told that the first mission had been the same except that they had some B-29s instead of 26s. Pyongyang was getting all the business and the aircraft doing the job were:

30	F-86
48	F-80
64	F-51
46	F-84
60	F4U
16	Meteors
70	B-26
334	Total

How many of these aircraft actually went on the mission, I don't know. The approaches to the target were fairly clear of cloud and before we got there the fighter-bombers were already at it with bombers and more fighters coming in all the time. Our 86s went into a beat back and forth from Sinanju to Pyongyang. With a raid of that size going on I thought the MiGs would sure as hell come out, but apparently none of the Antung crowd took any interest in the beat-up of their capitol. If they consider Ping Pong to be a stretch from their home base, they've got a lot to learn; a simple map reference shows that we stretch ourselves more than twice that distance reaching from our base to their front doorstep on the Yalu. Our total fuel including drop tanks is only 670 gallons and we would have a very handy reserve if we could meet some of them as far down as Pyongyang.

A chain of clouds went north and south over the target area and it was difficult to see just what went on, but talk about yak on the radio! Pilots were exchanging comments while trying to pick or identify targets and get lined up for a run or dive. Somebody called Mayday three times, a pause, another call, then silence. A different voice blurted out. "These SOBs have me zeroed in; do something dammit!" That one got my imagination working.

Another guy called that he had been hit and then said his engine had just quit. He must have gotten it running again though—with great relief, I'll bet. There was a lot of cussing, obviously hot work down there.

My section of eight 86s patrolled at the medium altitude of 20,000 feet and we all had itchy trigger fingers expecting opposition to this big operation. I was thumbing the sun again and called out bogies hidden in the glare at two o'clock high. As they became more distinct I counted eight approaching in a curve over us. At the point when they seemed about ready to roll down I recognized them as Meteors. Somewhat of a letdown, and it was frustrating to sit up there and not be able to take part in the action down below. A voice said he was going to try to make it to water beyond the coast, and as we departed another stated, "One down 45 miles south of Ping Pong."

When at last I came clumping back into my canvas home, Park, our new houseboy, asked, "Where you go? You fly?" And he made his hands go. I've been trying to teach this kid some geography, and after I answered, "Yes, we fly," I pointed to Ping Pong on my map and said, "Pyongyang—boom!"

Park replied, "Pyongyang? Oh, thank you."

More fellows that we knew in the Clobber College have come over for their start in missions and Charlie Mitson is in my tent now. Todd, Mitson, and I darn near cracked up while trading pidgin English with Park. Our attempts at conversation turned into a comedy of misunderstanding with all of us laughing and resorting to occasional sign language to get ideas across.

AUGUST 16th

I can never figure out what the peace conference is going to do from one day or week to the next. The Communists sound like they really want a cease-fire and yet they are pouring men and equipment into North Korea all the while the talks go on. While we occasionally discuss this, we know it's out of our hands—right now we have our own priority job to concentrate on.

I suppose that by this time next week I'll be heading back to my Squadron, the 336th. While I'm happy to rejoin my own gang, I don't look forward to returning to Johnson Field; I've had my fill of *that* routine. My hope is that the 336th will get back over here soon. I can't stand being in Japan *reading* about the war when I can be here *in* it.

Author in cockpit of F-86 at the end of a mission at K-13, Suwon, August 1951. The cockpit fit just right and with the sliding canopy closed, the visibility was the finest of any fighter—a very important factor in aerial combat. The "V" windshield was a feature of the A and early E models. The pierced steel planking for runway surfacing is visible behind the swept wings.

A new experience came my way on the 17th as I went to Combat Ops at 6:00 p.m. to serve as Duty Officer all night. A rat race is the best description of what that tour of duty developed into. We had two Blue Alerts and one Red Alert. I stepped outside the building frequently with the Army antiaircraft duty officer who was in charge of all the flak guns on the base. We would stand on the observation platform in our sandbagged enclosure listening for aircraft engines and attempt to spot the planes. Two armed T-6s and one F4U Corsair had been scrambled for night intercept, and while we were busy inside on our separate communications nets whenever one of these would go overhead, the Army duty officer, probably repeating his gunners' questions, would come off his phone and ask, "Can we shoot now? Can we shoot?"

I just repeated one stock answer: "No, no. Not yet." I was in a sweat because I knew if those flak guys ever cut loose there'd be no stopping them—and I only needed one guess as to who would be shot down, since the blasted intruder bogie that caused all the turmoil just milled around the base perimeter. Our GCA unit painted him occasionally, but he never came on in. I had to deal with 16 separate phones hanging in a row, each with a metal tag that dropped to indicate a call. That was so crude that two or three tags would flop on almost every single call and I not only answered the wrong line but couldn't keep track of who I was talking to as it seemed everybody in the world wanted to know what was going on. I got absolutely groggy running in and out and grabbing at phones, and even caught myself nodding off from lack of sleep. In spite of the seriousness of the job, I almost laughed at such comical confusion. It reminded me of some of the goofy actions suitable for a scene in an episode of *The Three Stooges*.

The missions of the 16th and 17th were scrubbed by weather, and though it opened up again yesterday, the night duty scratched me from the morning mission and I was glad to get some sleep. Upon waking up later I was anything but glad about the news the mission brought back that the MiGs had really come up and everybody had had a great fight. Dick Becker had shot down two MiGs, making four for his total score. Both MiG pilots bailed out. Hoot Gibson is behind now and really chafing.

In hopes of getting on the afternoon mission I attended the briefing, and last-minute aircraft additions got me a slot in what looked like sure action. When the other squadron got attacked by MiGs, my pack broke up to go after bogies and I followed my leader in speed runs around the area while listening to the fight talk and trying to figure out what he was chasing in such a hurry. We call Bingo fuel at 250 gallons and when he pulled out before that it was obvious that the only urgent business he had was back home. As a wingman you can sure get stuck with some choice prizes, and that guy is a fair-haired one in the outfit.

AUGUST 20th

Yesterday there was another red hot mission in the morning—damn, I hate to miss those good ones. Starkweather drove the weapons carrier and I accompanied him for pilot pickup. We went first to the end of the runway and watched the boys come by and turn off for the parking area. They had no tanks on, so we knew they had had some action. Presently, I saw this odd-looking 86 rolling by. It appeared sort of flat on top and then I realized the canopy plexiglass was blown out. But the tail—what a crumpled mess that right stabilizer and elevator were. When we drove over we could see daylight through holes in the aft section. The pilot was Todd, his hand was cut up and bloody, and as he got out he said, "That's a Purple Heart." He wasn't in the least shook up and said they had been in a turn when he got hit; it got pretty noisy and drafty, but that ol' 86 flew home real nice. We got a laugh out of his description, and a boost on the durability of the 86.

Hoot Gibson and I both made the afternoon team. The F-80s seemed slow in finishing their work while Dentist was calling in

The author suited up and ready to go on a mission at K-13, Suwon, Korea. The map in hand is still in his possession today, grease pencil marks and all.

46

trains leaving the station and operating in the Roulette area.[3] We patrolled along the Chongchon, starting by Sinanju and continuing well up the river. I figured in the briefing that the MiGs would not come down there to fight, and so did Hoot. And they didn't, not that that was any satisfaction, so we ended up with another ingenious lock-step patrol which I turned into another geography lesson, scanning the mountain country in that part of North Korea.

Today I was picked for a flight to Kimpo as copilot on the C-47 with ol' clanky. I explored a little around the base while I was looking for a friend stationed there who had gotten the unlucky job of Base Korean Labor Officer. When I found that he was away in Suwon on business, I went on about the trip and flew back to K-13. The slow flight up and back at a thousand feet was an enjoyable chance to scrutinize the countryside, and I noticed that there was a surprising amount of air traffic at K-14. I didn't bother to log the C-47 time—who needs *that* in a fighter outfit?

AUGUST 25th

I got used to the living at K-13 and it was sort of a wrench to see everything torn up for the move. Most people would consider camp life mighty crude, but just as I knew it would, the atmosphere of a fighter base in combat appeals to me. The mere sound of engines cranking up sets off my imagination, reminding me of the exciting days in flying school when everything was new. In that frame of mind maybe I expect too much, because I get impatient with the lack of innovation in some of our patrol beats and have to keep telling myself: "Keep your shirt on kid, you're learning all the time." My combat familiarization tour as an attached pilot was finished when I completed my tenth mission on the 22nd, and I figured that was that. But when I packed and attempted to clear out, I discovered our couriers were not running to Japan and my records had all been transferred in preparation for the general move to Kimpo, so I was stuck until the whole switch was over. I certainly was not going to leave without my flight and pay records.

That move yesterday was a real mad circus operation conducted in deep mud and rain, sorting and loading mountains of equipment. I finally bummed a ride by shuttle plane with Mitson, after sending our personal gear by truck. The situation at Kimpo was in the expected turmoil, and after locating our assigned tent we joined in the baggage-hauling, which got us all lathered in sweat.

Before I found my personal stuff, operations wanted me on the strip alert they were planning so I rushed off to locate my flying equipment. In the meantime, they must have considered my ten-mission quota, and placed Todd on the alert detail. Operations was putting together a good mission, and although I was not eligible I knew Todd was and wanted to get on it for his tenth mission, so I talked my way into relieving him from alert. I had a secret hunch that I'd probably get scrambled and that way get to sneak in some action and an extra mission.

Things happened faster than I expected. At the very moment I arrived at the alert site, a scramble was ordered. There was no time to check anything; while the alert leader fired up I dashed to the other plane, hopped in, slung straps and threw switches as I got the APU. The lead aircraft leaped off and I poured on the coal to get on the runway and follow. My gosh, my rudder pedals were all the way forward, but I was moving and it was too late for an opportunity to stop and adjust them so I just charged off on the run. What a takeoff! The runway was rough as hell and I lurched and bounced using what little brake I could stretch for as I didn't have enough reach to obtain nosewheel steering. I lost sight of the lead aircraft smoke trail and as we had been scrambled so suddenly with no briefing, I was completely in the dark about the score. I climbed out on a northwest heading and, several channel changes later, came upon the right one, went on north of Inchon, and orbitted the peninsula south of Chinnampo where I called for lead's position. He gave me some coordinates, but as I had not been given an alert map they were of no help, so he finally told me he was over Chinnampo. I steamed over at 15,000 feet and 100 percent, saying nothing more. When I picked him out below at 8 or 9,000 I shoved the stick forward and plunged down. We then dove together for the deck at Chinnampo and headed for the mouth of the Taedong River.

Control wanted us to search for four enemy boats in the Taedong that runs by Pyongyang down to Chinnampo. We spread out, keeping each other in sight, and charged along the river shore and out to the islands at the mouth. I sure wanted to find something to shoot up and though I eyeballed everything, our search provided no targets. I saw some small fishing boats and then heard over the radio that control was seeking some ships of 8,000 tons. What a joke!

As there was no flak seen, we were somewhat oblivious to

hazards and after buzzing all over the area we finally broke off the search with clearance to come home over the port of Inchon, which provided a close view of that usually restricted zone. Even though it didn't amount to much I enjoyed the mission. At least it was different. When we came in for my first landing at Kimpo I was still intent on making those slow short-field landings and cut it so fine I ran out of glide stretcher, dropping my bird in slightly short and hard. A rather embarrassing way to arrive—in a cloud of dust.

No sooner had we been refueled than we were scrambled again. On the second go we were directed to CAP east and west of Sohung, south of Pyongyang. I was so tickled about flying again I could hardly fit the oxygen mask over my grin and as we climbed north I had a good laugh at getting twelve missions instead of ten while my squadron was stuck in Japan.

My humor was quickly forgotten, for presently we heard many parachutes being called out and I thought, "What's going on, is the whole Air Force getting shot down?" Then I figured all the talking was about a bomber, and sure enough a B-29 was shot down with seven or eight 'chutes sighted. Another B-29 was heading for the sea and Japan with one engine shot out. We listened to some commentary by guys above who were observing the bail-outs. They could see that, as these fellows hit the ground, they were scrambling for safety while the Commies were gobbling them up. It made my sweat run cold.

Col. Preston came up on our GCI channel and called in one MiG destroyed—another good fight! Dentist Control told us to identify every aircraft and flight coming through so we dove down on F-51s and F-80s and called in types and numbers of aircraft. You should have seen those 80s break—I thought for sure we were going to get shot at. Those guys don't like swept-wing aircraft in their vicinity. To reduce our interference with friendly flights, we went over them with a full head of steam and zoomed back up after the briefest possible identification runs, but even so those boys were really bending wings and turning like cats chasing their tails. One gaggle of seven F-80s didn't even see us as we dove and curved behind them. This 86 is really a wonderful plane; what a joy the way it responds and when it's really moving what a difference in performance. All that cavorting around was pleasant exercise after the hole-boring of some of the missions. When I came in for that landing, I set down smooth and a bit faster to correct for my first dusty job. Not long after, darkness ended the alert duty and we packed off to our new tents. What a day! We were all pooped out and gooey with grime, and still had to sort out our baggage before settling in for the night.

Today, after collecting all my records and updated Form 5, darned if I didn't get stymied in another transportation snarl. That left the day and evening to watch the outfit settle in and discuss ways to start anew and spruce up these tents according to the tastes of each flight.

Author's father stepping from Curtiss F-Boat, Pensacola, FL. This was after his solo on July 21, 1915 and photo was signed with exuberance, "In the Air" TomE. Another rare photo.

50

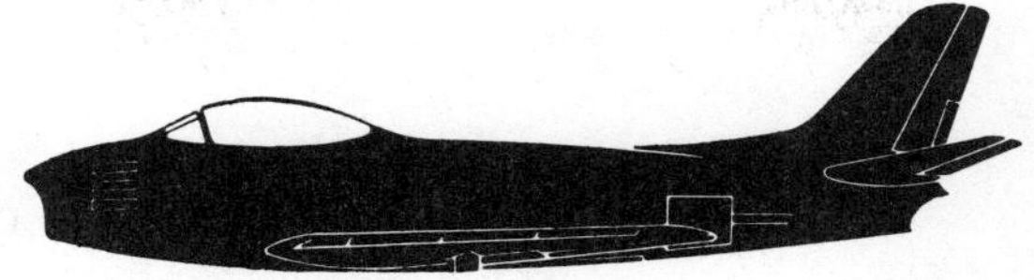

IV
Interlude along the Way

I'm not at all enthused about coming back to Johnson after a good start of twelve missions. This squadron rotation really fouls up the concentration you need in a combat tour. At least now I have the satisfaction of knowing the combat area and the procedures used over there.

Air transportation was still in a bind on the 26th when I departed Korea. While bumming my way, I onloaded and offloaded baggage between so many trucks and airplanes my proficiency became a very nasty habit. There was not just my personal gear but that of two other pilots who had to leave without theirs—in all, eight barracks bags, footlockers, and suitcases. This safari took all day and most of the night. By the time I arrived here long after midnight, riding a weapons carrier from Tachikawa, I looked and smelled like a real bum, and was in the mood for a dawn strafing mission using the baggage for bombs.

After these months of persistence, the Clobber College, and combat initiation with the Group, I'm glad to finally identify with my own squadron. It sure gave me a good feeling to see the fellows in the 336th again, and I know it will be great flying combat with my own gang.

No doubt about it, camp life promotes an appreciation of ordinary comforts. My clothes have been laundered, the shower is always available, and there is the choice of the mess hall or a menu in the O-Club. With no particularly pressing duties, I took my 'chute to the shop for some needed attention—the canopy has had a colorful way of dangling out of the pack that seemed to shake up folks when they saw that I had to frequently stuff it together. My remark has been that I only wear it as a formality; I sure don't intend to use the thing. Now that I'm settled for good in the 336th I also taped up my helmet for painting in the squadron colors—the last touch in membership.

During the course of what began as a normal day, those of us on the flight line began listening to the ops radio and the problems of one of the new pilots in Clobber College who was flying one of our F-86s. He had gotten himself lost in the dense haze somewhere in the local area. In spite of DF and GCI attempts he never did get squared away and kept calling in his fuel state as it went lower and lower until finally he was told to bail out before he flamed out from fuel exhaustion. What a suspense scenario that was. The pilot ejected okay and the doggoned airplane completed an almost perfect belly-in in a rice paddy all by itself. When they carted it into Johnson you had to get close to see that the bird had been bent.

The pilot's story was something: He bent forward in the seat to be clear of the canopy while checking the seat levers and trigger, and the seat went off causing him to almost swallow the joystick. He described the sensation of exit as having the plane falling suddenly away from him. As he wasn't prepared for departure, he hadn't yet put his heels in the stirrups, so he got terrible bruises on each calf and such a kink in his back he looked like he had a chair strapped on. We couldn't help but laugh over the comical aspects of the story, even though it means one plane less in our already skeleton resources.

My persistent heat rash and inflammation from scratching isn't about to clear up in this gluey climate so I went on sick call to get some medicine that might work. In the cool of the evening, when the sun goes down, the one medicine that works around here is bottled in bond, and in happy company the night after my arrival I met a guy named Bruce Iverson. We had a real session when we discovered that both of our fathers had been in World War I. How I love to yak about the planes and stories of that war. What makes the subject even better is that now I'm in that kind of flying myself.

SEPTEMBER 8th

On the last day of August I got off on two flights. The first was a scramble from strip alert to chase after a B-45, a plane I hadn't seen since the big performance demonstration at Andrews Field between the B-45, the RAF Canberra, and the Martin B-51 which I observed from the Air Guard ramp. We finally bounced this joker and I was impressed by his performance. The 45 seems to maneuver quite well and can really move along even though it does have straight wings.

In the afternoon I went up as part of a big escort gaggle for Prime Minister Yoshida of Japan who was in an Air Force C-97. We hear he was going to the States for the big treaty signing. The weather was terrible, but we leaped off a max effort of twelve ships and bored right over Tokyo in stinking visibility with a ceiling that was well below 1,000 feet. Then we proceeded to make many orbits in show formation—a real hairy workout. We finally saw the C-97 for a short time and then groped our way home where we all made two hot formation passes on the field before landing.

Saturday night there was a big smasheroo party thrown in the club annex. I went on an empty stomach directly from alert and by the time my buddy Panter got off alert and joined in, I was really wound up. The boys started a football game around the bar, tossing glasses back and forth and dodging around until somebody skidded on his face on the concrete and the game moved outside. The game broke up when two of the boys ran head-on into each other in the dark like two billy goats—it was painful enough just to *hear* the collision. The gathering then adjourned to the main club where for some reason the firewater changed from whiskey to champagne. I don't know where all the champagne came from, but I bought a bottle and drank plenty of what was available. I did manage to eat in the middle of all this—or should I say, I fed my face. We sure have a great bunch of kerosene cowboys and were pretty close to the speed of sound that night. After the quiet

Author in F-86A flying over clouds in vicinity of Mt. Fujiyama, Japan, on an air defense intercept mission, September 1951.

attached time in Korea, I was out of training for that kind of action. Needless to say, I had a lovely hangover the next day.

The situation is heating up fast in MiG Alley, according to the latest word, and the general feeling is that we might as well live it up while waiting our turn. We're supposed to go back shortly and I want to look around Seoul now that the Group is at Kimpo. The Australian outfit is there too and I intend to check up on the hospitality offered by those Aussies I met here in July.

I got my first flight for September on Monday, the 3rd, with "Swabby" Evans. We scrambled from alert and after the bogie was identified we tooled all over the area at 5,000 feet, using DF for fixes and position reports. Swabby pointed out old Japanese airfields he had strafed in WWII while flying F6Fs off of carriers. We did a loop in trail and then took turns in line abreast rolls and half rolls, eyeing each other's performance.

The next day I flew from alert again and Chris and I had a slam-bang toboggan race over the clouds. We practiced a high fast instrument letdown with all the garbage extended under the control of GCI; right at the bottom, while sucking up our gear and

Trying out the new Argus C-3 camera. Author's pal "High Mach" Panter poised to race the Sabre. Johnson Field ramp.

flaps, we got tangled up with F-51s and F-80s. We were so slow at that awkward moment that I laughingly compared our situation to that of a cougar falling out of a tree into a pack of eager hounds. Those boys were all over us. One hot tiger in a 51 glommed onto me so tight I expected to see his buzz saw make sawdust fly from my tail. I could just imagine their glee at catching 86s with their drawers down. They had us dead to rights, of course, but I was all primed for sport, and with nose down and full throttle, in two shakes I pulled away to play a few stunts of my own. With decent speed built up I zoomed into such a big loop that upside down at the top I could tell they'd lost me, so I came smoking down at their tails and went through their pack from one to the other like a ricoheting bullet. Boy, it's a great feeling to know that everybody is raring for a good scrap. The best school for fighter pilots is fun fighting—it exposes you to all kinds of crazy situations *and* promotes that all-important tiger attitude.

Yesterday Turner advised me that another bunch of cameras were on sale at our PX, so I raced over from the flight line and quickly made up my mind to buy an Argus C-3. With all the extras it came to $45.00. It looks like a real good deal to me. Now all I have to do is learn how to operate the thing, as I'm only checked out on box cameras.[4]

SEPTEMBER 10th

Last weekend, Panter called from Tokyo, where he is on a short leave; when I got the message I called back for a rendezvous. Torres and Griffith decided to go and Reeves joined in, so with the fare split to a reasonable amount each, we all piled into a taxi and roared off into the big city. Here and there in the center of Tokyo there are still evidences of the bombing during the war and the cabbies usually explain the Emperor's island-like residence as "Number One House." We dropped off at the Tokyo Electric Bar for a fast start, got a jeep ride to one of the other clubs to keep up the rpm, and then off to the Union Club where we walked in on a happy crowd. That was quite a thirsty gathering and we all got half gassed—especially since the time changed, giving everyone an extra hour for practice.

Our gang stayed at the New York Hotel and the next morning we ambled through the stores and stalls along the Ginza while waiting for the PX to open. It was a welcome relief to get a change of view from the airbase ritual.

That Tokyo PX is an amazing place, and I had a lot more time

Photo taken with new camera in front of "Clobber College" operations at Johnson Field, Japan. Left to right: Panter, McPherson, Kotok. September 1951.

available than on my first short visit. We shopped around over all five floors while trying to keep together in the constant rush of crowds. I don't believe there is a thing under the sun that the PX doesn't have—every necessity, trinket, and luxury was on display. A constant stream of uniforms of every branch of service were seen. In fact I believe every armed force uniform in the United Nations Command, if not the world, was represented. There were many service women, and service wives were there in force with kids scrambling about. The atmosphere was sort of overwhelming. Yes, the rigors of this overseas duty are tough to take. I didn't have much money to spare after buying that camera the other day and paying off my GI insurance for another year. Most of my dough goes home in the allotment because I figured I wouldn't require much in Korea and didn't expect to spend so much time in Japan.

After an interesting two-hour trip by train, we got back to the base in time for a smorgasbord. I felt starved and really piled into that chow, including some of the best prawns I've ever eaten. As the night was young, we formed a small group in the inside party room and soon some visiting homesteaders gathered with their attractive wives, which helped our morale a lot. Fortunately, we have a good gang and it makes up for our odd situation in this place. We really don't fit in with all these permanently based people and families—it's just a feeling you get and it keeps us closer together. That feeling warmed us up and I had a laugh-a-minute with Griffith, B.L. Smith, Bill Allnock and others—cowboy yells mingled with Smitty's "Fftooey!"

This morning I had a long bull session with Panter, after which several of us with time off decided to visit the flight line and take some pictures. It was a beautiful day and Dick Panter, Nick Kotok, Fred McPherson, and I got our pix and a little clowning around. I believe I'm transitioning well on my new camera.

TUESDAY, SEPTEMBER 11th

Most of our days are now spent on this endless strip alert or mobile control duty with flying cut to only a minimal essential schedule. There is the weather problem, too, which is so foul today we can expect no scramble flights from alert. So far this month I've only been on two flights. Our shortage of parts and airplanes is maddening. It will be murder it this war really breaks out. Actually, we should be doing even *more* flying than normal not *less*, to be in trim for combat. In all, I've been up about 60 hours in four months, which is about average for the pilots on my shipment.

After writing home good news about low losses darned if we didn't lose another pilot in combat—a good boy, too; I knew him real well. But, by golly, that sure was good news on the 9th: Dick Becker and Hoot Gibson making ace on the same day. How about that? That makes them the second and third jet aces of this war.

FRIDAY, SEPTEMBER 14th

I finally got another flight this morning, my third for the month—how hot can you get? Four of us F-86s escorted the C-97 carrying Prime Minister Yoshida to Haneda Field, Tokyo, on his return from the treaty-signing in the States. We were hanging at 150 knots and 70 percent in close formation. It all looked sharp, but we remarked afterwards about feeling on the verge of spinning in at such airspeeds. Another ship took pictures of the formation and I wonder what they'll do with them; we'd all like to see how they turned out.

Another bunch of the boys are leaving for home today or tomorrow. Those are the fellows who came over with the 4th Group. I see that I'm due for rotation in February or March, but I sure don't plan on anything as the lists change sometimes. In fact, I don't like forecasts; they get combat people thinking about things

F-86As lined up on the alert pad for air defense at Johnson Field, Japan, September 1951.

other than the job, and that's no good for your attitude or ability. At least that's the way I feel about it.

The fellows on the way home say the MiGs are really getting hot now—and why not, they've had all this time to get ready and acquire experience. We get reports that they are flying like crazy, training in the Antung area. They are all business now, know what they're after, and are putting up odds of three or five to one against us most of the time. It makes me think, especially when we must sit on the ground here sweating out parts for our few planes.

On the last two strip alerts the weather was so hopeless we were placed on 30 minute standby. Yesterday it rained all day, and though I had runway control I was able to stand by on call in the BOQ so I proceeded to get on with some writing. In the afternoon I played numerous hot rounds of ping pong and I'm happy to say my game is improving. There are some pretty sharp players in the gang, but I'm moving up. Regardless of what some people say about pilots playing ping pong during duty hours, I think it's a terrific way to sharpen up your reflexes. After all, what did we shoot skeet for in the Aviation Cadet Program in WWII? The same reason—and it payed off.

At the end of a washout day there was a small beer gathering in Dick Panter's and Al Reeser's quarters where we listened to the Ray Robinson-Randy Turpin boxing match. The fight sounded pretty good to us; maybe there will be a rematch. *Our* rematch will come up regularly when we return to Korea, so we have more excitement ahead than mere sporting events, which rank low under our interest in flying. Between rounds of the fight and while draping ourselves all over the available furniture, we talked about times back home, where Dick and Al will be going in November

Among the tents of the 336th Squadron living area. Dick Panter (left) and Al Reeser, Kimpo, Korea, fall of 1951. (photo from John P. Green collection)

with the last of the original boys. For the present, we have a close-knit bunch and I wish we could all get together in the same outfit in the future—a wish or dream that I suppose is as old as war. Many of these fellows got their wings together, and their recollections often cause me to think how great it would be to have some of my WWII buddies around; those who learn to fly together share a memorable bond. But in the fighter business you feel a mutual bond wherever you go—*if* you like the life and can get along.

It seems strange in a way to be around pilots younger than myself. I started flying so young I thought I'd never see anyone younger, and now here I am twenty-five, soon to be twenty-six, and some time ago I wrote big brother Tom, kidding him about turning thirty! From all these wars we are proving one thing: Experience is what counts, and the only way you get it is by adding flying years. I'm sure proud of the experience pooled in our family in two generations. We've had service in all the wars so far—*and* as pilots.

We got the word that Cliff Thompson got his face badly bashed in a crash over at Kimpo. It's a wonder he even got out of that one, with the plane breaking up and the fuselage ending up inverted in a canal off the end of the runway. A few of the fellows who are FIGMO are glad to be leaving here as there are some clanks from these latest missions. I still have a full range of curiosity to explore, and I want to find the answers for myself rather than get them second-hand.

SEPTEMBER 18th

Last Friday evening Panter, Shaw, and I decided we needed a change from Johnson Field so we took off for the Tachikawa O-Club. It was early in the evening so with our appetites, time on our hands, and me and my skinny wallet, we sat down to a steak dinner—how broke can you get? Things grew mighty dull and with a loss of interest in the Tachi Club we chose to switch to FEAMCOM where I believe Mike Alkire's dad was the Commanding General at the time Mike got killed in our Guard Squadron.

I'd never been to either of these places, so I was game for anything. After a long wait for a jeep taxi, we eventually made it over. What a plush place; they sure have a swanky club, although I understand there is generally not as much activity as at Johnson. Naturally, in such an established place we had to rent ties, and I suppose every place will eventually be back to ties and more formality.

While exploring around we strolled into the outside garden—a beautiful place, Japanese-style with a goldfish pond and arched foot bridge. Out in this garden pondering what to do, we detected noises that sounded like people were enjoying themselves somewhere. Our eyeball search landed on the second-story windows where it was apparent that a party was going on. This surely required an investigation, so we dutifully trotted inside and made the necessary inquiries, which uncovered the news that there was a promotion party in progress and new blood was welcome. Can you imagine? Wow!

We jumped right into the middle of this action. All the bourbon and champagne anyone could ask for *and* caviar—free! That was definitely the place for three wandering fighter pilots. Trying to catch up to the rest of the happy throng, we began on doubles with soda and stacking crackers with caviar. As we had finally heard definitely when we were returning to Frozen Chosen, we figured we'd better take advantage of this heaven-sent opportunity.

As that affair wound down, we were taken in with an endurance group and off to a continuation party. We sort of wondered who did the work around the place, but at the time who cared? There were a lot of late liver-uppers congregated around this session. In the middle of the fun, some guy started mouthing off about how he could lick any plane with a P-38. Naturally, this stirred me into a "discussion" which turned into a heated argument when he said he could easily wax a 51 with a 38. I was all set for a loaded gun test—what better way to solve the old air superiority argument?

Well, that party was more like several going at once. The three of us who had started out together pulled several more streamers through the place just so they'd know there were people involved in the war. I don't think we'll be invited again, but our time in Japan has about run out anyhow.

Saturday night the Johnson Club put on a Hawaiian show, and though it didn't come up to the advance publicity, it did draw in a fair crowd. Our squadron reserved four tables in the very front rank so we could have a compact little group. I wore a lei of flowers all night; it seemed the thing to do. After the show we had a real bottoms-up time singing songs like mad in our usual popular fashion. I was about broke and that performance finished off my finances. Being broke is one of those situations commonly known as a nasty break so I've had to pull in my horns for a quiet spell of reading and writing.

Yesterday four of us went up to fight in elements of two—myself and Neubert, Green and Beck. We had a fine slam-bang flight from which all of us were thoroughly beat out. We split off and reattacked each other again and again, zooming around clouds in the vicinity that we occasionally used for cover and surprise. That was a real strenuous go after so little flying for everybody this month. In fact, it was that flight that finally gave me my four hours time to claim flight pay for the month. Without the spirit that this outfit has, how could we make it under these conditions? When we landed after our much-needed exercise, the boys in operations said our radio conversations sounded like a real war had been going on.

Everyone is by now pretty well charged up to rejoin the real war. I know *I* am; this waiting while thrashing about the fringes of occupation duty is about to drive me ape. I will admit though that

One corner of the tent occupied by A Flight, 336th Fighter Squadron. Author's cot is beside table. Each pilot had a mosquito bar to hang over his cot. Due to bare facilities, most personal belongings remained packed in baggage to be taken out when needed. The table and cots with a stool or two were the only furnishings. Kimpo, September 1951.

this slack period, in between rounds so to speak, has been a lucky opportunity to get to know the 336th pilots better than I could have in any other way—a real benefit to latch onto in this nomadic life. The more a team knows its individual members, the better showing it will make against its opponents. We've had some good personal discussions comparing ideas about maneuvers and performance of the F-86 vs. The MiG-15, which I'm sure will benefit our coordination. I get more excited each day as the time approaches to put all this to the test.

SEPTEMBER 20th

Gee, yesterday was a swell day, or evening, or night. I was designated a troop commander on one of the C-54s that was to move our squadron over to Korea. Everybody spent the latter part of the day making sure their personal stuff and particular job equipment was sorted and packed, then assembled in the proper loading zone.

Before the late meeting, roll call, and briefing, I went over to the club where I was grabbed by each arm and swept along with the tide into a final party. I joined the forces: Smith, Bryant,

Hungerford, Thompson, Gibson, Reeser and so many others—all happy faces. Woohaa! I thought I was through after Saturday night, but it seems I can always stand one more. I was broke before this all started—that's why the boys hauled me in—so naturally I didn't get a chance to spend anything. Panter had a date and kept himself separate from us "quiet" fellas.

The club was staging another of their shows; this one started off with a Japanese simultaneously playing the guitar and har-monica while a bike-riding monkey skimmed the edge of the audience and seemed eager to bite anyone leaning out for a closer look. Then they brought on the dancing girls. We agreed that it sure was thoughtful of the homesteaders at Johnson to put on such a show—fiendish of them is a better description—dancing girls on the night we're returning to Korea! It was a good show and party, though. We said *sayonara* with doubles and then headed for the line where the roll call and briefing came off at 11:00 p.m.

I checked off umpteen pages of manifests making sure all my troops and share of equipment were on board my aircraft and we were finally all set by 3:00 a.m.! Panter rode with me and during the long dark trip we shared a blanket spread over some cargo boxes to get rather uncomfortable naps while droning across the drink.

We were all completely pooped when we arrived at K-14 at 7:30 this morning with the early sun shining brightly off our red eyeballs. After signing over the cargo and manifests I found A Flight and unloaded my duffle into my new little tent home. Good ol' Charlie Mitson is with me and we're already laughing about being in good company.

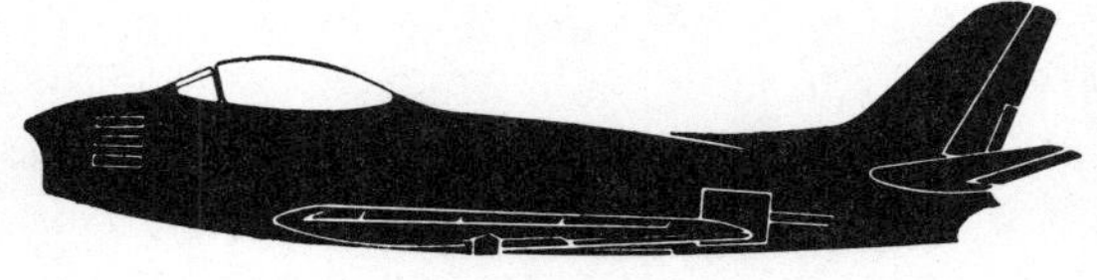

V

Bedcheck Charlie and Other Warmups

K-14 KIMPO, KOREA
FRIDAY, SEPTEMBER 21st

So here we are back in lovely old Korea, roaring like tigers—or is it meeowing like kittens? The MiGs are fighting like treed tigers now from the sound of all the latest war stories. This morning I stood air defense alert with Charlie until noon. Like the last time I was here at Kimpo, I figured I'd get scrambled as a hot mission had been sent out and this time I had the lead. After a long wait the mission turned into a fizzle. There were no MiGs, so no dogfight and no scramble. Nuts.

Later on, Charlie and I and two others went to see Yong Dong Po. I just absorbed the view as we rolled along through the farm and hill country. The town was interesting with plenty of dust and odors to share with visitors. Some of the thatched roofs were so thick and old they had melons growing out of them. Living conditions were pretty rough and parts of the town were barely hanging on. It's been a helluva war for these folks, but nothing seems to stop the carefree happiness of kids and there were lots of naked little ones running around. The high-waisted dresses of the women which seemed a bit odd required only short loose tops and this style made it all very simple to serve the infants their lunch. There was a congestion of little shops selling all kinds of knick-knacks, just about anything to make a little *won* and we noted prices to figure out the exchange rate. I browsed around getting ideas for an extra set of slip-on boots to wear around camp, but was leery of the tanning process as some of the leather goods had a powerful smell. The trip was really just a short excursion to get acquainted with the countryside around Kimpo. When time is available, I plan on making another trip to take some pictures and Charlie agrees to go with me. One advantage of being in Korea is the informal camp life and the wearing of fatigues, the only sensible way to go in this alternating dust and mud. The main disadvantage at Kimpo is that the showers are over a half mile from our tents, and the dusty hike fouls up the benefits of the battle of the bath. Hey, I hear we have a mission tomorrow . . . hope I'm on it.

SUNDAY, SEPTEMBER 23rd

Yesterday morning I went up for mission #13 and flew wing on Col. Preston, the 4th Group Commander. Oh, it was a beautiful day and the formation flying and maneuvering was a real pleasure except that my damned survival vest almost broke my bones. We all often wonder what genius designs pilot's personal equipment—surely no one who cares to fly. We couldn't locate any MiGs, but perhaps it was just as well as I needed a good patrol hunt and workout to get the accumulated rust of these last weeks off of me. My windshield frosted up in the traffic pattern and I landed hot as hell as I could only see out of the corners of the side panels and sure didn't want to land short and leave my wheels behind like one of the boys did at Johnson.

Late in the afternoon I read a little of Sherlock Holmes and after supper Walt Raby, who I had first met at Camp Stoneman, came by with a jeep and drove me to his tent in the 4th Air Base Group area. Raby works in Base Operations, and on the stopovers of his many C-46 and C-47 courier flights between Korea and Johnson we had become good friends. We looked at a bunch of photo magazines and had a few cool beers along with laughs about some of the highjinks back at Johnson Field. When I got to my area after the visit with Walt I crawled into my sack—a folding cot, and my sleeper for the duration. But just before doing so I moved it from the mid-tent position, opposite the red-hot kerosene heater, to in front of the door as I can't sleep in so much heat. This new location was to cause complications.

After really getting into a sound sleep I was semi-awakened by the drone of a plane and the weird tune of sirens. I wasn't sure if I was dreaming or just what until guys commenced scrambling around in the dark and calling out, "Hey, wake up—air raid!" And then we sleepy types gathered that an air raid was on. As I was fumbling into some trousers and probing for my boots under the bunk a terrific *bang* close by made me jump and then all the flak guns in the area were roaring away. What had been a scramble in the tent turned into a stampede full of boots, knees, and curses that proceeded over me as I was squashed into a heap on my sack in the race for the door. I was still damned if I'd run out barefoot in that slop outdoors and get fungus of the bungus or worse. I jammed on my boots and made tracks out to the zig-zag of sandbags that serve as a bomb shelter.

While shivering outside in our skivvies we got the obvious word that the big noise was a close bomb, one of several dropped by the boys from up north. The cold really got to us, so after awhile some of us said to hell with it and went back to bed, leaving the rest to massage their goosebumps.

I was almost asleep again when I heard engines—unsynchronized twin types—thrumming in our direction. I thought, "Hell, that couldn't be Bedcheck Charlie. That sounds like a B-26." At that moment it really hit the fan and everything cut loose again. I crouched just as I stepped out of bed and then another pilot in the tent and I dashed to the door in our skivvies. What a fireworks display! All sizes of tracers were streaming up through the night sky with flashes of explosions higher up. The pilot of the aircraft in question had put the cob to both engines and that added to the general din of the guns. You could tell the flight path of the plane by the flak along its route, and I also noted navigation lights on the

The 4th Fighter Group Combat Operations building under construction at K-14, Kimpo, after the move from K-13, Suwon. This was where pre-mission briefings for pilots were held, as well as post-mission debriefings.

aircraft, which was really hauling it by that time. We heard later it was one of our B-26s returning from a night mission and entering the traffic. This Army triple-A is sure trigger-happy and once they start shooting they are hard to stop. Though the 26 got away apparently unscratched, I'll bet the crew was in a monumental rage. I'd have been tempted to strafe the place after a reception like that, but of course it's very bad luck to fly into a base right after an air raid.

The flak was all very impressive and the two of us sat around yakking about it before crawling back into bed. The all-clear came a bit later while I was already snug in bed, and the only disturbance was the cursing of the returnees from the bomb shelter when they found the two of us comfortable in our warm bunks. A few of us felt that pneumonia was a greater danger than Bedcheck Charlie, and you might break your neck falling over or into something in a dash in the dark. They accomplished their job though, as we were all pretty sleepy when we got up for the day's work.

This morning, all bushy-tailed for action, I taxied out for a mission and had to abort at the last minute when the tailpipe temperature went overboard and the aft fire warning light flickered on during the run-up—of all the blasted luck. As I then had time on my hands, I went to look at the bomb craters from last night. While they weren't very big, a couple of our 86s did get some damage, and one obvious dud made a nice clean hole as it buried itself in our immediate area.

Yesterday afternoon after the mission, I took a walk around

Meteor Mk.8s of No. 77 Fighter Squadron, Royal Australian Air Force (RAAF). These British Gloster-built twin engine jet fighters are being refueled on the alert pad at Kimpo, K-14.

Meteor Mk.8 of No. 77 Fighter Squadron, Royal Australian Air Force (RAAF). Gun ports of two of the 20mm cannon are visible in nose.

our working area and finished up my first roll of 35mm film. I talked to the two Australian Meteor pilots on pad alert along with our planes, and snapped their ships among other subjects. It gets quite warm during two or three hours of the midday; the rest of the day is cool, with the nights cold. I sure like autumn weather; it's too bad it can't remain just as it is. One of the fellows is now getting a haircut from our traveling Korean barber. I have to see the outcome of *this* operation. The radio is also entertaining us with a war story—what a thrill.

A couple of fellows in my tent have shortwave radios and by the news broadcast, when we got up this morning, we heard that three aircraft raided the Seoul area last night and one was shot down in flames by a night fighter. The Reds are building up a terrific air strength in Manchuria, and we wonder if they will really come over in earnest. Peking Radio says they are going to hang all the pilots in the 4th Fighter Group from the frame of the old burned-out hangar on the field. This used to be Seoul's municipal airport and was badly beat up as it changed hands in the ground fighting. I'm getting some pictures of the shot-up administration building, hangar, etc.

SEPTEMBER 29th

On the evening of 23 Sept., while I was on strip alert, the demolition boys detonated the dud bomb. They built up a circular pile of sandbags around it like the structure over an old well. We pilots were watching from close by on the alert pad as the charge was set off. What a blast—there was a big flash and dirt and rocks went up in a column followed by some of the sandbags. Those sandbags were what worried me—one of them on the head would drive you into the ground like a tent peg. I was ready to dive under my plane if they came down among us—better my plane than my head. They came slap-bang down around the bomb area and gave all the watchers a thrill. The close explosion was just like the slamming of a giant door. I'll bet the demolition charge was a hell of a lot bigger than the bomb, as the results seemed a bit larger than expected. It must be a hell of an experience to be under a really *big* air raid with thousand-pounders dropping around you. Holy smoke!

I believe it was Monday, 24 Sept., that a bunch of us took our weapons carrier (3/4 ton) for a short tour of Yong Dong Po and Seoul. We took a bit of our personal whiskey with us as we had heart it was good barter for boots and other junk and we were still short on issue stuff. We weren't very keen businessmen, so decided during the trip we would keep our hooch to cheer up our tent life. We stopped on the Han River bridge (the others were demolished in the fighting over the area) and took some pictures. While trying to adjust his camera one of the boys dropped his fifth on the bridge in one of those wincing crashes. The rest of us got a laugh out of that, but he was a bit slow in coming around to our sense of humor.

After the bridge interlude we went on into the city of Seoul for

U.S. Army anti-aircraft gun emplacement, quad .50s mounted on a halftrack (M16). Parked F-86s and the old Kimpo hangar and terminal building in background.

my first look at the place, so I was taking in everything. You sure didn't have to be told that a real shooting war was on. There were some real modern imposing structures beat all to the devil, slashes and big gaping holes in many that were struggling to stand with sagging walls. On close scrutiny we found many buildings were just shells in which the interiors had collapsed. Other structures had been pocked all over by shell fragments. One tall tower that we guessed was for fire lookout had been zapped by some high-powered sharpshooters. There were blocks and blocks completely pulverized with a few people here and there going in and out of basements like cave dwellers. We made a circular tour about twice around the main part of the city. The capitol building was sure impressive at the end of a broad avenue—somewhat damaged, but there were repairs underway. Some of the boulevards were quite wide and we noticed a number of Korean women working as traffic cops while standing on little islands at the intersections.

We then looked for 5th Air Force Headquarters and found it out of the way amongst large trees behind a wall and fence. It was made up of very nice buildings with no evidence of damage, like a hidden sanctuary. Some said it had been the University before the war. I figured both sides must have used it for the same purpose—Headquarters—and each had spared it for high-level accommodations as it changed hands.

The burned-out hangar and bullet-pitted terminal building at Kimpo. F-86 boresight target in center.

A scene on the tour of Seoul, capitol of Korea, in September 1951. Artillery or rocket holes are evident in what we assumed was a fire lookout tower.

Next we located their club (naturally); what a deal. We were told that it had at one time been a shrine or temple and it had great carved wooden beams, wide double doors, and even mirrors—quite colorful. It had a great long bar and plenty of plush furniture with all the best brands of liquor—some layout, a real live oasis, as I called it. We sensed that our crowd of fighter pilots was getting the evil eye from the staff people, what with out flying suits, fatiques, BO, and muddy boots. So after a couple of fast ones we piled back into our "limousine" and roared back to Kimpo for chow. It's quite a long trip, actually, and all our behinds were sore from sitting on the metal compartments and bouncing around in the stiff-jointed weapons carrier. Our mess had steak and I was so pleased I got on the outside of half a cow.

On the 25th there was a good mission. We had several aborts enroute, and after the necessary reshuffling I ended up on Capt. Paul Bryce's wing in lead of the squadron. The two of us proceeded way up north of everybody as the outfit went off hunting in several areas. Dentist called many trains in the area and this was all I needed to really get my head on a swivel and as I looked up—*oops*—four MiGs about one thousand feet over our heads going southeast. I thought for sure we had a fight as they were in a good position to bounce us. We wheeled around in preparation, but the MiGs went on into the sun. Then we observed flashes in all directions, with the usual comments back and forth over our radios. Four more appeared right on top of us with another flight of four off to their side. We were turning and weaving all the time, and chased after four more crossing high in front of us; we couldn't close as they went north hell-bent for home. We were kept on our toes all the time and I found it exciting work, but as we were both getting low on fuel we finally pulled out, climbing on a good Mach. We were the last two of our people out and though there were still MiGs all over, our fuel state prevented any more fooling around with those guys. Dentist warned to watch our tails as MiGs were around Ping Pong. Just north of the city we saw six MiGs on our left (the east) turn on our tails so Bryce dropped his nose slightly and we left those boys far behind. I felt it was a good mission because for me it meant building up more experience in seeing quickly, maneuvering properly as a wingman, and gaining confidence in general. We had heard one of the boys having trouble earlier and found out he made it home okay.

That night Charlie and I had lots more to talk about. Of course there are really only two absorbing activities around here: flying, and talking about flying.

There was another big mission the next morning, the 26th. The schedule was a little mixed up and as some changes were made I got put on element lead. Before we even got to the target area MiGs were called out below Sinanju and we dropped our tanks. A few guys had tanks that wouldn't drop so they pulled out, and as I began moving up on Blue Flight we all started the first turn on our patrol course. At that moment, looking back to clear, I saw there were MiGs all over right above, which promptly tipped over and came down on us in a great swarm. Man, they look ferocious when they shoot all their cannons. Their whole nose lights up and great blobs of fire flare out of the muzzles, pushing streaks of very nasty looking tracer shells. What those streaks can do if they hit—hmmm! They blaze away, throwing out a shower of shells even though their aim was off.

Blue Flight dove away in a curve and I let them go as I didn't care to lose altitude with so many MiGs right on top of us. I went into a fast weave, searching like mad until I saw four MiGs approaching on our level and cut into them as their path went across our noses. I fired at one of the four but couldn't hold a track at that altitude and angle-off and they scooted away.

Though the sky appeared suddenly and surprisingly vacant, we kept turning and clearing ourselves. The radio was a babble of fight talk as a lone MiG came high across in front of us. I started my nose up and changed my mind as I saw how fast he was going. Two

Front quartering view of MiG-15 flown to Kimpo Field, Korea, by defecting North Korean pilot shortly after the armistice in 1953. The MiG is in USAF markings for testing at Okinawa. Note the high distinctive T-tail and the three cannon barrels protruding under the nose intake (gun camera housing on top of intake). Two 20mm cannon on the left and one 37mm cannon on the right side of the nose—the dangerous view of the MiG. U.S. Air Force photo)

others that I decided to chase kept their distance, so when I spotted two closer I turned left and went after them. The hand spanning and ranging mechanism of my gunsight was out of whack, so the sight had been fixed at 1,000 feet (and pegged with a cotter pin!). Anyway, I squinted through it and took a shot at the wingman before they chandelled away.

There were so many MiGs and 86s going through our vicinity in fours, twos and singles that it was a bit confusing to decide which MiGs to try for a shot or which to look out for that were trying for a shot themselves. I'd see some to go after and then have to turn to throw off others diving on us from above. There must have been over a hundred MiGs involved in the action. I caught glimpses of planes going round and round while voices were shouting, "Break!"

And, "Look out for those two!"

"Hang on now, we'll take these guys."

"Heads up gang, there's more above, some coming down."

"Let's get those jokers, way over there."

My wingman, Hays, and I weren't saying beans. I was looking around too much to do a lot of talking. Instead of calling when I went after a MiG, I just headed for him. Two more showed up on the left so I turned left and then right to cut them off. At 30,000 feet we couldn't turn tight enough, so they had slipped well out as I got at their six. The MiG wingman was rocking wings, evidently watching and not liking us back there. I tried estimating range and lead with my "stone age" fixed sight and let go a blast. They simply chandelled and as we couldn't match that I just let them go and looked elsewhere.

Suddenly a MiG was coming head-on and slightly low—too late to duck my nose and fire, and he didn't shoot either. I don't know if he saw us, but he went by between Hays and me just a few feet below our level. This all took the snap of a finger, and even at that I got an exceptionally close look at him. I concentrated so intensely that the passing appeared like slow motion. What a beautiful shiny airplane! As some of the fellows have said, it looks like their noses are painted with blood, they are so vivid red. You can sure see those cannon jutting out under their noses, even at a distance.

More turns, each of us covering the other. Then Hays yelled, "Break right!"

We whipped around and down and over my left shoulder I caught a glimpse of the MiG, which kept on going. I had been turning on four MiGs approaching on our right and Hays had been on my right and behind, covering the left rear, where the MiG came from. He said later the first he knew of the MiG was the red cannon shells going over his head and he just broke as he called me. Hays cut inside of the turn while I kept getting a sharp right wing drop from sticking leading edge slats in the hard turns so I came around behind him to start a crossover. We dove for a little more airspeed, and just as I told him to continue turning until he locked on me, I saw four more MiGs behind which were gone before we could bend around. I dove on another four way out in front that must have seen me as they broke early and simply scattered out of the picture.

I didn't see many MiGs making very tight turns; they reminded me of sharks cruising through the scramble (cruising on the Mach, that is). Everybody was going like blazes. When aircraft approach each other at a combined speed of 1,000 miles per hour or therabouts, it's damned hard to turn back around and do any good—plus you have to be a hell of a lot quicker in your recognition than you did when everybody was flying prop jobs.

I jumped four more planes, then saw they were 86s, and as I pulled sharply back up, you should have seen them break. They thought we were MiGs and were yelling at each other. I didn't have much difficulty identifying MiGs and 86s, but two 86s jumped us and I watched them closing, met them in a curving head-on, and

Rear view of captured MiG-15 test firing its cannons on Okinawa, 1953. The large rudder, high T-tail, and mid-positioned wings are very distinctive identification features. The *best* view of the MiG. (U.S. Air Force photo)

ducked underneath. I don't think they identified us until the last second—another good lesson in taking nothing for granted.

I climbed again to get better altitude and, as our fuel was low by that time, we went home riding the Mach downhill. What a mission—woohaa! There was a big bull session at debriefing and we heard the bad news that young Barnett had been shot down in the fight. Darn near every mission in the last week or so has been a madhouse. Considering that we are often outnumbered three or four to one, we have done well. On yesterday's missions the gang got five MiGs—talk about a good show. For a morale booster and touch of humor, in Combat Operations there is a shelf on the wall with two small bottles labeled, "Pink Pills for Pale Pilots."

There are so many hundreds of MiGs now available up north that they send some south of the fight at high altitude to jump us on the way home. Dick Panter was going home by himself low on fuel sometime after his wingman lost him, and got jumped by eight MiGs that cornered him in a hell of a bind. He managed to maneuver them into a high angle-off, then pulled tight into them, dodged under before they could recover, dove toward the deck at full blast, and got away. I got the full story right after he got to his tent, where I found him laying on his cot—still hyperventilated and so infuriated at his wingman that he was considering shooting him.

The morning of the 27th, those of us not on the mission clustered about the operations radio listening to the gang as another serious fight developed. All of us were so tensed up that when we heard Dick Panter cry out an emergency break we nearly jumped out the nearest window. We could hear many trains being called out as the fight wound up with the usual sharp tense clamor of fight talk. In this case, not being personally involved, we could concentrate on each call and identify voices and individual problems that you don't catch when you are in the middle of it yourself. Having been there, the listening pilots could visualize what was going on. It gave me a prickly sensation; just sitting there listening made it seem hairier than when busily involved.

As soon as we heard someone was hit we looked at the flight lineup and found it was Kenny Rapp. He had spun out and no one knew what happened to him. We figured he'd had it as he wasn't on the radio. But, by golly, Ken appeared in the pattern and came in for a real find landing with his whole left aileron shot off and fragment holes in the fuselage, through his canopy, hard hat, and into his head. Boy, did everyone swarm around his plane when he parked. He was pretty bloody and completely pooped out. The troops helped him out of the cockpit and he just sat down on the ground in relief for a moment.

Ken said when he was hit he was dazed and didn't really know what was going on until he found himself in a spin. He had a real struggle recovering and it took all his strength to keep his left wing

Rapp flew this F-86A home minus the left aileron, which had been shot off by a MiG. An aileron is half the span of the wing and more than the chord of the flap. The large loss in lift and control surface is evident. The ground crews are assessing damage and repairs. "Frenchy" Richard under wing with fatigure hat. K-14, Kimpo, September 1951.

The crowd of pilots and crew chiefs thickens around Ken Rapp's shot-up F-86. Kimpo.

up when he pulled out, so he thumbed on aileron trim. As this didn't help his situation, he looked at his left wing to check the trim tab and saw his entire aileron was missing. Since there is no tab in the right aileron, he then knew he'd have to wrestle the bird all the way home.

After all that determination and effort he was still sharp enough to check the slow-flight characteristics with speed brakes, gear, and flaps down before landing. By some miracle his hydraulic lines were not severed, so he had boost in his right aileron to help, but it's amazing to see how much wing and lift area is missing when the aileron is gone. Ken did a great job of flying to get home from that one, and they hustled him off to the hospital to get the holes in his dome patched up.[5] Panter said he had seen him get hit right after he called the break, then things got generally mixed up in the wild dogfight.

I got on the afternoon mission, but the weather must have screwed up the MiGs. Either that or they just stayed home with their vodka. Later I visited with Ray Trebilco of the RAAF whom I'd first gotten to know on his July visit to Johnson Field. He was on the alert pad and gave me a good cockpit check on the Meteor. I'd sure like to get a chance to fly one of them.

Ray came over in the evening in his C.O.'s jeep and took me to their pilots club (No. 77 Fighter Squadron, RAAF), a quonset hut they had fixed up themselves. Since a good percentage of their pilots are sergeants they all have the same club. There were early introductions all around and I was always in the middle of constant company with someone making sure my glass never got below the half mark. It seemed like we each drank at least a gallon of beer. I listened to a lot of funny stories and hilarious songs with loads of laughs. Those guys are sure fine company. They all like our F-86 and were interested in anything I had to say about it. Their former C.O., Cresswell, is flying some missions with us in our 86s as he is to return to Australia and work on the Sabre project down there. Australia will build Sabres as Canada is doing now. After a great time they furnished me transportation back to my area. Now that's what I call real hospitality.

We had another air raid alarm in the early hours, about 2:00 a.m., with the usual stumbling around in the dark to and from the shelters. I really flaked out when I finally got back to my sack. After all that, yesterday we had an early mission, too. Though some MiGs were reported to be in the area, the clouds were gathering to obstruct the view. We capped at nearly 40,000 feet and everyone pulled those long advertising contrails. It was just like watching skiers on distant mountains of white, vaulting the chasms of blue . . . endless tracks in the sky. Occasionally the earth would appear in gaps in the cloud mass, resembling brown stains melted bare from the depths of the snowy cloud valleys. I just enjoyed sailing along. When I was looking in directions other than the clouds and streaming contrails, I had that high-altitude feeling of being suspended in space on nothing more substantial than a sort of floating imagination.

The afternoon mission got scrubbed because of the weather and after that I almost got checked out in one of our new F-86Es. I managed to get pretty well squared away on all the cockpit poop, especially their weird hydraulic system and flying tail stuff, and then the deteriorating weather even cancelled the checkout.

Some of us planned to go to the Seoul HQ club again if we could get a vehicle, but Commie guerillas were reported active and since a raid was expected last night, the Han River bridge was closed. Dick and I decided we'd get a change anyway and hiked around the field to the Aussie club, as they are the only ones here with a supply of beer. Evidently, we are being saved from this contamination, which means we have to buy hooch in Japan and bring it over ourselves—some situation.

I found that Ray Trebilco had gone on leave to Japan and we were invited in on a small party they were having for one of their pilots who had completed his 100 missions. We got some great flying stories circulating along with that swell beer. Those guys really turned on their vernacular and neither Dick nor I could understand everything that was said. In the middle of this good gathering a Blue Alert was sounded and the lights were put out, leaving us all groping in the blackout. While this roused some hearty curses, the party continued right on—the Aussies could care less, and quitting at that time didn't suit our mood. In the search for refills, occasional bottles and glasses were knocked over with a clatter of glass and comical collisions in the dark stirred up laughs all around. After the all-clear we were able to hoist a few under the lights before departing.

When Dick and I stepped out into the night and considered the long walk by perimeter road, we decided to cut straight across to our side of the field. So in the pitch dark we set out for another experience of groping our way. The engineers have been busy grading the mid-field area and it's like a no-man's-land of scattered equipment, muddy holes, and mounds of dirt. At our pace we darn near got lost, but by some miracle kept our directions; luckily, I had my small penlight which I used only

Major Dick Creighton, the fourth jet ace of the Korean War and commander of the 336th Fighter Squadron, in his F-86. (Air Force photo)

sparingly. It was a strenuous trek and we were glad to crawl quietly into bed when we got back.

Today it is pouring rain so all flying is off. Unless they have additional duties that require attention, the pilots are having sort of a lazy day. I'd better use this time to get some of my paperwork, historical reports, etc., out of the way. I really lucked out and after a long blank spell got a batch of mail just in time for my birthday tomorrow. Though the mail situation is periodically fouled up, with all this commotion and frontier-like, make-do existence, I guess it's a miracle the mail gets sorted out at all. There is an obvious relief back home now that Heather is completely out of diapers. She and Tom's little Cynthia must be becoming quite the young ladies by now. A card from Tom and family jokingly described my moustache as "jungle rot."

On the way back from evening chow I ran into the former group adjutant who informed me that the pilots of the 4th Group, because of our air-to-air mission, will no longer go on Forward Air Control duty with the Army, cut off from flying. Yippee! As different and probably interesting as that duty might be, I just can't get enthusiastic about two or three months without flying, especially after the frustrating time spent in Japan. On FAC duty you fall way behind your buddies in the squadron for chances at lead positions, lose out on the missions—the very reason you learned to fly—and your fighter proficiency goes all to hell.[6] Besides, those crunchies don't want any part of *our* job; it would make them so airsick they'd throw up their socks.

The Armed Forces Radio Service is playing some of my old favorites of the last war. Those great songs sure do something to you as each one brings back its memories of special times and places.

OCTOBER 1st

Only a few personal thoughts paid to my birthday yesterday; that just isn't important here, but I did get on the afternoon mission to spice up the day. As the mission schedule had remained the same for two days because of the weather, there was no chance of asking for an element lead. I was flying the C.O.'s wing though, and figured he'd hunt up some action. Maj. Dick Creighton is a tall, easygoing sort of guy, but a real eager fighter jock. As we walked together to our planes he already had those intense blue eyes of his busily checking on the sky condition to the north.

On the way to the target area we saw three B-29s approaching Anju with black puffs of flak around their formation and trailing them. They were to the right of our path and 10,000 feet below us. We proceeded to set up our patrol in this area and in short order the Stovepipe boys called that there were many MiGs to the north.

With that word we dropped tanks although I felt it was a bit premature. Maj. Creighton got a hung tank and I knew he was boiling mad as he slammed his plane around and even fired his guns a couple of times trying to dislodge the tank, which clung like a burr.

"Number two, I'm going to pull out and find another hung tanker. You fill in with the squadron, over."

I replied, "Roger, lead," and watched his plane peel off and head for the west coast. While I remained momentarily as the third ship in the flight, I looked around and saw another flight with an odd number of three so I pulled out to drop back and fill in the fourth spot.

At the moment while I was figuratively out in the "void" between flights, everybody broke in all directions like hot popcorn. As the formations split up I proceeded to do some adrenalin-propelled gyrations of my own while clearing my tail. I saw various twos, fours, and other combinations of planes at several angles accompanied by the spontaneous radio yakking of bogies, warnings, and instructions. As long as I couldn't positively identify MiGs about to bounce me, I couldn't see leaving the scene, even though I was alone.

Some lone 86s put out calls for others at the mouth of the Chongchon River by Sinanju. I began a wide orbit at 30,000 feet and though I saw a single 86 go by head-on, we were both going too fast to attempt a join-up. I then saw four bogies coming up on me at four o'clock so I turned into them and recognized them as 86s. The leader appeared to be smoking more than is normal for that altitude and I had a strong suspicion that he was firing at me. If so, he was way the hell out of range. Inquiries about such possible mistakes invariably draw a blank.[7] I turned into them, threw them off, and ducked away—trying to join up in a fight can develop into a real riot. Three more 86s appeared, and I called them to keep things calm. They answered me, I identified myself, and cut hard to join them. Due to the very high speed I had been maintaining, I had to pull a whole bunch of Gs to get into them and felt as if I was going to pull the stick out of the floor. Since they were all E models and I was flying an A I took over the element lead. We settled down to a regular area patrol and when our fuel got low with nothing exciting happening, we made for home. I kept thinking as we coasted on the downhill, "I'm here . . . in the middle of things I wanted to find out about . . . a lot of work and a long way . . . but I'm here." It gave me such a good feeling all over I couldn't help grinning to myself just looking at the planes in formation.

Today I got on another mission flying Ken Swift's wing in the element, while Charlie flew wing on Paul Bryce, leading the flight. We patrolled up to the Yalu and though MiGs were called out north of us in the Antung area, we didn't sight any. The scattered clouds that were below most of the time cleared off completely up around Antung, and all in all it was a beautiful day to be flying. As often as I could, while we were banking around in our patrol turns, I would sneak a look below and watch our fighter-bomber boys at work. They looked like busy gnats going up and down the roads north and south of Sinanju scouring over the enemy supply routes. Our altitude and attention to our own lookout business prevented me from observing the results of their work.

The MiGs didn't interfere with anybody, so after we all got bingo fuel our flight pulled out and the rest of the pack followed us home. As we got near enough to commence a long let-down, we slid into a loose trail and then into a roller-coaster tail chase to keep everybody properly motivated to the last minute. Looking back, I could see the whole gang following suit, the planes appearing like an undulating stream of water from a hose with the nozzle being swung up and down and around.

It was all thoroughly enjoyed and appreciated by everyone, the sort of harmless but stimulating whoopee that has always been completely beyond the comprehension of non-fighter-type people. We had a good time discussing the tail chase after we climbed out of our cockpits to collect together on the ground, and particularly laughed about the last-minute echelon join-ups in each flight just before entering initial. There were comical positioning problems presented by such challenging attitudes as . . . upside down? . . . one more roll? . . . which way? It sure is a great life.

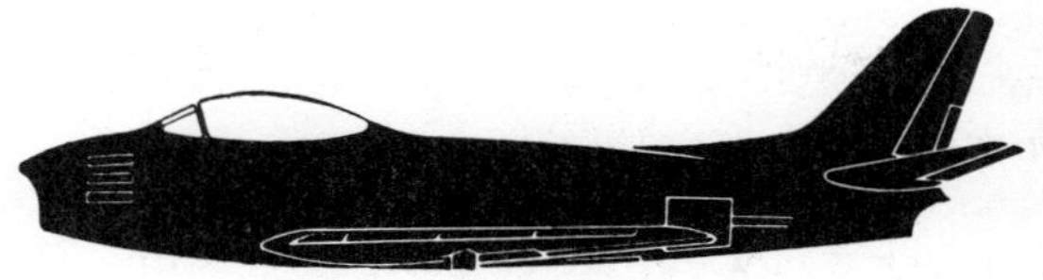

VI
Fast and Furious Fall

OCTOBER 4th

Ken Swift, our Flight Commander, made out the schedule for October 2nd and was generous, so Charlie Mitson and I got to fly together as an element. We patrolled on up to Sinanju, and then, as many MiGs were called out, we got rid of our tanks. My blasted right tank hung up so I gave a couple of full thrusts to the right rudder pedal while honking back on the stick and the tank flew off to the side—swell! Thompson, in the lead, also got a hung tank and called he was pulling out with his wingman so I moved my element up toward Blue Flight to form a six-ship. As I was closing on Blue, the squadron commenced a turn to the right, which required me to swing to the left and the outside of the patrol turn.

Just at that awkward moment the whole squadron broke to the right like a school of fish. There was no radio warning that I recall, just eight or ten MiGs diving right into us at between one and two o'clock. They went past so close that they seemed to brush our formations as all of us bent it around to the right. I intended to keep up with the squadron, but as I looked back for Charlie in the turn, I saw him spinning down like a leaf below. That scared the hell out of me. I thought, "Holy cow, Charlie's bought the farm!"

I figured he'd been nailed by those MiGs, but I didn't want to ask him if he'd been hit, so I asked him what I later considered to be the ultimate in ridiculous questions: "Charlie, are you in trouble?"

He proceeded to answer with the understatement of the year: "Negative!"

To my great relief, he recovered in another turn as I went down after him. He called again, "I don't have you in sight."

I replied, "Okay, I have you. Turn left and I'll cut inside and in front of you and you can tack on."

But fouling up my plans were four more MiGs high on our left angling in on us, so I tightened my left turn into them. Charlie said he still didn't have me and I took a quick look over my right shoulder. Damn! "I don't have you either now. Watch it—more MiGs coming in at eleven o'clock!"

As hairy as things were developing my head went into full swivel, clearing in all directions. About this time Charlie called that he was in the clear, but alone and pulling out west. Since I was still in the middle of it at the moment, I kept maneuvering around trying to keep track of the swirl of 86s and MiGs. The attack of those first MiGs so impressed me I recalled it in the middle of this mix-up. As they met us, some of that first batch had hauled almost straight up over us and they were pulling streamers off their wingtips—*at 30,000 feet*—some aircraft!

As I continued clearing to protect my fanny, I saw two MiGs crossing in front and above my nose. I pulled up in a curve and fired a good burst at the leader while tracking from a rather high angle-off, which caused them to pitch-up and zoom out. Not caring to delay hanging on my side, I went over on my back and pulled through, heading for the vicinity of Sinanju and the mouth of the Chongchon—or "Hey Rube," as we call that locality.

I felt I had overstayed my welcome by myself and it was time to say *sayonara*. Slightly nose-down for extra departure speed, I headed south at 25,000 feet. Suddenly, I happened to spot three swept-wing jobs that appeared to be about 10,000 feet below and in front of me. They were MiGs.

After carefully clearing myself all around, I pushed over and down in a steaming dive, leaning in the shoulder harness with the go handle still at 100 percent (the usual setting when along in MiG Alley). I rode the Mach on the way and gave a beep on the trim to level out behind these guys—slightly too *much* trim as I damn near went through the bottom of the cockpit. Maybe it was the adrenalin. I figured these guys would see me coming and bend around at me; in that case, rather than get cornered alone, I'd take a quick shot and dive through. But they didn't break! I just bored right up their tailpipes. I sure wanted to shoot, but kept telling myself, "Make damn sure they're MiGs."

I closed in and positively identified the T-tails and mid-wings, then picked on the number three man, who was straggling, and spanned him with my manual Mark 18 sight. A short burst and hits! The jerk never moved, so I held the trigger steady, and did that buzzard light up. There were flashes all over him with rips appearing in the metal skin along with puffs of smoke and hunks of metal flying off.

I can't really describe the sensations I felt, but I suppose they were the same as those experienced by all fighter pilots in all air wars at their first kill. I was tremendously excited—tight as a knot in the guts, mingled with an odd feeling of awe that all this was happening. As if I was sawing wood I just sat behind him (I was trying to do everything at once and didn't span properly), held the trigger, and clobbered him as my nose moved around.

I felt I was going to overshoot him as I had had a tremendous overtake speed and I could just picture myself sliding in front of their cannons. I popped my speed brakes and honked off some power while continuing to knock flashes off of him. Some of these flashes were up his tailpipe and even on his turbine wheel; then the whole interior of his tailpipe turned gold and spurted flame, just like a hot start on the ramp. More puffs of smoke and he snap-rolled left to upright.[8]

In this short space of time I had worked myself up to a regular jungle fever. I had also lost sight of the other two MiGs—they may have pulled away in a split; I'm not at all sure. Hell, I was hypnotized. I did notice I was dropping back slightly and remembered to pull in my brakes. As I gave him another long burst, he flopped over on his back and seemed to hang there with his wings wobbling and more smoke puffing out of him.

Then I felt two heavy jolts to my ship and thought, "You boob, get your head out—those other two MiGs must be shooting!" I split-essed immediately (I hated to leave my sure thing, but I knew I'd concentrated on him too long) and made another terrific vertical dive from about 15,000 feet. I twisted my neck left and right, looking behind and jigging my ship on the way down. My tail appeared to be clear, so I leveled out at low altitude about 30 miles southeast of Anju, just north of Pyongyang, my head still swiveling in all directions. Then—*blam, blam, blam,* and a jolt with each. I really ricocheted around the cockpit and can remember saying to myself. "That damn wise guy must still be back there popping away at me!"

I just about pulled my insides out in a 360-degree turn and still could see no MiGs. What the . . . ? Then two more hair-raising explosions with black smoke right in the middle of my neat 360. "Damn flak! I'm right on top of their guns." I didn't like a bit of that low altitude and started zig-zagging and climbing. More jolts, but the flak was all behind now. That Ping Pong is a hell of a hot area, so I climbed out and away toward the Yellow Sea, as I had no desire to fly right across the city which was directly south of me.

I called Charlie as I neared Chinnampo and orbited once, but I was low on fuel and couldn't hang around. My climb took me over sixteen F-84s and I carefully watched for them to turn on me as they often mistake us for MiGs. Evidently they didn't see me and I proceeded home alone.

As I climbed out of that low flak area I noticed I was boiling and soaked with sweat—the trombone and all heat was full on from high altitude, but I sure hadn't needed that assist in working up a sweat.

The debriefing after the mission was quite exciting; we had one of our best days so far. Col. Gabreski got a MiG—his third, I believe. George Dunn got a MiG and shared another one with Charlie Spath. Paul Bryce, Lloyd Thompson, and Lt. Col. Ola each got one. As I didn't see my MiG crash I was told to claim a probable, which was okay by me—I know I'm earning my pay. I didn't get hit, so I don't know what caused those initial jolts to my ship unless it was the flak, which I discovered at lower altitude.

I felt restless that evening while thinking the mission over, so I went for a walk. It was a dark, quiet night and I stepped out along the tent rows. Somehow, I like the feeling of living in a tent community, there is a sense of simple, friendly closeness—like camping out—that just doesn't exist on a fancy "established" base.

What concerned me was the thought of being off guard and shot all to pieces like that MiG I'd nailed. I just couldn't imagine anyone simply sitting there and taking a blasting like that without some effort to escape. The MiG pilot must have just frozen on the controls. Well, I'm sure he won't do that *again*. It must be terrible for a guy's morale to be waxed in a dogfight and shot down to boot—especially if you end up being a prisoner, like our fellows, with the rest of the war to think about it. You sure can't dwell on stuff like that; after solo thinking and fresh air, I rejoined the boys—the finest tonic.

Yesterday I was pulling Mobile Control as the gang roared off in a cloud of smoke. I watched until the last traces disappeared and then had practically no other traffic until the boys came slicing down from out of the blue nowhere in small formations, with their gun ports sounding off their familiar long-drawn moan resembling distant organs. They said plenty of MiGs were snooping around, but in the hunting nobody got bounced or within firing range. Later in the day we went through a practice alert drill for possible ground attack on the base. I've got 20 missions now; this afternoon will make 21 if it goes. Speaking of hunting . . . I made a sieve out of that MiG, but I can see now that, as excited as I was, I sure needed improvement in my gunnery. And, as more than one guy has found out, jets aren't as fragile or easy to shoot down as we thought.

OCTOBER 5th

Yesterday evening I felt in the mood for some partying, so I got Charlie and Dick, and the three of us launched the operations errand bus (the weapons carrier) and went around the perimeter road in the dark to the Aussie club. We still aren't familiar with that part of the field and had some difficulty finding the place with the usual bouncing around over the scratched-out, unmarked roads. Dick was at the wheel with the rest of us throwing in our two cents' worth of navigation advice. We make a great trio. Charlie and I are the same sporty laugh level, medium size with moustache; Dick is the tall, dark, and handsome member—so he thinks, but when we get to living it up we all think we're ten feet tall.

As soon as we walked in the Aussie boys handed us quart bottles of beer and glasses while we got together around a table. We swapped a few war stories and introductions and I'm glad that I'm getting to know quite a number of them by now. We began by playing "bottles." That brought a lot of laughs and got the ball rolling. Some of the Reccy boys came in from the 67th Group (also on that side of the field) and the singing got started. Sonofagun, what songs! Those Aussies sure know a pile of them, and talk about funny! I laughed 'till I damn near cried. I'm going to have to write some of them down, they are just too good to forget. Those that were familiar to all became voice volume contests with veins and eyes popping out. Ah, that fine one that ends each stanza with, "Oh, there's none so fair as can compare with the boys of the RFC . . ." Talk about tradition—that's back to World War I!

After each song we'd all give thunderous yells and I contributed my cowboy or rebel yell. Right in the middle of it all I felt that there is nothing, absolutely *nothing*, like being with a bunch of fighter pilots in combat—the best there is! What spirit and what a good feeling to be with such fellows. Through the uproar, Charlie and I were happily slapping each other on the back and shouting into each others' faces to communicate our joy.

Some fellows stood on the tables to lead songs and others climbed on to jump off—everybody was pulling streamers like crazy. We were all getting roaring. After all, a barrel of the stuff makes anybody roar. Those guys are tops for my money and Dick, Charlie, and I had an A-number-one time. Their hospitality and friendliness makes me embarrassed about the occasional cliques, killjoys, and holier-than-thou types in some of the outfits I've known.

When we finally decided to head for home the Aussies told us, "You good party boys come around again soon or we'll beat your bloody heads in!" With that for a send-off I drove the carrier back home right across the airpatch like Barney Oldfield. Dick and I were woohaaing like Indians and still laughing; Charlie was worried about the guards but we didn't get shot. At least we weren't sneaky about it, and must have sounded like an Apache raid on a cattle drive—I think the ack-ack boys hit their holes. We continued to pull streamers into our tents, still laughing before going to bed.

As I woke up in a fog this morning I found I was on the first mission and so were Charlie and Dick—they must want to get rid of us. Believe it or not, I was all bushy-tailed by the time the mission came off. I was to fly wing on the C.O. again, and before we climbed into our planes the last words Maj. Creighton said were, "Call me if you lose me, but *don't* lose me!"

I came right back with, "Yes, sir!"

As we flew up the peninsula, trains were called leaving the station, and later called entering our now general combat area around Sinanju and Kunuri up the river, so we dropped tanks. It was good timing because we saw a big gaggle of contrails coming at us from due north and then more aircraft way out west along the coast—slightly below our altitude, but much too far away to be recognizable.

I called them out: "Some flashes at nine o'clock, a little low—bogies going south."

An answer came back, "Those are just 84s going home."

Well, since the primary T.O.T. hadn't occurred yet I just didn't agree that anybody was heading home at that time, but I knew better than to get into an argument over the radio.

We kept patrolling north towards the big gaggle and then contrails were sighted south of us. I know damned well they were those bogies I'd called out, *and* these cons were now coming in behind us.

Another voice: "More cons coming in at three o'clock high. Looks like about forty." *More!*

Holy cow, I guessed about 30 cons were at six o'clock and those at twelve o'clock high were developing into what appeared to be four squadrons that were stair-stepped upward behind the lead squadron; each contained 20 MiGs—80 in one blob. An awe-inspiring sight—in fact, I was so awed I figured we'd all had it.

My squadron of twelve ships, and our other squadron somewhere east of us on the mission, were all below the con level. About this time the contrails of the lower MiGs ceased. This indicated the Commie ground radar had warned them they were closing and they were dropping down to our level to engage. Immediately all flights spread out and commenced arcing around with frequent heading changes. Nobody wanted to get hit with a surprise bounce and you could sense everybody straining to see what was going to happen. My head went into a full swivel while we were banking around.

Then suddenly they were all over us like a net in the con level and below it. Try as I might, I just couldn't keep track of the swarm and felt the grip of that jungle fever again. The way those flights of MiGs whipped back and forth right on top of us was very distracting—your head and eyes make a sort of jerking reaction to each separate motion.

Creighton was checking threats and opportunities in slashing, max rate turns. Anything I called out received this attention and it was a good thing I had flown with him before as I was aware of his style, although that certainly didn't lessen the job of anticipating and sticking with him. Part of the MiGs swarm came down right into our level and came tearing through from several directions. We made terrific turns into these flights, parrying their passes and keeping ourselves clear. Things were getting so wild our flights split up into elements, while all the excess high MiGs were diving into us like bombs trying to catch somebody napping, then zooming back up with their friends for another turn.

A flight of MiGs came across our noses in a sort of head-on angle from right to left, and directly in front of us the number three MiG seemed to drop out of his formation as if he were left hanging out there in space. I was going to call him out to Creighton, but I figured he saw the MiG as he was in a left turn, and he did. The radio was so choked up I couldn't get in a word edgewise. He really started to pull in on him and the MiG continued in that peculiar hanging appearance in a steep left bank. This gave us a sudden surprising overtake. As I was trailing, I had a fleeting thought that I was in a better position to latch onto him, but in this business you do not try stunts like cutting out your leader—especially when he's one of the hottest.

I followed the overshoot on the pass and slid across like a slalom on skis into trail as Creighton cranked hard over to get back into position. At this point the MiG turned over and down with the two of us eagerly following. I saw the MiG do a beautiful barrel roll as we headed below and then it was hell-bent for the earth at 100 percent. Judas, were we moving—my aircraft got rigid as we hurtled down. I could see a pull-out was commencing and Creighton was tracking his prey. The dive had gotten so close to vertical that to avoid negative Gs and keep us clear I did a couple of rolls myself, looking back on the way down.

I was getting kind of far behind as we pulled out and could not catch up, but I watched them both and kept calling all clear as I was asked. As we started north I saw Creighton firing twice while making sharp, short turns after this joker. This MiG was really working and the G forces made our quick calls to each other a series of grunts and gasps. The MiG pulled up steep into a vertical roll with Creighton right on his tailfeathers. I just followed up, clearing behind us. The MiG went over on his back and pulled down again; they both sort of ducked sharp and I half-rolled down on their level.

At this awkward moment I caught sight of three aircraft closing at four o'clock as the C.O. got right up on this guy. I was figuring during the chase that the MiG pilot was probably screaming for help and I was watching for any of his pals. I identified the three bogies as MiGs boring in on a pursuit curve.

"Lead, I've got three MiGs coming in at four o'clock!"

Right then the target MiG appeared to stop still and went over on his back. I called again, "You'd better turn right."

Creighton exclaimed, "This guy just bailed out!"

I saw an object separate from the MiG while I was trying to cover both the action in front and the bouncers curving into my five o'clock who were pulling hard to get deflection on me. The three MiGs were close on my butt now and I called, "Lead, break right, *now!*" They're right on us!"

Creighton just started a left wing down—yipe! "No, no, *right!*" I yelled.

He really whipped to the right (he said later that he caught on in time and used both hands on the stick) and I broke also to the inside as hard as I could turn with those MiGs snapping at my heels. What a spot, especially as my trail position made me slide past and way back in a tail-end chase as we cranked around to throw these three new problems off our tails. Thankfully, they only followed around part of my reversal breakout, so we get enough separation to light out of there.

A quick orientation and I could see we were northeast of Sinanju about over Kunuri at 12,000 feet with my gauge indicating only 110 gallons and something like 150 miles to home—sweat, sweat! I could see the MiGs trailing us as we bent the go-handles over the firewall climbing flat-out for home.

Our radio conversations had brought us assistance—the very best. Maj. Bill Whisner called that he was in our vicinity and looking for the MiGs. He found us and dropped behind to hunt. I just continued a straight climb for home and noticed as I passed over Pyongyang that I had only 80 gallons left.

The MiGs must have seen Whisner's flight as they disappeared and he couldn't find them. Maybe when their MiG pal suddenly went off the air they developed thoughts of home.

When I got enough altitude, I pulled my throttle to idle and began playing glider with all my concentration centered on getting my fanny to Kimpo. I got plenty of encouragement from Creighton, but both of us knew that it was one of those situations where you're on your own—nobody can hold out a helping hand or carry you home in the fighter business. What a feeling of relief when I sailed into the pattern as my fuel gauge passed through 20 gallons. Whew!

After we got together on the ground, we figured one of my external tanks didn't feed before jettisoning as I had almost 100 gallons less than Creighton, and had called low fuel while we were chasing that MiG. He was kidding me about his visions of me going down up there out of fuel and HQ jumping down his throat.

I said, "I was only thinking about all those unfriendly cannibals below and a rotten rice diet."

We looked each other in the eye with the relief and understanding that can only come through such a shared experience. He slapped me on the back and we both laughed as we went to debriefing. The MiG kill on that mission was number three for Creighton.

Some private thoughts: These flights home after a hairy fight when you're very low on fuel seem to be unending—slow motion—as if you are merely floating toward friendly territory. Meanwhile, making an agonizing survey of too-familiar terrain below with all its unhappy possibilities and watching the needle on your fuel gauge drop to the empty mark makes a very empty feeling in the stomach. You feel like you're over a vast map and you wish you could reach down and pull it under and behind you to speed up the passage. *Where is the bomb line? The front line? Ah, there's the Han River. Come on baby, just get across that strip of brown but beautiful water, and then I know for sure I'll be around for another day.*

This afternoon I was scheduled for an element lead, but some of our aircraft couldn't get refueled in time so we were short of birds and I ended up on wing again—*#*&%*!! No sooner had we arrived in our working area than there were MiGs in all directions again. They got right on top of us, chasing back and forth, some pulling cons—sort of like the start of the morning mission. More of that reaction of jumping around the cockpit and maximum G repeated turns. We didn't get down to real close-in lead-swapping with these guys, but I'm sure everybody was using their share of adrenalin. I saw some of these MiGs dive on a few of our guys but I was so busy flying wing and checking six I don't know whether they got in any shooting.

On the way up to our patrol area I saw some B-29s leaving Ping Pong and vicinity well covered in smoke and dust clouds. They were followed by persistent bursts of flak. From our view, as we went over them, it looked like they had done their usual good job of pounding the place. It sure must get noisy down there.

Our business with the MiGs continued in this round-and-round stuff, watching the buzzards so they couldn't get a shooting position on us, and then as everybody got low on gas both sides sort of eased out for home.

OCTOBER 15th

Again, somewhat of a lapse in writing this stuff. On Oct. 6, as I didn't have to get up early, I was in my sack when I heard the boys leaping off on the morning mission, then I dozed off. My tranquility was really interrupted when two guys burst in with the chilling news of the mission. They got into a hell of a fight—a hair-raiser. I guess I really missed a wild one. Two of the gang got shot down and bailed out while two others got their planes shot up. Things were really ape. I led an element that afternoon—full of anticipation, but we didn't get into any fight. That made 22 missions and I'm getting to feel I can at least carry my own weight in this combat business. There is so much to learn and analyze; I watch all the action I can in a fight and thankfully know something about teamwork and throwing an airplane around. Also my aircraft recognition is damn good, if I do say so myself. I've learned now how you can get that load of adrenalin and as tense as a big spring. It takes awhile for it to wear off. These guys who like competitive sports so much ought to try a real dogfight for a match of wits and skill—nobody dares lose.

Oh yes, during the last ten days the big splash came out in the *Stars & Stripes* about our big day on Oct. 2nd, so I clipped it and sent copies home. We've also learned the new setup of flights in the squadron since Torres, Lloyd Thompson, and Ironmonger left. Hammond got D Flight and I got assistant A Flight.

I opened the mail from home and lo and behold—those blaring *Times-Herald* headlines. I had no idea the fighting here would make much news back there. Man, was I embarrassed. Then I thought, "Watch this," and put the headlines and article on the tent door and awaited the reaction. It came quickly. I could hear guys outside saying, "Who the hell is *this*?", followed by other raunchy remarks and hero comments. They'd come charging in my tent as if to kick my tail and we'd all end up having a great laugh out of each other's headlines.

In the following mail there were pictures along with articles from every D.C. paper—wow! What publicity. It seems everybody at home must have gotten excited over the whole business—what a lot of noise over a fight and a MiG. It made me think that there are probably certain embassies in D.C. putting clippings together on some of us—shades of the last war.

At last I have a plane assigned to me; it is #240 and has been in the shop a long time at Johnson Field, but now it's back and carries my name on the side, by golly. I've put two missions on it and feel real fortunate that I have a Number One troop, Hulin "Frenchy" Richard, as my crew chief.

On the 8th I pulled a "Stove Pipe" mission (ugh) in our experimentally painted "green dragon" bird. Ragland flew with me and we varied our orbit from over Chodo Island to over the coast of the mainland. To relieve the boredom and frustration we got in some acro and tail-chasing while straining our eyes to pick up any cons to the north or northeast where the group was patrolling. The F-84s called us to say they were being bounced by MiGs so I changed channels to our group and relayed this info to Dignity

Red Leader. The 86s couldn't find the MiGs, but the MiGs also ceased bothering the 84s in their interdiction job so maybe we accomplished something. Anyway, if I can avoid it, I'm not going on anymore of those Stove Pipe jobs. There are others who eat that stuff up—anything to log a mission.

I flew several missions with MiGs in the area but we didn't tangle—just more hunting in and out of the weather. These missions involving prowling in weather can keep you tensed up and on your toes as you never know who you're apt to run into around the next cloud bank. I've led six elements so far and today I was the spare on mission #30. Boy, we had perfectly beautiful weather—and couldn't find any MiGs. What can they be thinking about up there? I'll bet we all had eye strain trying to see 100 miles in all directions at once to locate some business. That's a tiring exercise as it must be continuous; you can't afford to relax.

In a letter to Tom I passed on our opinions over here that the airpower situation ceased to be a joke a long time ago. He knows that, but I've gotten a personal look now myself, and I study all the available information besides. I can't say more but I'm sure he gets the idea. To cast a bit of humor we have some good cartoons around. One in Combat Ops shows two MiGs flying along with the Yalu River in the background. One pilot says to the other, ". . . and stop calling me Ivan. Remember, there's nobody here but us North Koreans."

Lately the MiGs merely sail around the area, keeping us all jumpy; we aren't making the hard contact or mixing it up as frequently as we did the last week of September or the first week of October. That was a rugged session for everybody. I've acquired a feeling though—if I have a choice I'll take air-to-air, that's for sure. This aerial combat is way out in front of slugging the ground with bombs and rockets. We discuss at length, but can't really describe the sensations of seeing a flock of planes approaching, realizing they are MiGs, and watching them churn around, each side maneuvering for a good shooting opportunity. At first it's hard to realize that that MiG boring past carries a pilot who is an enemy—and he's trying to kill you. You know they are watching you and both sides are poised to blast the hell out of the other. There may be an instant of wonder about what you're doing in the middle of all this while performing flip-flops in the cockpit trying to keep track of all the action.

One of the fellows got a newspaper article from home with the heading: "Wanted—A way to get more Red jets." Did we see red and have a case of the tight jaws when we read that. These damned armchair tacticians. Other articles on this subject have been coming out, too. In so many words: "When a hundred or more jets get in a roaring dogfight all over the sky, shooting like mad, why aren't more planes shot down?" Considering that 80 percent of the "battling jets" are MiGs, we'd like to take up some of these experts and show them how easy it is—man, oh man.

So we sing our little song carried to the tune of "When it's Springtime in the Rockies," which goes:

> *When it's springtime on the Yalu*
> *And the MiGs come out to play,*
> *When the contrails run in circles,*
> *Fighter pilots earn their pay.*
>
> *When it's springtime on the Yalu*
> *And the napalm is in bloom,*
> *When the fifties do the talking*
> *And it's just a MiG and you.*
>
> *Then we'll hold our glasses ready*
> *When they pass the beer and gin,*
> *And we'll hold our triggers steady*
> *While our sights are zeroed in.*
>
> *When it's springtime on the Yalu*
> *And my fuel is running low,*
> *Then you'll hear me softly whisper*
> *That it's time for Kimpo, go.*

I have a very particular feeling about that one. It just seems to have that special tang, and I guess I like it the best of all our songs over here.

Then there's a catchy little one to the tune of the jingle, "Super Suds":

> *Sabre jets, Sabre jets,*
> *Lots more MiGs with Sabre jets.*
> *Smoother, hotter, swept wings too,*
> *They're the jets that super do!*

We particularly delighted in loudly singing that ditty at Johnson Field. The song goes over real big with pilots of other aircraft, of course.

I got my first hop in an F-86E on the 13th. The all-hydraulic flight control system seems pretty complicated and I don't quite like the idea of my fate in the hands of hydraulics without a manual backup. Anyway, I had a hell of a slam-bang flight as I prefer to have on a checkout. I like to know as quickly as I can what kind of a bird I've got strapped to me.

It's really not a bad aircraft and that new flying tail simplifies turns at speed. I bounced four F-80s out of K-13, Suwon, evidently on a training flight, and I was going at terrific speed as they saw me coming in. I thought I was going to pull something apart, but not only could I say on those guys, I cut inside to track. We had a real good lash-up and can that beauty turn! Those aileron reversals were just as smooth as you please. The gunsight in it showed me nothing though, and I noticed that bending that E around in a hassle takes muscle—like an 84.

My moustache is coming along swell. It bends right up at the tips—with coaxing, that is—and is as stiff as wire. I never knew I could grow such a bush and get a kick out of working on it. Lately I've thought I wouldn't mind an R&R next month with Dick or Charlie, but if I can't go with my pals to hell with it; I'd rather stay right here.

OCTOBER 30th

On the 16th we got into a big fight. We kept the two sections and each of the four flights together for quite a while as the action developed. Things really got cranked up as a stream (or was it a big squirt?) of MiGs passed right beneath our formation going from right to left. I felt it was a golden opportunity to roll over to the right and drop on top of them and was literally hopping with excitement trying to call out suggestions, but the radio had erupted into such a babble I couldn't get in a word. I wanted to break out with my element on my own but our orders were to maintain formation and as I could see the other flight in our section right on our tails, I sure couldn't break out with them still in position.

What a maddening moment! What an opportunity! Evidently Maj. Frank Fisher took this bounce with his Blue Flight and got two kills. During all this radio yak and wild looking around I saw a MiG going down in flames at five o'clock and it must have been one of his.

The squadron divided down into flights for better maneuverability and Maj. Creighton and I, as Red One and Three, took our elements down on a lone MiG we spotted and then lost below the rim of the horizon, so we pulled back up to regain our altitude.

Nick Kotok (Red Four) and I saw two planes going around below us and I called Creighton and Pat Green (Red Two) to make a 180. When they did they both yelled at *us*, "Break left! There's a MiG right on you!"

Pat later told me this MiG was right on our tails and evidently out for blood, as he fired damn near point blank just as we broke and must have snapped upright trying to follow our tight turn, then just hauled it straight up and out. Pat said it sure was a close thing, but ignorance is bliss and I had replied over the radio, "I don't see a thing, no sweat."

Nick and I then went off to investigate some distant hassles. We had gotten down to minimum fuel when Blue Four called for help in a big bind at the mouth of the Chongchon River near Sinanju. We dove down to the deck but couldn't see any MiGs and then we saw Kulengosky racing right over the mud flats with flak popping off right behind him. We told him he was clear of MiGs on his tail but to watch the flak. Then new MiGs appeared—six above on our left paralleling our course south and two above on our right over the beach. What a nice little sandwich to be in with our fuel state. We damn well couldn't engage those guys and since they didn't choose to come down, we raced for Chinnampo before commencing our climb for home.

Our fuel situation was an emergency by this time and as Nick reported he was in worse shape than I, we elected to split so each of us could concentrate on our own best fuel solution. I decided to stay at full power longer than usual, climb higher, and get the maximum forward airspeed before pulling the throttle to idle. From the radio talk, it seemed the whole group was in a real sweat for fuel. I glided at idle for 70 miles and arrived at the field with my fuel gauge indicating empty and a very clammy feeling all over about getting on the ground. I still did not touch my throttle as I commenced a 360 spiral down to land and was told to widen my turn as a deadstick was coming in under me. Nick had already flamed out some miles back and gone off the air, so I didn't know what had happened to him.

My airspeed got too low while I noted by the red and green lights my landing gear were not indicating all down and locked. I dumped the nose for more speed and then a sharp pull on the stick popped the gear down and the lights green. At this point, I flared out of a near wing-scraping final turn to a kiss-on landing—whew! There were two more deadsticks coming in at that moment so I coasted off the runway as soon as I could turn and had enough fuel still in idle to make my parking area. As soon as I could I inquired about Nick and hear he had made it across the Han River, but couldn't stretch the glide to Kimpo and had bailed out into a Marine line outfit area. They later brought him back to us in a jeep—somewhat bruised and scratched up, but still full of tiger blood.

Later that evening we had a serious meeting of all the fighter pilots in the Wing. The meeting sort of centered on the subject of minimum fuel and getting out of the combat area at the right time according to your gauge. Any way you cut it, though, with ranges we have to fly over enemy territory, and the fights in which we get wrapped up, we're always going to be skating on mighty thin ice if we're going to show these Commies anything. That was our biggest news day so far for MiG business—claims were put in for nine MiGs.

There are supposedly thirteen unusable gallons of fuel in the F-86; I found I had used six of those getting home. We have a joke going now about changing the name of the outfit to the 4th Glider Group.

On the 17th we ran a sweep all the way to the Yalu River where we could look down on Antung and see flashes of MiGs taxiing out, but we made no contact with them. I wondered what kind of a bunch they have down there. They claim they are going to run us off of Korea into the drink, yet they haven't got the guts to get with it when we've had to travel 200 miles over their own guns to damn near invite them up. There was another mission of escort of photo reccy and I suppose it's just as well we didn't get mixed up in a fight as the responsibility of keeping track of those guys is enough of a job.

On the 19th I got another hop in the E model. Charlie Mitson and I got on our G-suits, natch, and boy, was it a relief to leave all the rest of the usual personal equipment junk behind and fly a rip-snorting local. As we were suited up to go, Al Simmons sized up our moustaches and quipped, "There go the two Gold Dust twins."

I had been with Al in the same fighter groups at Grenier and Kirtland, and the kidding was just an indicator of our feeling that this is the life. There are several of us here who feel something special about these times and experiences in which you just don't ponder the future other than as a continuing flight of the present. These thoughts often draw me back through the haze of memory to some summers of my boyhood, which seemed so wonderfully long and full of endless explorations that such tiresome subjects as school were totally out of mind.

The two subjects of the comment, "The Gold Dust twins." Author at left and Mitson wearing G-suits ready for check out in F-86Es.

In this cool temperature of a fine fall day Charlie and I went up in a flight of three and took turns leading and flying left and right wing positions. I found it takes a bit of real work to get the hang of that irreversible hydraulic system and the moving stick when you use trim; it's kind of weird in a close wing position with turns and speed changes. We got our blood to circulating in some real good wring-out rat racing.

On another mission, MiGs were reported which got us all excited for nothing as we made no contact. The B-29s were up pounding something. That night I got to see John Castle who had to RON in one of our tents. We hadn't seen each other since Kirtland days when we were in the same squadron together. He's doing damn good work flying F-84s. We had a good chance to talk and he had some generous compliments about my activities.

On the 22nd I had 24-hour Airdrome Officer duty and the press of air traffic (about as bad as National Airport) kept me up dashing around all blasted night. If anyone in the States had told me I would pull AO in Korea I would have laughed in his face. I got a few winks of sleep here and there in a chair in Base Operations, signed more clearances, and got more confused than I had in all my previous tours of AO over the years.

Some of the transport Aircraft Commanders pulled their rank (the higher the rank, the lower the cooperation), and some wouldn't wait their turn—just signed and threw down their clearances and departed without filling all the damned squares. That left *me* holding the bag, supposedly knowing weight limits, destination weather minimums, alternates, range, and fuel limits on all this conglomeration of trash haulers. What a rotten prize job to give a fighter pilot in combat. On top of it, we hear that all these multi-engine drivers get combat time boring holes between Japan and Korea while we don't even log combat time on a local test or tactics hop while cruising down the front line watching artillery duels. I guess it's like that expression the boys picked up in WWI—*C'est la guerre.*

Author flying and photographing from the F-84C in the 121st Fighter Squadron prior to duty in Korea. Author's wingman is Mike Alkire, who was killed in a crash not many weeks later. The F-84 became the primary fighter-bomber in the Korean War.

One of the damaged B-29s that landed at Kimpo with wounded aboard. MiG shell strike is evident in flap at wing root. October 1951.

On the day part of my AO duty I missed two good fights. A lot of F-84s came into Kimpo low on fuel—the usual thing after a surprise engagement with eager MiGs. I went to meet them and see who the pilots were as I know fellows in the 49th and the 136th Fighter Groups, both of which are equipped with F-84s. I found Cicala among the bunch. We hadn't seen each other since I had shoved off from our D.C. Guard Squadron. He's in the 49th Fighter Group now. I'm telling you, he's as funny as ever, especially describing that hairy "horizontal flak" flying out of the noses of those MiGs. It was great to see him and enjoy his humor. The Reserves and Guardsmen are really in strength over here.

As I got no real sleep on night AO, the wheels wouldn't let me go on the next morning mission—**#&*%!! I watched the boys off and headed for my tent, but as I soon heard there was trouble returning home I went to the line with my camera. Three B-29s were limping in all shot up with wounded aboard.

I joined Pat Green and some of our guys who had just returned from the mission and we gathered by the side of the runway to observe the first 29 come in with an engine burning. As he touched down we noticed the tires on his left main gear were flat and evidently shot out. He bounced and another tire exploded as he swerved to the left and went into a sideways skid, going off the runway right toward our crowd. I don't know about the rest of them, but I scratched out on a new world's spring record and the big bird skidded through our spot in a thunderous cloud of dust. As

A lot of people went to greet the shot-up B-29s that limped into Kimpo from the great brawl in MiG Alley.

it came to rest our crash crew and medics were right there and helped those poor shaken-up guys out.

The rest of the shot-up 29s came in, though not quite in the same hair-raising fashion. The wounded were rushed off and we noticed some of the equipment they unloaded was splattered with blood. One of their pilots was really worked up and indignant over the contest: "Those SOBs, they came in so fast we could hardly shoot. What a lousy deal!" As he explained it, the CFC (central fire control system) could barely hack jet intercept speeds.

When we looked over the MiG cannon shell holes in the B'29s we didn't envy them a bit. You could crawl through some of those holes—37 mms, I guess. That's the kind of fireworks we dodge in our dogfights; if a MiG nails an 86 like that it won't be coming back, that's for sure. Three of the B-29s were knocked down up north by that stuff.

A share of the returning mission excitement was furnished by the escort 84s coming in from the same mix-up in a big sweat— very low on fuel, landing hot and blowing tires in their hurry to get on the ground. A real able sugar mission.

Since I wasn't scheduled for the day I had time to sit and think. It's amazing what aerial opposition does to Headquarters' well-laid plans or to any over-detailed mission. It seems to me there are a lot of outfits that need serious air-to-air thrashes in their school-work before they come over here or they are going to be in for nothing but unpleasant surprises. To be honest, I realize that in our group our daily bread is air-to-air and we are fortunate in that we can generally avoid wallowing in flak like the boys working over the ground targets. But too many people appear to have *never* encountered—or even *considered*—an aerial contest, even in fun.

The Navy has the same problem; whenever the MiGs invite themselves into their missions it screws up their fuel and carrier
recovery time and they use Kimpo as the alternate carrier. Well,
we've got a bunch of planes sitting around on our airpatch now
waiting for maintenance, repairs, or new tires.

I guess that was the biggest air battle yet on the 23rd. Whenever the B-29s go north of Pyongyang the MiGs come out in swarms
and go hog-wild. They really smothered our guys on that mission;
we lost planes of every type except 86s. That MiG is probably the
best bomber interceptor there is—those poor 29s. These bomber
boys aren't beating their chests like the strategists in the Pentagon. I keep finding out things about this war that amaze and
infuriate me—like close escort of prop bombers with jets, and
carbon copy missions at the same idiot times.

I hope we are learning something; if only our pilots discussions
could be heard. One thing I do know: *The best day fighters decide
air supremacy.* I don't give a damn what other aerial brainstorm
doctrines are around. We have a damn fine plane but not the best
on every point; what makes the difference is that our pilots are
better by far. We wouldn't have *that* skill if we didn't take each
other on in contest dogfights.

It wouldn't surprise me if the Russians have more ships of the
MiG-15 type *alone* than we have total jets in our entire Air Force.
With all the fighting we've been doing lately, about all we can
think and talk about is combat, tactics, and aircraft, at all hours
into the night.

The U.S. May think the Pacific is a sideshow and feel we
should commit only minimum forces and equipment, but the
Commies don't think it's a sideshow. The end of this war is not

Side view of the captured MiG-15 under test on Okinawa, 1953. Note the
chunky fuselage and large sweeping rudder. Behind is a B-29, often the
adversary of the MiG and target for its formidable cannons. (U.S. Air Force
photo)

Crash crews assisting B-29 on smoking arrival from fighting in MiG Alley. Three shot-up B-29s barely made it to Kimpo and three others were shot down in North Korea and lost out of a formation of eight B-29s—a bad day for the bombers.

going to slacken the Commie Far East aspirations. They've got long-range plans and Korea is part of them—they'll get Korea later if not now. They've got to have it; this isn't the first war fought over this strategic peninsula.

On the 24th I got off on Al Simmons' wing as White Two and we got into a hell of a fight. I never saw any difficulties in distinguishing a Meteor from the rest of the fighters that are flying up here, and I know the Aussie boys are probably the best bunch on aircraft recognition in the war. They can tell an 86 from a MiG easy, and a lot of us in the 4th think it's a snap too. But anyway, a mix-up started over Meteors and MiGs coming through our formation at the same time from different directions. That caused a commotion on the radio, naturally (did you ever witness a *quiet* barroom brawl?), and for reasons I couldn't understand, the cross bounce of one section over the other got screwed up. I thought it was clear who were MiGs and who were Meteors, but my words didn't carry over the general excitement and everything split up into a real churn.

Simmons must have had on all the trim available on his bird. I was hanging onto him in the twilight zone on the verge of a blackout half the time. We went around so tight, so many times, I thought it would never end. It was a bad day—Wicks and Irish got shot down and are missing, and Ragland's plane was all shot up. He barely made it back. Man, were those MiGs tigers.

After that wild prolonged hassle I finally got my plane on the ground with the fuel gauge indicating empty—again. When we pitched into the pattern I was sweating as I showed only 20 gallons, and then a gaggle of planes just crowded in and cut me out, and I was forced to go around. Talk about mad—blast, I was boiling. I figured I'd have to bail out over the field; the traffic pattern looked hopelessly crowded with everybody low on fuel. I just stayed clean, pulled the power back, and floated around beside other planes. On final I dropped gear and flaps and touched down in close formation with a landing Meteor.

I'll say one thing: Flying as wingman in a wild dogfight is the toughest combat job there is. I practically bent my ship in the middle on that mission. I can get as bewildered as anybody, yet so far I've always been there on wing from start to finish. Maybe I gyrate around in the cockpit, but I don't trust anybody to see for me and it sure is paying off.

Dick Panter and "Spider" O'Connor finished their 100 missions that day and man, that night the whole outfit got roaring drunk—and I mean *roaring*. Dick and I pulled streamers in all the tents, which didn't go over too well with some people. Several of us got the word the next day.

I got up at 6 a.m. after that lovely bash and because of some last-minute aborts while northbound I had to make a switch from an element lead to fill in a wing position in a forward flight. This put me on Dave Freeland's wing in our standard shuffle forward, and as I got into combat position I noticed Dave was flying an E model. As we were just about to tangle with approaching MiGs, it was too late to discuss this problem. Anyway, I was flying my own trusty old A model, 240, and really got a workout staying in formation. Several MiGs tried to get in position on us and Dave was really cranking around to keep us clean. He kept checking with me to see how I was doing and our radio coordination was going fine until I suddenly went into a partial blackout—the tunnel-vision kind. I couldn't get enough compression on my guts to even talk on the radio.

After that sudden surprise I realized that my G-suit had come unplugged right in the middle of a squashing turn. While struggling to stay on Dave's tail I fumbled around with my left hand trying to replug the hose—which I just couldn't manage—and all the time could hear the worried pitch of Dave's voice as he failed to get any replies from me in the turning scrap. I kept thinking over and over, "Please Dave, level out for just a second."

That moment then came and I jerked my hands off the throttle and stick, ducked my head to the side, made a quick frantic plug, and then back on the stick just in time for the next gyration.

Dave called again, "Blue Four, give me a check. Are you okay?"

Author's brother Tom in cockpit of his P-47 Thunderbolt, 405th Fighter Squadron, 371st Fighter Group. Photo taken in November 1944 in France.

With a great lung full of relief I got out, "I'm okay, Blue Three. My G-suit got unplugged; no sweat now, I'm with you."

The fight finally ended and both sides just evaporated for home. When we got back, Dave and I had a good laugh over the mission. What with the last-minute formation shuffle, the hectic start seemed to continue through the whole scrap. When I had gone off the air, Dave thought I'd had it, and my recount of my cockpit troubles and pleading thoughts really hit our funny bones. I flaked out on my sack for awhile and a short nap caught up the sleep I missed at night.

On the 26th I leaped off on two red-hot missions—woohaaa! I wrote home a good description of them to pass around, particularly for Tom to compare with his P-47 experiences in the ETO.

I must recount these latest doings: Charlie Mitson and I were together on both missions. On the morning mission I was scheduled to lead a flight (my persistence must be paying off), and as the weather has been good the last few days, I figured on a good flight for each mission. The MiG activity has changed again; now whenever the weather is flyable we fight on every mission.

At the briefing for the morning job, the Group C.O. sort of knocked my flight as he needed my element for two spares. I led the element of the tail-end flight—this tail-end stuff is getting familiar.

We went up for a fighter sweep in the Sinanju area. The MiGs were there waiting for us and we watched them turning way out in three directions from our position. Some were pulling contrails as usual with many others lower on our level, moving about and giving us fleeting glimpses. As our squadron turned to keep the MiGs from a bounce position, bogies were called coming in at eleven o'clock level—said by one of our flight leaders to be straight wings. I identified them as MiGs immediately after, and they came right through our formation head-on, eight MiGs vs. eight Sabres.

I guess everybody was excited, including the MiGs, and each formation wheeled around to get on the other, but the MiGs broke away before we got all the way around. We then broke into four more MiGs and they hauled up in a zoom over us and rolled back for a diving pass. It was really interesting to watch and I called, "Let's not let these guys yo-yo on us."

Our formation ducked under and back of their perch, which foiled their setup. We were supposed to keep as many planes together as possible so I stuck on the tail end and sort of line abreast of the other elements. As we made another turn I looked up at six o'clock and—eeeyow! There were eight more MiGs diving down on us in more of a gaggle than a formation and just spraying our flights in general. There was gun smoke streaming back from the MiGs' noses, muzzle flashes, and those big red cannon shells streaking around us. Keeping my eyes on these guys, I whipped around and ducked under them before they could latch onto my tail. Naturally everybody, including the MiGs, then broke into flights and elements and round and round we all went—boy, these Korean merry-go-rounds!

Charlie and I got into a short maneuver duel with four of them, each of us doing some fancy reversals and crossovers until the MiGs climbed out. I was about to twist my head off looking up at six for MiGs on our backs and trying to keep us together at the same time. Charlie lost me in one quick diving turn and I tacked on his tail, then wheeled right so he could get back on me. We separated again in the confusion but I caught sight of him turning away on my right so I yelled, "Turn left and you'll have me."

While we had been racking around I had seen three MiGs way below (we were at 28,000 feet), but after rejoining I lost the MiGs. Again I saw two swept-wingers turning below, and as we were clear above at the moment, I dove on these guys. I heard somebody yell "Two bogies at ten o'clock!" so I broke off as they were Sabres and we charged by each other.

The sky became miraculously clear except for far-off contrails of MiGs. By this time I was browned off as I could hear fight talk, so we went on a lone patrol of our own looking for MiGs. As we were

Pilot and crew chief beside F-86A-5-NA 49-1240—ol' No. 240. Author at left and "Frenchy" Richard with star for first aerial victory overhead. October 1951.

south of Sinanju I made a 180-degree turn and drove straight north until we crossed the Chongchon east of Anju. I called a left turn to Charlie and then there were two . . . no, *four* MiGs in front of me. While I pulled around behind them to line up, still at 28,000 feet, they went into a zoom. I picked the leader and followed them up firing my guns—they were out a ways and just pulled off and left me. I couldn't see any hits but gave them a parting frustrated burst. Nose down and there were two more MiGs on my right. Calling Charlie, I hauled around on them but couldn't make it tight enough at that altitude, so they too got well ahead before I got my sight on. I blazed away at this leader and thought I saw a little smoke without clearly seeing any hits, but did notice two or three brilliant flashes in that last shooting and Charlie called, "Did you get hit?"

That startled me and I glanced toward him. "No, why?"

"I saw a flash on your nose."

It occurred to me that it must have been those damned incendiaries exploding in the barrels. To hell with it—I just ignored that problem. Those MiGs left me sitting, too; I was boiling mad by then. I glanced at Charlie again—he was still right there and so were more MiGs. We seemed to be in with a stream of them going

108

north. There on my right were two more very close. "Look at that!" I yelled at Charlie and cranked over. Again that slow turn at altitude (by this time 33,000 feet), and again we observed the amazing acceleration of the MiGs. I just couldn't believe it. I really thought I had one of these in the bag and he scooted off as I blazed away. Charlie was lined up on his wingman and gave him a parting blast too, after I had called him, "Look out for his buddy."

We began hearing all kinds of radio calls as everybody wanted to know where the action was—like: "Where are the damned MiGs?" The big laugh I got out of that improved my humor because we were the last guys to get into the middle of them and everybody else was running around an empty sky. Apparently, all the MiGs were real low on fuel and carefully avoiding any mix-up on the way out. Those last MiGs headed for Antung like scalded apes and everybody who heard me mention that was disgusted—but not near as much as Charlie and I were at the way those MiGs had left us sitting. Again I say what an airplane that MiG is.

Charlie and I scooted for home waving to each other and porpoising up and down as we flew side-by-side. We were greeted on the ground by a bunch of people who, by the radio transmissions, thought we'd shot down the MiG air force. What a lot of yakking went on while we related our experience. Boy, it's great to have my own airplane with the best crew chief I've ever had. Frenchy gets as excited as I do over a good mission.

We were all hopped up for the afternoon mission. Again Charlie and I flew as an element. We've been trying to get together as a team for some time and took off as Three and Four in Red, the squadron lead flight.

No sooner had we gotten north of Sinanju and across the Chongchon than we saw gaggles of contrails approaching again. I counted 22 MiGs in a squadron formation going by on our right and 16 more further behind, but while my attention was on them, Al Simmons, who was Red Lead and must have really had his eyeballs extended, called eight MiGs down on the deck. He ordered the rest of the squadron to cover us and continue the patrol and then called, "Red Flight, let's go!"

As we rolled over and headed down I could see the MiGs but in the curving dive we lost them under the low cloud deck that hugged the ground. We leveled out momentarily, straining our eyes as those MiGs looked like gnats down there. Then we sighted six more (evidently trying to sneak in low on our fighter-bombers) and Red Lead called, "Keep your eyes on those guys now."

We put our noses practically straight down in a terrific full-power dive. I got going so fast I wasn't flying an airplane anymore, just a rigid bomb—the fastest dive at the ground I ever made. I had to use both hands on the stick to maintain control. Meanwhile, *all* the MiGs had disappeared under the edge of the cloud deck, but we saw a hole and went tearing down into it as if it were a crater, the earth within expanding in our faces like a scene in a movie with a train roaring at you to fill up the screen. I had a sweat for an instant as I just managed to pull out before bashing the ground. Nobody thought of slowing down.

It was after dive recovery that I noticed the cloud base was only 1500 feet and I was setting my own personal low-level speed record. We were practically scraping through one of the hottest localities in North Korea—the main supply funnel and heavy flak area of Sinanju. The scream of our passage must have been ear-splitting to the enemy on the ground. In the gloom under the clouds I could see two MiGs way out in front with more beyond them. Simmons fired a shower of sparkling tracers at these MiGs while inquiring for his wingman, who had lost us in that dive through the hole in the clouds.

I called out, "Go ahead Red Lead. Red Three and Four are right behind you."

Our attack must have had an unpleasant surprise, because when Al fired the MiGs made an obviously startled break and I racked to the left after the nearest two. I chose the left MiG, ignored everything else and concentrated my gunsight on him while we were all going like bats out of hell in a curving crossover. I flat cut inside of this MiG, but before I could fire, cannon shells were streaking over my right wing. Since I was already in a steep bank, I went on over on my back to expand my view behind and saw this second MiG, who had just fired, pull up into the clouds.

Charlie later told me he had found himself 20 or 30 feet directly under this guy in the crossover—so close he could see the oil stains on the belly of the MiG. He saw him shoot the burst at me, but couldn't call me as he needed both his hands on the stick for control. Before he could do anything about the MiG on top of him, that guy popped into the clouds and Charlie stayed with me.

I snapped my attention forward again to see the first MiG also duck in the clouds—blankety-blank the luck! Then my feelings changed as in those seconds, still upside down, I went into the overcast—just great at that speed and altitude! Gently easing the stick back, I came back down in the clear and—talk about meat on the table—there were two more MiGs smack in front of me right under my nose. With both hands I rolled around upright onto their tails and then they must have seen me as they yanked up into the clouds. I didn't take time to do any thinking, I just yanked up right after them. Disregarding the instruments, I stared through the windshield; there was a moment of darkness and at about 3,000 feet the sunlight hit me in the face and there were those two MiGs under my nose again.

After all that crazy cloud-dodging this looked like the moment. At the rate I was still traveling (just under the Mach) I knew nothing made was going to get away from me that day and I horsed my plane over and down in a roll that put me right on their tails. I steadied my gunsight on the MiG leader, pulled the trigger, and my trigger, and my ship shuddered as I let go a blast. There were strike flashes all over him and the MiGs pulled up hard to evade. I followed up, sight on and clobbering the leader. With the aiming lead required because of the Gs we were pulling, the tracers were making an arc before smashing into the MiG, sending pieces flying and fire and smoke streaming out of him. I was so intent on nailing the guy I didn't pay any attention to whatever maneuver he was trying to pull off until I saw we were all going straight up. This sort of surprised me, but I wanted a MiG and this guy was it, so on over

First flight of the captured MiG-15 with American test pilot at the controls. An F-86 chase plane is behind at the point of takeoff on Okinawa in 1953. Some of the different design features of each of these fighters can be compared in this view. (U.S. Air Force photo)

into the top of a sloppy loop we went. I was still hosing him while he shed pieces and showed more flame. As we passed over the top and were going down, still upside down, I remember saying to myself, "Well nuts, blow up or something."

After all the pounding and roaring my guns had been doing I thought something definite ought to happen. It did. As we headed for the clouds down the backside of the loop, the MiG canopy popped off and *ha*—out came the pilot like a hopping frog. I released the trigger and while rolling around upright thought, "That's what it's like when you have to give up."

I quickly looked for the other MiG and saw him close above on my left, cued up and curving down for a shot at me. I ducked under him to spoil his pass and watched Charlie latch onto him with all guns working. The MiG reversed down with Charlie pumping lead into him.

As I turned after Charlie, I saw my MiG jockey close by my left side, hanging in his parachute and settling to the cloud tops. Up to that time in the fight we hadn't spoken a word over the radio; we had been too busy handling our stiffened controls in those high-speed gyrations.

"Did you see my clobber that guy? See his parachute at nine o'clock?"

As busy as he was, Charlie replied, "Yeah, I see him. See me shooting this guy?"

"Yeah, yeah, boy. Get him!"

I guess we were sort of excited, but the positive way to confirm a victory is to have a witness—we were making sure of that. Charlie was blasting flashes off his MiG and they were almost inverted. The MiG then sort of fell off like it was out of control and still going like blazes, plonked straight down into the low clouds streaming fuel. Charlie wasn't about to go through and crash with him, so he yanked out of the dive. I was following and pulled off abruptly too, calling, "Let's go, boy!"

Charlie answered, "I'm going, boy!"

Our fuel was mighty low and as we had been fighting right over Sinanju, a long way from home, we lit out of there like two scalded dogs. We couldn't resist trading a "Yahoo!" to each other over the radio as we flew home in formation, waving to each other and jumping around in our cockpits. Man, what a mission.

Before we landed the thought struck me: I wonder what all those Commies on the ground are thinking? Jets screaming around, bullets and shells flying in all directions, and then two of their own fighters crashing into the ground right among them. Some airshow.

We were about the last 86s home and the only ones that got into a good fight. What a pleasure that debriefing was—everybody wanted to hear the story. Among many others, Col. Gabreski came over and shook our hands and congratulated us. It's a great feeling to discuss a kill with the big aces. What a day! That was perfect teamwork between Charlie and me—you just can't beat it. Frenchy was elated and was going to get that red star painted on our ship, good ol' 240, right off.

My whole flight got into the celebration. We really got with it in the "Swig Alley" quonset club and charged around the tent area with plenty of that issue mission whiskey for ammunition. We made ourselves very popular, of course. Another spree like that and I imagine we'll all be shot—especially me.

On the 27th I got my 40th mission leading an element on an escort job. In the evening, in the Group pilot assembly for film review, I got to see my gunnery film of the day before. It came out good for a change; I really clobbered that MiG and we could see the pilot bail out. Everybody chorused, "There he goes!" That loop sure looked funny on gunnery film. I wish to hell the film had turned out on my first MiG—blast the luck.

On the 28th we had two terrific fights. Judas, that morning job was something. Charlie and I flew again as a team in one of the trail flights. As we had 16 aircraft, we flew in sort of a box of flights or two sections of eight in parallel, with Red and White flights in one, Blue and Green in the other—kind of unwieldy, but that was the system we were using.

When we had gotten situated in our briefed patrol area we made a swing from northeast to west and saw MiGs approaching on the right, one o'clock high in the contrail level, 30 of them. We made a right turn toward them, but not as far as I thought we would and the MiGs continued by to our two o'clock as we held our new course. When they got to our three o'clock they laid over in vertical banks and peeled down on us in a tight curve. Those tigers must have been the first team and were *not* fooling around—they meant business!

They goofed their pursuit curve though, and ended up in trail, dead astern of Green Flight, which was on my right. All 30 of them came boring in, and were evidently excited as they began firing too far out. I had been watching them all this time and could not understand why nobody was calling a break so I called Green

Flight to break right as the MiGs were firing behind them. They really broke all right, and I could see their wings shuddering and wobbling under the strain. I followed that by calling White Flight (the flight I was with) to break right across and into this pack of MiGs. Sabres and MiGs were then going through each others' formations with MiGs pumping out cannon shells as we screwed up their bounce.

I had seen as many—in fact more—MiGs at once, but never so many so close up at once—in every direction. They sure are pretty birds but all these MiG boys were evidently Antung's hottest and they were looking for some scalps. It became a terrific duel with each side trying to beat hell out of the other. We were doing yanking turns and full rudder rolls right around with MiGs, looking into their cockpits while struggling to get behind one another. What a lot of wild, furious maneuvering—pop-over and push-under close ones, wings at every angle. The violent pulling and ruddering was so intense neither side could get in the saddle for a shot, about like a tight bag full of wildcats—whew!

The fight was too hairy to keep track of more than Charlie and myself. I saw a snap opportunity to line up on two when Charlie called that he didn't have me. I flicked on my back looking and saw him turning under me, so I told him to pull left and he'd have me— he did and I completed a roll down which rejoined us, but the two MiGs in front had vanished.

With some elbow room now in the fight I saw six MiGs in beautiful formation turning hard right to get on us. In response I turned hard right to face them and attempt a head-on, but the hot rock MiG leader, starting from a better position, evidently had the same idea and beat me to it, putting his nose on me as I was coming around. I called Charlie to pull up; at that the MiGs opened fire, the leader blasting into my face on a point-blank closure. In spite of concentration I involuntarily ducked—*mama mia!* Those three cannons looked like flamethrowers. He must have fired just behind or under me and our formations went through each other like two combs. Man, what a close one. We all passed at terrific speed and I don't see how we missed each other as the MiGs kept a close formation. For a long moment I held my direction with a hell of a squeeze on the controls. I heard Charlie, almost in a whisper, give a low, relieved "Holy smoke!"

I really couldn't say anything while I was swallowing my heart back in place. Then, as I started a turn around, the sky cleared of aircraft—crazy business.

I could hear fight talk over the radio and went patrolling with just the two of us. Four more MiGs went over our heads about 2,000 feet above, but they didn't turn or indicate they saw us and we didn't bother to try climbing after them—no use. Even after a long dive and low sweep along the MSR (main supply route) below Sinanju we didn't flush up any more MiGs. It was as if everybody had scattered to let their wind back after that first mad lash-up.

When we got back the hairy stories were going thick and fast. Maj. Creighton, who had been leading Blue Flight, had had a real shaky one with some roaring tigers who had gotten on the tails of his wingman and himself and clung right on them down and around, turning and shooting like mad. They couldn't shake the MiGs until they were all practically down in the weeds. We all knew we had met the best of Antung—they think only of attack and are keen fighters. We are betting though that the MiG pilots are saying they also had a hairy time of it; Bob Moore nailed one that didn't get home.

The afternoon mission got underway with everybody expecting a hell of a fight. We weren't disappointed—or is that the right word? No sooner had we arrived in our patrol area than the other squadron came under a serious attack with a lot of yelling and frantic calls. My squadron went to full bore and, riding on the Mach, we raced in the direction that was called to us. I was already full of adrenalin, had been before we got our wheels rolling on takeoff, and knew I was sharing the tenseness of everybody as the twelve of us steamed toward the action in formation.

Then—eeeyow! Just as if someone had stripped aside a curtain, there they were: some in the con level, but beneath it the majority now materialized from three directions, diving and firing right into us. All three of our flights went into hectic breaks, violent turns, and two-handed reversals dodging this swarm which was spraying showers of very large, bright tracers among us. Puffs of what I assumed were exploding MiG cannon shells (37mm?) were scattered in blobs through the dogfight space. I got a good look at the Aussie Meteors going through this action as they also got involved. Those Aussie boys knew what they were doing; the rest of the F-80 and F-84 outfits shoot at us almost every time we get near them, because of our swept wings.

Moments later I saw Meteors again whipping by under us. Like everybody else, they were going full-tilt. I was sure busy looking around during this maneuvering and noticed my wingman, McPherson, was lagging behind for some reason, so I broke off from Red Flight and cranked back on him. His speed brakes were cracked open and would not fully close, so I reminded him of the emergency procedure as we got together. We went hunting on our own, and during a turn I spotted two MiGs also in a turn to the right—hot dog! We only had a slow closure rate cutting off the turn; then like an idiot I got overanxious and fired at extreme range. What a mess of tracers came pouring out—the biggest batch that ever came out of my guns. They must have double-dosed me with the blasted stuff and of course this stream I hosed at them gave our position away, if they weren't already aware of us closing on them. They tightened their turn and started up while I got further inside in a right chandelle. That first burst had merely hosed a lot of fireworks that fell off below and behind them. As the MiG wingman was on the outside of the turn, I had concentrated on the leader. I was still not at the best range, but I was afraid they would climb out and away as usual so I tried to be as smooth as I could in hand spanning and steadying the pip.

We kept in this chandelle through 29,000 feet right over the Chongchon River while I got tracers all around the number one MiG and some hits. I saw what looked like fuel streaming out of him and was at a most eager state when I heard over the radio: "Blue Three . . . (pause) . . . *Red Three*, MiGs at six, break left!"

That first call had sounded like Mac and I figured he had meant Red Three before he corrected himself. In that instant of correction I took a quick look back over my left shoulder through the tail area and got an awful shock: There were two MiGs with great round red noses, windshields clearly visible, closing right up our tailpipes—the crafty buzzards. They had almost joined formation with us, holding their fire—like I *hadn't* done on the two in front of me, which I promptly forgot about.

What an all-out break I went into—sudden back stick while simultaneously cramming full aileron and rudder, a sort of rolling breakaway to throw off their aim and put everything I had into a nose-low max-G turn. That has been the recommended procedure when caught in an extreme emergency, which is what we sure as hell were in.

I was pulling my guts out while thumbing on more trim, which intensified the strain of trying to see behind, and there were those tigers going round and round with us, clamped on our tails. I don't mind admitting I really felt the worst clutch of my life. Though I beeped the trim somewhere past 5 degrees those guys stayed tucked right in there and both shot a squirt of bright red high explosive shells showering past us. No matter what I did, those MiGs were still there, but I knew they were having a frustrating time because I did things I never did before, and they didn't hit us. In one wild reversal I nearly went out of control throwing off their aim; they had been pulling enough lead to show their undersides . . . very bad news.

Passing through 15,000 feet, I could only keep track occassionally as they were slipping back, losing their close range. We were running out of altitude and in a glance back I saw one of the MiGs blaze off a burst that seemed to surround Mac, who was under my left wing. Our voices had become only grunts and gasps over the radio, but I thought Mac said he was hit and expected to get mine at any instant. I made two more squashing spirals with violent reversals, one to the right and then to the left, struggling to check our tails. I noted we were below 7,000 feet, over the beach, and at last couldn't see any MiGs still with us.

My G-suit was on high pressure and had damn near cut me in half all that time; I felt internally as though I had been ruptured. As I called Mac we were clear, I thought I would fold up in the middle. We recovered at about 5,000 feet and began the long climb to regain altitude. In the middle of the struggle I had called for a hand, but could only gasp out our position in the Hey Rube area, and now I could hear some of the gang calling out as they searched for us. I explained that we were out of our bind and climbing out. Boy, was I shook up on the way home. The Han River and Kimpo sure looked good. I landed rather mechanically.

McPherson wasn't hit as I thought. When we all got together for debriefing we heard four others had had similar experiences, but not as violent or prolonged; the MiGs rarely ever hang on with that much determination. I must have looked like death warmed over. Maj. Creighton saw my wilted expression and after hearing our tale he said, "I know damn well I'm keeping that R&R schedule now!" He could vividly remember his similar terrible bind on the morning mission.

Somehow, some of the "joy" seems to have gone out of this business. I still have the clanks and can't figure out why we're still alive. I know one thing for sure now: To hell with that high-G *spiral down* stuff, the Gs practically paralyze your ability to maneuver and you waste all your altitude options too quickly. I'll fight to stay upstairs where I'll have room to yank and roll, thank you. What a lesson, but as it is I suppose we did a good job, considering the fight started with the MiGs camped right on our butts. A bunch of us went to the Swig Alley O-Club that night and got hold of some of that tiger juice to loosen up the knots. We got into some serious discussions and everyone agreed that we had had a hell of a brawl with that gang of hot MiG pilots.

Two more missions today. One thing about these days: You don't have to sweat the past; there is too much new action coming up. The morning job was rather quiet, relaxing enough to be considered a joy ride. Of course we kept our eyes well-peeled keeping in mind the surprises we've been having lately. Antung and the MiG fields were under a wide river of fresh-looking cloud that had formed or settled in the Yalu valley. Evidently it kept the MiGs on the ground; we didn't sight any.

In the afternoon, still a bit jumpy, I thought we were really in for it. What a sight! We were patrolling over fighter-bombers working the western MSRs and saw four MiG squadrons in trail in the cons. Two other squadrons were reported to be with them below the cons. Obviously, we didn't know their intentions, but in short order Able squadron reported they were under attack. They were separate and considerably northeast of us and before we could get engaged the whole affair ran out of fuel, so our squadron

Left, "Frenchy" Richard, crew chief of #240; center, author; armorer on right. The access panels have been removed to expose the .50-caliber machine guns (three per side). This was right after the hairy mission McPherson and author had in dogfight with two MiGs. K-14, Kimpo.

withdrew also low on fuel; the MiGs did likewise. There are a number of drawn faces these days.

I get mad as hell when I think of the odds we have to contend with, plus the superior climb, altitude, and acceleration ability of the MiGs. Just what does the home front expect of us anyway? The government may think this is an unimportant sideshow out here, but damned if we do.

One subject we discuss: Who is flying these MiGs? Well, we can guess. Among the probable pilots, the Chinese Commies have not yet had the span of time to accumulate any real proficiency, nor have the North Koreans. One obvious clue is the source of these MiGs—the Russians—who have been operating MiGs for as long as we have Sabres. Our success has been due to our fighter background with F-86 experience added to it—and topping that off; the desire to go up and get with it. When we run into guys who know what they're doing and can really handle the MiG, we know they've got fighter time under their belts and didn't just check out yesterday.

Why can't we learn who these guys are; what experience level some of their squadrons have, who leads them? In fact, why aren't we *told* as a matter of course? It's vital information to us; no football fan expects his home team to play the big game against a team about which they know absolutely nothing. That's the situation we're in, except that this is no game.

It's starting to get cold as blue blazes now and I can picture a "lovely" winter ahead. I wonder if my letters are getting to sound too bloodthirsty lately. Sometimes I get carried away. When I sit down to write I seem to drift into a sort of conversation in which I project my thoughts, yet I can't express everything. Once combat experience sinks in, you feel most comfortable with those who share it and less able to relate to outsiders though I still feel the urge to talk about it on paper. But then, our whole existence is wrapped up in it now. This is a lot different air war from what it was when the 4th Group first came over here.

I'm getting some boils or something on my tail that are really bothering me. To take my mind off that, I hear I've got two more missions tomorrow—44 so far. And in the midst of all the current activity, we've gotten the word we are going to move to the old building area that has been under reconstruction. We knew the move was coming eventually, but we are also going to change the people around in our flights. I hate that because I know A flight and feel at home there. My morale takes a drop and so does

Charlie's. Dick Panter is on leave in Japan, soon to go home, and Charlie is leaving for several days with some of the fellows. I guess I'm just not in the mood for these changes. They really get me down.[9]

NOVEMBER 11th

Those two missions I had scheduled for the 31st were cancelled out due to weather. I was glad for a change. We've had so many serious dogfights so regularly that everybody was getting a bit twitchy. I have some wallet cards that I use to keep a sort of personal log of missions and fighter time and I see that between 25 and 30 October I flew eight missions, most of them wild fights.[10] Now when I compare events with my favorite reading of the past, I realize that through all the wars, aerial combat is still about the same: a lot of thought, sharp eyes and sudden reaction, and hairy as hell.

The 1st of November was also a day of crappy weather so we all had two days of goofing off, fighting some whiskey in the evenings and enjoying each others' company in laughs and songs. Except for getting out to the chow hall for meals, in which we could take our time instead of gulping down on the run, everybody sort of stayed holed up in their tents. The frigid weather has discouraged going out except for essential squadron duties—and of course, answering those necessary calls of nature.

The visits to our outdoor latrine are a real torture. As the fellows say, the exposure encourages you to hold it and bake it as long as possible. The latrine hut has screen all around with board from a foot or so above the floor to shoulder level to establish a crude privacy—a practical arrangement for reasonable temperatures, but something else now that we're so neighborly with the North Pole—or worse, Siberia.

On top of our flying suits we pile on sweaters and jackets for any outside activity, so when the latrine calls we have to remove the outer garments to peel down the flying suit. It's at those moments that you appreciate the grim humor of the old joke, "Cold enough to freeze the family jewels off a brass monkey." Whoever dreamed up the term "rest room" certainly didn't have this drafty misery in mind. Why can't they design a flap in the back of coveralls or flying suits like kids' pajamas? To help relieve these discomforts, those of us who may be huddled there usually crack jokes about what a worse disaster it would be to be caught like that while trying to evade out of enemy territory. You can't help but laugh as you

Colonel Harrison Thyng, commander of the 4th Fighter Wing, who became
the 16th jet ace. Col. Thyng has one of the most unusual score records of
any American ace. In North Africa in WWII he got one Vichy Frenchy victory
and four Germans. Then in the Pacific he got one Japanese victory; going
on to Korea, he got five MiGs. (Air Force photo)

struggle back into your clothes to run like a demon for the tent,
where you can crowd the space heater and thaw out.

Even with the cold I took the opportunity in our two-day break
to hike around and visit each of the other flights. There is usually a
new story to hear or pocket book to swap. And always there is the
subject of flying, which we never tire of nor wear out.

On the 2nd of November we leaped off on a cagey mission. The
idea was to send up our two squadrons on the usual fighter cover

and area sweep, and when they got with the MiGs, a special flight, which would start northeast, would then head west to jump on top of the hassle. The special flight was to be led by the Wing Commander, Col. Thyng, and had a call we had never used, "Fox Flight." What a deal—I got to fly the element in Col. Thyng's flight.

When we got well up into North Korea, we heard over the radio that the rest of the gang were really mixing it up with the Antung crowd. Col. Thyng went to the firewall and we headed straight for the action. During this time we had not made a transmission and the call sign Fox had not been used. When we arrived, there were MiG formations scattered all over below us. Col. Thyng pushed over and we all took a high dive right into the mess—yippee! Gosh, that's great stuff. We were curving down looking for suitable targets and then—ha! Two MiGs in a left turn below, the wingman trailing his leader. What a setup. The best part was the coordination: Col. Thyng wanted the leader and I knew my job was to take the wingman. We didn't have to discuss the situation; every man knew his business and the tactics were everyday reflexes. "Rags" Ragland was right with Col. Thyng and Nick Kotok was tacked on to me.

When I had climbed into my ship for the mission I saw it had a radar sight, which I had never worked before. I called one of the pilots over for a little info on it and he said, "Just turn on the sight and gun switch. When you get on something, the diamonds will snap onto radar ranging to span, a yellow light will come on to show radar lock-on, and you just have to keep the pip on target— nothing to it." With all that background on radar sights I proceeded to fire up and get in the taxi sequence.

Anyway, down the chute we went on those two MiGs—what a beautiful bounce. Although I felt a little uncomfortable in a different aircraft, everything was going great. I put the pip on MiG number two and the diamonds opened and closed and then spanned perfectly; that lock-on light sure looked pretty when it came on, slobber, slobber. I could just see us slapping those red stars on the sides of our cockpits when Nick's voice came out loud and clear: "Fox Flight, break right!"

The urgency of that call meant *now!* What a shame to break off such a sure thing. I put everything into the break and, looking over my right shoulder, saw a formation of MiGs diving down like bombs falling right on top of us. We went into a violent right spiral and threw them off. When we were clear I couldn't help but laugh over the whole thing—here we were ready to slap on red stars and I know those guys who jumped us were all ready to stick on white stars. Everybody went to bed hungry, yuk, yuk.

In Fox Flight we had retained our tanks until after this scrap; then we punched them off, but Col. Thyng had one hang up. He didn't give a damn, just kept charging around and we ran into the Aussie Meteors again and started bounces on 86s until we recognized them. We couldn't really get on anybody after that, so when our fuel ran low we pulled out. As we were cruising home in fingertip formation I heard a very clear voice come up: "Fox flight, look out at six o'clock."

Naturally this got a rise out of me. I swished my tail around and started checking six like mad. Then another call: "Fox Flight, break left!"

I was already carrying the element left and was checking six so I crossed to the right and back to left again, giving me wide coverage to our rear. Nothing. Col. Thyng and I discussed these transmissions and I called, "Who's calling Fox Flight? Identify yourself."

The unidentified voice had had no foreign accent or British inflection—just straight American-type lingo, but there were no more transmissions. When we got back for debriefing, the Intelligence folks were interested, but I never heard any more on that subject. I also brought up some white puffs we saw near our formation at the start of the mission as we had climbed out over the Han River. I had a strong hunch they were flak without tracer sneaking a few shots at flights climbing out, as our field is very near the front lines. I'll bet that's how we lost two of our 86s due to unknown explosions and fires. The pilots had bailed out behind our lines, but their planes were chalked up to accidental operational losses.

In the afternoon I was White Flight Leader—hooray! My first flight lead. The squadron got a poor bounce and Blue Flight took it as they were in a better position. Red Leader reversed in the sun, which dazzled us, and I kept to the left. As I bent it around further I discovered White Two and I were alone, but started cueing up on two MiGs at three o'clock when White Two called that two others were at nine o'clock coming in. When I checked left I saw four MiGs and ordered a hard left turn. What a rate of closure those MiGs had, and they wanted scalps. I was then really cranking left in a vertical bank. They were too. Their leader had his nose on me and fired, very bright muzzle flashes pushing out red balls. I tightened momentarily and shuddered my turn reacting to these high explosive shells, but as he was not pulling lead on me for his angle-off, I just held my turn advantage, watching him shoot. I thought, "Okay you . . . now try a turn contest." At that I really dug in on them, which apparently changed their minds because after 180 degrees of turn they hauled out. I looked for Bob, my wingman, and saw him still spiralling down with a G-voice: "Are they—still—with—us?"

He was just starting missions and had never been hosed with cannon shells—a hair-raising first experience. I called we were clear, went down after him, and got us rejoined. Setting out again, I passed up a couple of possible sucker bounces as their pals were right above and behind just waiting for us to take the setup bait. Most of those MiGs appeared to have red rudders—evidently a new or different outfit.

We milled around with the scattered fight but couldn't get real close to anything, so we patrolled as a lone element. At the end, we met and joined up with Red Flight for the cruise home.

Along with all the combat mission activity, the pilots and the rest of the officers had to find time for the mad scramble of moving out of our tents into the building area. Packing, loading, hauling, and locating, *plus* flying combat—what a pain in the neck.

As I understand it, the buildings were used for occupation housing between the wars and are located on a hill off to the side of the south end of the runway. Since we moved to Kimpo, American and Korean construction people have been working on these structures, which had been badly beat up in the ground fighting that went on back and forth through here. "Buildings" *sounds* good, but we're not overly impressed with the facilities compared with our tent arrangements. For one thing, you can't hang much from a cement wall. For another, these places can be cold soaked without heat, whereas at least the sun warms up a tent pretty well during the day. In addition, we are now about a mile from the mess hall and showers—real swell. The repairs have been just enough to get us settled for the present. The other buildings, which are still torn up, provide us with a refugee atmosphere. We call it "Nob Hill."

To further stir up the confusion, the 335th Squadron has come back over from Japan. Of course they don't have any more planes to offer or operate, it just means more pilots to compound the aircraft shortage. The only consolation is not having to rotate squadrons back and forth anymore. Now we are to stay as a Group.

I managed to find time to see the Flight Surgeon about these boils or whatever they are that are bothering me. He said they were probably just due to the lack of proper bathing facilities as our showers have generally been out of operation. He gave me some ointment to apply.

On the 3rd a sweep with *skoshi* weather. We could see Antung and went almost to it as it goes under your nose at that altitude over the Yalu. Some MiGs were reported operating in the area, but none were sighted or contacted so the mission became more of a relaxed sightseeing flight for everyone. That gave me a chance to notice new details in the scenery up the river and on the Manchurian side; there is never time to really scrutinize the mountain country up there. I was leading Green Flight and felt great to be able to conduct my own maneuvering in the formation.

In the afternoon I led White Flight. As we hit the patrol area, we could see contrails all over and some MiGs diving out of the con level where we lost sight of them. Several of us saw about twelve MiGs over Long Point, level at twelve o'clock, and the squadron made a 180 at this time, putting them behind us. After I called them far out coming after us, we made another 180 and a flock of MiGs came diving into us from our right side. Everybody went into another one of those round-and-round deals. I figured on keeping White and Red flights together, but in the hassle, ended up on Red One and Two. I goofed and missed a good bounce on two MiGs while waiting for Red to take them. I felt like kicking myself and decided to break out of that circus, but we didn't accomplish much. There were so many MiGs going around in the cons over our heads they nearly socked in the area—a regular spider web. You just can't afford to ignore a situation like that, even though most of them appeared to be boobs. We got back home with very little fuel to spare. Nick was in there all the time; he sure can fly a good wing position in any situation.

I got on the pre-dawn alert section (ugh) at 5 a.m. on the 4th. Man, what a miserable Siberian cold in the pitch dark. We had to preflight and check out the birds; when we were all squared away I reported our status into Ops for 5th Air Force. You don't dare touch anything around the planes without gloves unless you want to leave your hide stuck on the metal parts. All of us, pilots and crew chiefs, were so stiffened with the cold we moved around like zombies.

With alert duty to start the day off, I at least didn't have to prepare for the morning mission. After alert, my flight had gone back to our room and I just took a break on my sack with all my

First photo of two-photo pan. Pilots of the 336th Fighter Squadron, 4th Fighter Group in their briefing room waiting on the word to go out to their planes. Left to right: Freeland, Panter, Beck, Ragland, Merook, Cabana.

gear on and waited for briefing time. By this date, with winter upon us, my gear was continually gathering: Long Johns, G-suit, then wool flying suit so I could utilize its pockets for a hunting knife, signal mirror, extra gloves and socks, first-aid kit, compass, chocolate bars, and an extra signal flare.

When I left for briefing all I had to do was grab my shoulder-holstered Colt .45 and flight jacket and charge out the door. Due to the added distance from the flight line because of our move to Nob Hill, our squadron uses a boarded-in weapons carrier for transportation. The pilots have dubbed it "The Tiger Cage." How we all cram ourselves into this poor clunker I'll never know. Of course by this time, after being together so many months, nobody notices trifles like BO anymore.

During the briefing I felt, well, sort of proud about leading a flight again—my fourth so far. Maybe that's why all the details stayed with me. After the main briefing, the squadrons split to their own buildings and we had the usual last-minute discussions with our own gang.

Good ol' Frenchy was waiting for me by our ship, 240. I passed on some of the briefing dope to him as I was climbing in so he would know what the team was supposed to do. I took another look at the

Second photo of two-photo pan. Pilots left to right: Cabana, Banks, Mossholder (behind), Merrick, O'Connor, Hays, Kulengosky. Kimpo, Korea, October 1951. Door in center leads to pilots' Personal Equipment room—parachutes, crash helmets, Mae Wests, etc. To the right is a briefing map of Korea with MiG recognition sheet.

sky while I was buckling in the cockpit and it didn't look too hot. The view appeared very dull with a solid overcast. We had been briefed it was clear up north; we could only hope.

I kept checking my watch as start-engine time approached, and with Frenchy standing by on the wing I went over the cockpit again to make sure I hadn't forgotten anything. Even though the preparation has become routine, each mission gets you keyed up as your watch finally says *now*.

Throughout the parking area, jet engines came to life with the low rumble that settled into the familiar whine of idle power. More hasty checks of instruments and then I could see helmeted heads turning to watch as, with a roar, the first ships blasted out of their parking spots with a swirl of dust and heat, the smell of jet fuel penetrating everywhere.

My cockpit canopy closed over my head with the hum of its electric motor and I was sealed off to the peculiar whines and whispers of my own aircraft. The hiss of air and pressure on my ears indicated my cockpit was sealed and pressurizing okay. The only sound from the outside world then came sharply over my earphones as the squadron leader called for us to check in. I was leading the trail flight, Green, and pushed the throttle, taxiing out behind the rest of the squadron. The flights lined up in order on the runway: Red leading, then White, Blue, and Green. The whirling forefinger windup signal was passed down, followed by the thunderous smoke cloud of the mass run-up, the planes shuddering in the jet blast like a team of sled dogs trembling in their traces before the call "Mush!"

Following Red Leader seconds apart in elements of two, we released brakes and tore down the runway. The J-47 engine really smokes at low altitude, so the squadron exhaust pouring onto my windshield and swirling past my canopy gave an added sensation of speed as I kept my eyes on the two ships rolling in front of me.

Kimpo's runway was still rough as a cob from all the old bomb and shell crater patching and endless repairs, so there is never any doubt when you break ground. I signalled gear up and checked to my right and Cabana, Green Two, was tucked right in. The rice paddies went whipping by under us as we picked up speed for the climb.

When my element, Green Three and Four, had closed in I headed for the overcast to follow the rest of the squadron through. Concentrating on my instruments, I poked into the gloom of the cloud ceiling; in short order we bored through to pop out into the sunshine of a beautiful day. Ahead of me, gleaming in the sun, I saw the rest of the squadron streaming those familiar twisting smoke trails and moved the flight into position as we climbed north over the Han River. We could see the clouds breaking ahead as we set course for MiG Alley.

As enemy territory began rolling by, I went through the ritual of making myself comfortable: unlocking my shoulder harness, loosening my safety belt, squirming my rear end around in the seat, shifting my back pack and beginning the endless swivel of my head and neck. Considering the free-for-alls we had been having, it was a ritual I took mighty seriously.

While I got that necessary feeling of elbow room, I noticed we were passing just to the east of the west coast port of Chinnampo, partly enclosed by the sharp sweep of the Taedong River—a most familiar landmark on our regular trips to and from the combat area. At this point I flipped on my gun switch and pressed the trigger for a test burst. The plane shuddered with the recoil and although the roar was as loud as ever, I didn't notice it compared to the start I got on my first missions. From the altitude we had then reached, I looked to the right and could make out the harbor of Wonsan on the east coast with the Sea of Japan glinting in the

Squadron of F-86s of 4th Fighter Group lined up for start of mission. The first aircraft are commencing takeoff roll. Kimpo, Korea, fall 1951. (photo from John P. Green collection)

morning sun. As it often did, without any design or intention, the thought came to me that only with flying can you actually grasp the meaning of geography, so denied people rooted to the ground.

Proceeding north in Korea, the view presented other sights: the Taedong sliding under the nose of my F-86, snaking its way from the dark, forbidding city of Pyongyang off our right side; the frost-rimmed brown patchwork of rice paddies waiting for the summer; the jagged mountains of central Korea masked with snow like drifts of smooth ice cream stretching into the dimness of Manchuria. Then came the glistening tidal mud flats of the west coast facing the Yellow Sea and pointing out the approaches to the Chongchon River—our area of heaviest work and the beginning of MiG Alley.

Ahead and slightly below I could see that a thin layer of cloud seemed to be roofing the area of the mouth of the Chongchon and inland east and north of Sinanju. Right then Red leader called, "Red Lead here; let's let down and stay under that stuff."

We were all now on the lookout for activity as the squadron slanted down, ducked under the cloud shelf, and bored over Sinanju. In a way it was a pretty good deal: No high MiGs could jump us, while we were at 26,000 feet—just under the stuff with perfect visibility to cover the fighter-bombers. It was like plunging under water to skim along beneath a calm but scummy surface.

The squadron swung west in a turn to the coast and I ducked under and crossed wide to the other side to balance out the formation. We had begun our patrol and I concentrated my scan across and past the squadron, with some reserved for my side and

all that empty space to the rear of my flight. As we neared the coast
I looked down at the tiny islands dotting the Yellow Sea—brrr!
That water looked cold. I sure didn't dwell on the consequences of
going down in the drink or those snowy mountains to the east. I
banked my ship over, changing position as we wheeled around to
the east, and in the turn my eyes traveled momentarily to the dull
brown mouth of the Yalu River. Ol' Antung sat in its sanctuary on
the other side. I noted that the cloud shelf didn't extend to the Yalu
and wondered what kind of a whirl we could expect from those
"slope heads"—one of the names we hung on the "who-are-they?"
characters flying the MiGs.

My headphones livened up: "Able Leader, this is Baker. I have
four bogies at three o'clock, way out and level."

"This is Baker Three. There are eight more coming at five
o'clock—they're MiGs!"

"Roger gang. Able Leader here, drop tanks! Hard right
around."

The 334th Squadron had made contact. We were now heading
in the direction of the scrap and Red Leader called up: "This is Red
Lead; full power, gang. Drop tanks—*now!*"

That tingling sensation of expectancy came over me as I
punched the jettison button and the ship lurched as the drop tanks
flipped away. I could see other tanks falling away, turning end
over end as fuel vapor plumed after them like smoke. We were
really moving out.

My element leader called me: "Green Leader, this is Green
Three. One of my tanks won't drop, over."

"Green Leader here, pull out to the coast with number four and
try to shake it off, over."

"Green Three, roger. Let's go, Four."

I moved to an outside trail with Blue Flight and just then I
noticed eight bogies coming in on our right, out beyond White
Flight. Before I could say anything—"White Two here, eight
bogies coming at three o'clock. They look like MiGs—yes, they are!"

A quick check to the left—uh-oh! "This is Green Lead, MiGs
closing at eleven o'clock, level—four of them."

"White Flight, break right!"

"This is Red, hard around on these guys."

"Blue Flight, down and left. Six more—unh—at—unh —nine
o'clock!"

Mama mia, it started with a bang all right—MiGs diving in

under the clouds from four directions. The Commie GCI radar must have put them right on us.

As Blue Flight cut into the MiGs at nine o'clock, I closed with the four at eleven o'clock. You felt you could almost hear the swish as we steamed by the MiGs; six hundred miles per hour each way equals a 1200-mph pass and that's quite a swish.

Everybody went into a general dogfight, Sabres and MiGs churning around everywhere I looked. Green Two was right there with me as I pulled over onto two MiGs, but they saw us coming and broke hard into us. As I pulled around, I saw two others closing at nine o'clock and, quickly reversing my turn, I broke into them. There was another swish. It seemed like no matter who I started after, there were always others coming at me to keep my eyes from my gunsight—a very exasperating situation. While I was in one of those hard turns I noticed two MiGs below going hell-bent for the Yalu with two 86s hot on their tails. One of the MiGs was trailing smoke and they were out of sight in a wink. I thought to myself, "Well, by golly, somebody got onto one."

Seeking an opportunity, I went into another right turn and swung a look along my right side to the rear—two MiGs coming in at five o'clock. "Pull it around tight, Green—unh—Two. Unh—we've got two at five."

I pulled like mad figuring no sweat, as those guys were coming at us so fast they couldn't make the turn and would overshoot. What a laugh. That MiG leader was a real tiger and brother, did he suck that crate around—the tightest corner you could imagine. Bingo! He was right on my wingman. Green Two was about 300 feet below and behind (we were both in vertical banks) and this MiG leader got about three ship lengths behind him and opened up with his cannons. Flame licked out of the muzzles and red cannon shells streaked by my wingman. Yipe! I expected to see the Sabre and ol' Cabana go blooey, but the MiG driver wasn't right on—and missed! One burst was all the MiG jockey got before he snapped out; that turn had been too tight for them after all and must have been a desperation shot. The second MiG got slung out of the turn and disappeared.

It really got my goat to see that MiG shoot, and in that instant of the burst and snap I was right above him on my side, close enough to make out the pilot through his canopy and notice that some of the red paint had peeled off the nose of his plane. I really wanted to nail this guy and just as I was about to pop my speed brakes and do a quick roll under to try to get on him, I caught a glimpse of two more swept-wing jobs coming right up our tails—blast it! In that second of decision I wasn't positive if they were MiGs or 86s, so rather than take a foolish chance, I grunted out for Green Two to keep pulling until we were clear. In fact, upon pulling up my nose, I couldn't see the fight anywhere.

I was still sore about not being able to fix that wise guy in the MiG and took out for the mouth of the Chongchon, as the radio indicated a fight in that vicinity. I couldn't locate a thing and swung around to head back up the river.

Somebody called, "Where the hell's the fight?"

Good—that's what I was trying to find out myself.

Another voice: "We're among 'em just north of Sinanju."

I checked to the rear as we barrelled along and saw Green two crossing over behind me—all clear. Aha, there was a mix-up ahead; now to find out who was who. There below were two MiGs turning hard, the one on the tail end smoking. Two 86s were after them but not having an easy time in the tight Lufbery. The MiGs had quite a separation between them; in fact, the lead MiG was way around the circle from the others, so I figured maybe I could tap him while the other 86s were whacking away at his wingman. Try as I might, at my entry speed I just couldn't crank around enough to fit in and got slung out of the tight circle. It was sort of funny, like trying to jump on a merry-go-round going full blast.

Whoops! "Hard right, Green Two. Check those guys at three o'clock."

Something had made me check to the right outside of the circle where I noticed a line of aircraft sweeping in under the clouds from the north. The thought came: "Are they 86s? We're all supposed to be engaged."

To make sure, I reversed right and went in head-on, leaning close to the windshield for a better look. Uh-oh, twelve MiGs driving in in beautiful line-abreast formation. I'd had enough experience with cannon fire right in the face to feel that twelve of them was too much. We were closing at a terrific rate and I aimed for the middle to hop over at the last second. Maybe their recognition was slower than mine because we were just into each other when their whole formation lit up with a blaze of cannons and they passed right under our bellies. What a sight!

They were still firing as we passed and then I saw something I didn't like a bit: The MiG formation split in a break—six to the right and six to the left in big sweeps to come around and box us in—what a spot. I had the feeling my hair was trying to stand up under my crash helmet as I thought, "Which way to break?"

I called Green Two for a max right and put on so many Gs that the top of my oxygen mask slipped down under my nose and over my mouth. With a quick swipe I pushed it back as best I could with my head twisting around watching those MiGs.

Then, what had appeared as the closing of a trap suddenly evaporated. Before the MiGs completed their turn-around they split up and scattered in all directions; that surprise meeting must have shaken then up. Swell—now to latch onto one without all his gang aiming at us. That overcast felt as nice as a roof overhead. No additional MiGs had been able to dive into us and take advantage of that bad situation when we had had twelve to consider.

Two MiGs passed under our right in our direction; as I broke right and down on them, they went into a hard, steep right chandelle. I was right after them, pulling for all I was worth. In the first moments I closed slightly, concentrated on the wingman, and began hammering away, but my blasted gunsight was out of whack—set with a cotter pin in the fixed, pegged position—so I was forced to guess range and lead. There were only occasional tracers to use as a crutch with my sight and I noticed a strange rattle to my guns. I hit him with two or three flashes out of four or five bursts, but we had gotten into such a steep spiral it was tough to maintain any steady aim. Those boys were working to get home. I was steadily losing ground until it seemed like we were falling backwards. My controls were mushy from the low airspeed, so I checked our tails before a last squirt and rolled over and down— talk about frustrated, and those two MiGs, going right up like elevators, disappeared through the overcast.

As the weather at Kimpo had been lousy and the action had faded, I figured we'd better head home with our remaining fuel for a penetration. We headed south under the overcast when all of a sudden a surprise lone MiG popped out of the cloud ceiling above in a steep dive. We must have seen each other at the same time and he opened fire. It all happened so fast I didn't have time to pull my nose up and as his aim was way off anyway, I didn't worry about it. The MiG whipped by over us, still blazing away like crazy the last I saw of him—some kind of a nut. Maybe he was in a hurry to empty his guns and get home to tell how he shot us both down so he could collect his "Hero" medal.

That sort of crazy firing has been witnessed on missions by a number of fellows. I like to see it, frankly. It means the buzzards are all clanked up.

As we approached the Han River I could see cloud breaks in the Seoul area and toward Kaesong to our left. I signalled for speed brakes and we made one of those refreshing high dives through the clouds like plunging off a cliff into the surf. We mingled with the rest of the gang dropping through the clouds and got into the pattern under the breaking overcast.

While filling out the Form One, before I even got out of the cockpit, I heard my armorer swearing like a pirate. He already had the gun panels off and had discovered that four of my guns had jammed. That many is rare—no wonder my guns had sounded strange. Then this parts shortage that shafts us with pegged, stone-age gun sights—what a lot of crap. On top of that, my film didn't come out again. It makes a man feel like a jackass to have no film to show after a good scrap.

We all say there's nothing like flying a quarter-million-dollar airplane with a two-bit sight and camera. Even with all that, I still feel like a lousy shot. Anyway, the good news was that Bill Guss, the Marine pilot with our squadron who had been leading Blue Flight, got a MiG and so did Al Dymock in the 334th. The debriefing was a real lively discussion that just about matched all the yakking over the radio during the fight.

That afternoon we went off on what became another hot mission. After all the usual tedious preparation, by the time I slung on my parachute it just seemed like a bag of cement. I felt beat walking out to our aircraft and down to my own. We had sure been going at a heck of a pace lately with all these long-range hassles. Just imagine fighting in sight of your home field like those MiG drivers. I compare all that Commie territory to flying hundreds of miles over cannibal country. My stomach was in a knot of indigestion from smoking all those weeds during briefing and I had that tired feeling that I was just dragging my tailfeathers, but it was too be my 50th mission, so what the hell. I had also received the word I was to ferry a bird to Japan the next day and pick up another from maintenance. At least that would be something different to think about later.

Anyway, I went off as Blue element with Nick Kotok and we got an early call that MiGs were interfering with our fighter-bombers. The squadron made a fast curve down onto the MSRs to identify aircraft and went west to the coast. We turned back again low over the roads with a mess of flak around us. Besides the usual puffs of smoke, I could distinctly see bright flashes as the stuff exploded. In our first sweep we had passed on over fighter-bombers; this generated a controversy as to whether they were Navy Panthers or Air Force F-80s. My feeling was: They were ours, so why were we fooling around?

Finally the flights scattered out to hunt better. Blue Lead didn't answer when I asked him if he had his eyes on anything hot, so I climbed into the "Race Track" area up past Kunuri toward Huichon. Oh yes, as we went deep and up to 25,000 feet, we found MiGs all right—plenty above, and no 86s, at least none since I had sighted two 86s on two MiGs streaking for the Yalu, tracers from the lead 86 and smoke from the number two MiG. I tried to climb at some of the higher MiGs, but they had too much speed up and appeared to be going all out for home in elements of two.

Earlier in the mission I had seen 20 contrails heading in the direction of Pyongyang and thought perhaps I could get up there and meet them on their way back. For all I knew those traveling overhead might be part of that bunch. One sharp guy split-essed on us from a passing element, flashed by, and faded away. Two other MiGs came into view that I thought had possibilities, but as I tried to cue up on them, I found I hadn't ginned up enough speed after my climb to match them. This had put me on a north heading and I was rocking from side to side, looking carefully around. This brought two more MiGs above us to my attention. Just by chance I scanned to the rear and there at five o'clock was a big red nose. This surprise MiG was behind and to the right of Nick, who was on my right wing, thus we were all in a sort of echelon. At that angle, Nick hadn't seen him as he had not called, so I eyeballed him before breaking.

Though the MiG wasn't closing, he was right in firing range and rolled on his left wing and then on his right as I figured which move to make. It was actually strange to have these seconds of deliberation, but I guess he was trying to anticipate our actions too, plus clearing himself. When he went into a left vertical, still at five o'clock, I yelled for a right break and around we went at max trim. Though we beat the MiG to the break as we bent around, that tiger stayed with us in a mad Lufbery. I almost snapped on my back, then settled into a more workable turn as Nick and I continued around. The MiG was trying to get on Nick, but couldn't quite hack the turn while I had worked around to the opposite of the circle from him. I noticed all three of us were shuddering in this circle and the MiG was pumping lead at Nick, yet didn't even have his nose on him—a good sign: overeager and firing out. Our airspeed was getting low and Nick called in a strained G-voice, Let's—unh—spiral down."

All I could say was "Keep turning."

As the two of them went lower, I started making money on the MiG. He fired once more. Straining with expectancy, I was pulling my nose slowly around to him when, as he next got to a north heading, he suddenly broke out. I involuntarily said, "Now let's get this wise guy," while I finished hauling around to his flight path.

That sonofagun shot away and left us sitting. We had ended up below 15,000 feet at a little over 200 knots, and the MiG, with a beautifully timed break-out, accelerated surprisingly. I didn't even bother with a parting burst the range spread so quickly; we just did not have the poop to scratch out like that. We dove out to regain speed and headed home low on fuel. Nick and I were both worn out and my mouth was dehydrated with a terrible taste from all the Gs and fast breathing of oxygen.

That night we had a little get-together and shared some private stock. I got into a relaxed mood and couldn't help but think this was swell company to be with and compare experiences of the day. For an intermission there was an air raid alarm, so we trooped outside to watch the flak display down Inchon way.

The next morning was another of those hectic scrambles to get ready to ferry the two planes to Japan. Ragland and I completed preflighting and packing our stuff in our two birds and were ready to go when maintenance told me they wanted me to take another plane. They said they couldn't get one of the 120 gallon drop tanks to feed and since I was experienced they wanted me to take it. I asked what my experience would have to do with making the tank feed, but got stuck with the substitute anyway. That's a mighty long haul from Kimpo to Johnson Field even with *good* tanks, but it was a beautiful day and I looked forward to a scenic trip.

I hadn't been able to observe much in my previous trips in the back end of cargo planes, so this was different. It was my first look at the length of Korea as we flew down the peninsula. The fighter-bomber boys made that long haul every day from Taegu to the front lines and beyond. While still attending to my flight plan, I followed our route on my map to observe points of interest. Some of that south country was pretty roughed up with hills and winding roads; that sure was a mess down there last year with the troops jammed into the Pusan pocket and then fighting out and back over all those hills.

136

I got a good look at K-2 at Taegu and wished we could drop in to visit some of my pals—I've got a lot in that place. It wasn't possible to distinguish all the fields around Pusan because I got busy setting course across the Korean Strait for Honshu. The bays and inlets on both sides looked like they would be fascinating to explore by boat. The blue sky, the sea, the islands, and the whole change of scenery were a pleasure to view, and I took it all in. Ahead of us the cumulus clouds were growing a bit more puffy over the mountains in the direction of Tokyo.

It was in the middle of this reverie that I discovered my one supposedly good tank wasn't giving me much fuel to speak of. Rags was concerned and asked if I wanted to land at Komaki, but I figured I had just more than enough and went into an idle, on-course let-down ending up in a spiral into Johnson Field. By the time we taxied across the ramp and around behind the hangars I was ready to flame out.

Upon completion of the delivery paperwork, Rags and I wasted no time in getting into those BOQ showers for a super hot bath and long soak. I stood under it as I would a waterfall—to hell with the water bill. It seemed like the greatest of luxuries. After donning a clean uniform I went to the base flight surgeon about these infernal itching welts. The Doc said it was scabies and pretty bad, too—the first I'd ever heard of that. From the way he explained it, no wonder I was a scratching maniac. Evidently, they burrow in like the chiggers I've gotten while tramping and hunting in the woods back home, only these are a hell of a lot worse. If that stupid Doc at Kimpo had figured out I had these super-cooties they wouldn't have gotten so bad. We figured I must have gotten them by turning my clothes out for hand washing in Korea, where they got mixed with a scroungy pile. The Doc gave me some special strong lotion to apply.

I chowed down a big juicy steak, ran into some people I knew at the O-Club, and wound up in a party. Hard to believe the different life around there. I had tried to make a long-distance call home after I ate, but just couldn't get through. That is generally a pretty impossible job.

On the 6th I felt like I was really living it up. After a real sleep in a real bed I had another long hot shower, a big meal, and shopped around a real PX. The change of pace made me feel like I had been turned loose as one of the idle rich. I didn't feel like going to Tokyo or anywhere else by myself, so by early evening I was loafing around the club. I was having some cool ones at that long curvy bar when I ran into Brownell, who was with his Red Cross girl from the States. By this time I was really getting with the program and feeling no pain. What with Browny and I yakking about old times back in our stateside squadron, I told a few war stories about the 4th Fighter Group. This brought on some smart remarks from a half dozen pilots (F-51 and F-80 Johnson Field jocks) at the other end of the bar.

When jets first came out we got smart remarks from jet pilots; when I was flying straight-wing jets we got smart remarks from swept-wing 86 pilots, and now that I'm flying 86s in the hottest assignment in Korea (or anywhere, as far as I'm concerned), I was getting remarks from jealous prop and straight-wing pilots. It was just too damn much. I had been in a fair mood till this stuff started, and along with this scabies medicine that had me in flames, I got in a foul mood. I told those Tokyo Guard types, as we call them, where to shove their propellers and straight-wings and then went among 'em to make sure they understood. I feel I've finally made up for that awful waste spent in a pilot pool watching World War II end. Some of those that did make it over consider that that alone makes them supermen and no other war counts, when they never saw an enemy plane and had difficulty finding any target to get a whiff of gunpowder. I'm not impressed by that "Big War" line anymore and told those guys I could shoot down the whole lot of them. I was at the teenth-gringing stage and must have had smoke coming out of my ears because nobody took me on.

Though I rejoined Browny for some more firewater, the evening just wasn't the same. However, I did feel satisfied that I got off some steam and told some irritating people off for a change.

The next day I bought a light meter to help my picture taking. Then I got a cowgirl suit for Heather and a nice string of cultured pearls for Lu. No planes were yet ready to ferry back, which I guess was okay except that I was getting bored.

On Thursday, the 8th, I got a ride in a GI 2-1/2 ton truck to Tachi, took some pictures and bought a set of hot-looking short black leather pull-on boots for wear around the base at Kimpo. They had some kind of white fur for lining—rabbit, or maybe some stray cat.

That night I got in with a pretty good group back at Johnson Field. I suppose you could call it a party, but I think we overdo the word—especially in Korea. Rolling horses for drinks and talking about flying is hardly what most people would call a party. I kept trying to get a call through to Lu in the States and finally at 3:30

138

a.m. the next morning, Friday the 9th, I was roused out of bed as the call got through. We sure had a wonderful talk, but I could feel the tremendous gulf between two worlds when I had to hang up the phone. You want so badly to place the call, and yet it really tears you up when it's over. It was 1:30 p.m., Thursday back in D.C.

There were quite a few of the boys showing up at Johnson on R&R or ferrying as I was. Due to lousy weather and sorry aircraft status, I was able to spend five days before I had to ferry back, so that was mighty good without formal leave. There were some real carefree times in the club and everybody got a charge out of my bushy Sabre mustache. Each night after chow, while at the bar with any of the gang that happened to be around, I kept trotting back and forth to the phone working on that long-distance call while continually scratching. I must have looked like a real nut let loose from Korea.

I've heard a number of compliments (some indirectly) like, "Gee, you can fly pretty well." I'm pleased to hear that I have a good combat reputation; it sure takes a lot of effort in each outfit I get into to work out of the new guy stage (FNG), but it's a great feeling to have made it again.

Though I appreciated those free days, I was getting so I could not get any decent sleep with the torture of those scabies and the lotion that was setting me on fire. There were still no aircraft on Friday, and as I was too miserable to walk around much, I went to bed early and tossed and turned all night. I went to the flight surgeon again Saturday and he gave me some ointment to counteract the lotion, which had painfully inflamed my skin. After that I went to our Maintenance & Supply Group to check on my personal plane—good ol' 240. It's coming along and they fixed up my gunsight so it will manually range—whoopee!

Rags and I finally got packed in two ships that were ready to go and leaped off for Komaki. Since it was a rather short leg, I decided to stay under the weather and we skimmed over the mountains, dodging the clouds and bouncing around through the turbulence of the peaks and valleys. The high country scenery was wonderful—really absorbing. How I'd like to take a ground trip through those mountains with their winding roads, pretty villages, and dark forests.

When we got out of our 86s at Komaki and walked into base ops to file for Kimpo, everybody just gaped in awe at us. After all, we were the only 86 Sabre outfit in the war, the big MiG hunters, and considered very hot stuff wherever we went—especially heading back for combat. I had on my new boots with my flying suit tucked in them and felt like I was really hot stuff—in the best outfit and best assignment in the world. Boy, it was a great feeling, and I made the most of it.

Then it was off to K-14 through some more weather to altitude where we picked up headwinds of nearly 150 knots. My aileron boost got screwed up and I had a hell of a job crowbarring my ship the rest of the way. When we landed at dusk my arms were worn out from two-handed flying. Back in our little home we naturally got into a large bull session with the boys and told stories about living it up. I broke out my new supply of DDT powder I'd collected at Johnson and proceeded to shake it all over my personal gear, especially in my sack before I got in it. I dreaded the thought of more scabies, but I put in so much DDT powder it was like laying down on a sandy beach. The Doc at Johnny had jokingly told me that if the scabies don't drive you nuts, the cure might. I didn't need any more laughs on *that* score.

Today I was up early for the first mission but it got scrubbed; I did get off this afternoon though. There was some weather to consider up north; a sort of shelf of it projected south from Manchuria to Sinanju. We got on top of all this stuff and patrolled to Long Point. The Commies usually don't fly when there is any weather so as we cruised along I kind of doubted we would find much action. Were we in for a surprise!

Out of the deep blue ahead suddenly appeared a squadron of MiGs head-on. The abrupt sighting and rate of closure was sure startling—evidently to the MiGs too, like someone jumping out and yelling *Boo*! They were slightly above us and dropped their tanks right in our faces—some commotion. Everybody reached for the panic button at once and we punched off our tanks while dodging theirs, which flipped through our formation. The whole squadron wheeled around to the right at full throttle to chase after these guys who had gone straight over us. We never saw them again. To the southeast we spotted cons and charged over, thinking that was the bunch. As planes materialized in the contrails I was bent over looking through the gunsight, finger extended over the trigger. I was flying an 86E and it sure handled nice and easy on the Mach with the wings slick. The planes ahead proved to be 86s and Meteors north of Ping Pong—what a let-down. While we were clean we swept the area awhile longer, then went on home, making high dives through the clouds to the landing pattern. Man, this 86 goes downhill sweet.

From the mail I wonder what the story is on Tom and the 121st Squadron. They no go Alaska? (Pidgin English again.) I guess they hope not.

From the latest on the peace talks (which started up again on October 25th), it looks like the end may be near as they were talking about a cease-fire and demarcation line. Of course, anchoring the front line doesn't put barbed wire in the sky. We don't go underground so our combat will not change. I don't imagine any combat outfit is exactly eager for the conditions of another winter of war in this frozen place. For us, the prospect of getting shot down way up there in the middle of the deep-freeze is enough to shake anybody up, but we don't pay much attention to all that peace babble the Communists put out.

I don't yet know what Lowell Thomas said in his radio broadcast of October 26th, but a transcript was mailed home and they'll send it to me. I'm pleased and proud that he mentioned me personally in one of his regular newscasts. That is a real pat on the back from a highly respected man.

I just finished some tasty night snacks with the boys in my flight; we're chewing and talking and after all this writing I'm pooped. It's kind of a chore, but I enjoy writing down my thoughts and activities. You may only get these chances once in a lifetime and I know damn well this is my time. I'm going to have a beer and then turn in.

NOVEMBER 19th

The days sort of sail by. Some of this time drags a bit as none of us are doing much flying. Each of the flights have collected assortments of books and magazines and I've been looking over the paperback stocks for new reading material. Our flight gets visits from the others looking for a swap or book loan. All conversation may cease while each one is buried in some story. We had about three days in a row of really lousy weather, lots of rain and thick low clouds, so we took advantage of the situation and became sack rats. It's a shame you can't store up sleep to draw on in the hectic periods, but in the service you soon learn to grab extra shuteye when you find it available. The weather broke on the 16th, but I didn't get on the mission. We may be seeing a lot more red noses, as they were out in force.

The new pilots and additional rank haven't materialized, so for several days now I've been Flight Commander of D Flight; I may be able to retain it too. They tell me that if the additions come in they will have an E Flight again and I'll command that—good deal! Charlie Mitson had to move to another flight, but most of my flight has been the same for some time. I still have the same plane and Frenchy as crew chief. Things are looking up.

I hadn't done much imbibing with the boys since I came back from the ferry trip, and on the night of the 14th, during the terrible weather, the whole Fighter Group went Able Sugar in the Swig Alley Club and came back raising hell by squadrons. All our squadron was bombed except my flight (we missed the word somehow) and did they give us hell—with particular attention to *me*, on account of my past escapades. One of our flight commanders and a guy from the 51st Group broke out one of our windows, and they were so plastered it's a wonder they didn't cut their throats or wrists aborting a try to crawl in through the broken glass to make a raid on us. Guys would charge in and continually throw us out of bed. Poor Kotok. Nick never bothers anybody, but he sure caught hell anyway. Then McPherson and Neubert jumped (or sprang) on me in my sack. My poor canvas cot—in the resulting struggle it snapped and collapsed. The place resembled a small riot—funny as hell, really.

The next night, the 15th, it was *my* turn to get rip-roaring on red eye. With some others for company I really whooped it up; what a hangover I had the next day. Guss woke me up for Mobile Control and I spent a good part of the day on that in the radio jeep. Laughing about this crazy but great bunch of guys and great life was rather painful to my head. It was Siberian cold outside; I figured my marrow was liable to fracture. Our immediate business is the boys from the 51st Fighter Group at K-13, who are here flying our 86s like crazy, getting recurrent for their conversion to Sabres and the Counter Air Mission. We will then have two Groups hunting up north, which ought to change the odds we have been up against—if we can keep a decent number of planes in commission.

We had a very interesting (and I hope productive) pow-wow that included the Wing and Group wheels, Creighton, and ten of us experienced pilots with a Col. Sykes from the Pentagon. He is one of General Vandenberg's boys over to get the straight stuff and we held the session in Combat Operations. We discussed our tactics, the MiGs, the guns, instrument flying, equipment, etc. Then he got a personal war story from each of us while his secretary took it all down. The war story part sort of embarrassed us, but all in all it was very interesting. I wish we had a lot more discussions of that sort with key people.

Wednesday evening we had a show in the open theater on the other side of the base. With the tremendous mass of men assembled it looked like half the troops in Korea were there. The big affair was Danny Kaye and his show, which had flown in from the States. Monica Lewis was with him and you should have heard the yelling. Several of us got an early close seat so we could enjoy the view. The show was pretty good, but some of the loud-mouthed troops sounded off too much with the crude stuff and the program seemed to be cut short. I really could care less about some stage entertainment, but stuff like that burns me up.

On the 16th, Glen Stalker and Smith, from the 49th Fighter Group, dropped in on me. They were up here to pick up a couple of F-84s that belong to their outfit. Glen is a Capt. now and he's got the extra sack in my flight room for the night. We got a sack for Smith also in our building. I asked Stalker to stay over the next night and I'll take him over to the Aussie Club—Saturday night, yahoo!

Gee, we had a great bull session about old times back in the States—and, of course, combat. I wish I could visit all the fighter outfits in Korea and see all the guys I know over here before we're all shipped out or bumped off. Smith's wife lives next door to Lu at Barnaby Terrace and they see each other a lot.

While we were yakking that first night, one of the boys had his Zenith Transoceanic radio on. That lilting Stateside music does things to you, songs like: "A Little Bit Independent in Your Smile." We usually listen to Tokyo or Nagoya AFRS; they have real good programs, mysteries, music, news, sports, etc. Sometimes we had to stop talking to listen to Tommy Dorsey's "I'm Getting Sentimental Over You," and then there was Bing with "I'll Get By."

I'm glad the weather broke for a change. The steady rains made a sinkhole out of the place—ankle-deep mud like glue. We can imagine what it must be like at the front.

The next day, the 17th, we went off on a big sweep mission up to the Yalu and then started hunting back and forth. We saw lots of contrails and figured there were about five enemy squadrons in the area, but they didn't fight for some reason. I thought they would eat us all alive by mobbing us when we were stooging around across the Yalu from Antung. Col. Preston and Beck latched onto a lone MiG and shot him up some. I had the element in Creighton's flight, but we couldn't locate MiGs we could get onto— all that adrenalin for nothing and the weather was perfect after all these dud days. That sure is rough on the system when you go up charged to capacity with expectation and then return with it bottled up in you—enough to blow the cork. We thought Col. P. had bought the farm or something from all the yakking on the radio.

That evening about nine o'clock I borrowed a jeep from the squadron and four of us went over to the Aussie Club across the field. I took Stalker for the experience, and Mathews and Beck came along, too. After blundering up and down the muddy roads we found the club. I have to hunt for it every time I go over, what with the black nights and the new diggings going on.

I got with Ray Trebilco and then everybody got introduced all around. We all started by swapping our latest war stories. The ones that got the biggest laughs were about the toughest fights (getting cannonballs from a MiG or something as hairy) and the whacky radio transmissions during a hassle.

Then the visiting Aussie Wingco put the squeeze on his accordion from the bar, everybody held up their glasses, and the singing started. We were really muzzle-loading that Asahi beer and outbursts of singing developed into shouting contests at times. What an uproar and what happy faces: "Oh, There's None So Fair As Can Compare to the Boys in the RFC," and "Old King Cole," and "Cats on the Rooftops," and "Jolly, Jolly England," and "Sing Us Another One," to name a few.

Music? Ha, ha.

The singing became so violent we all got hoarse; we call it "firing out." Then the Wingco jumped off the bar and formed the lead of a sort of train that trooped around the quonset club. Each man would put a hand on the shoulder of the man ahead of him and hold a glass in the other while they stomped and chanted along the route. Anything in the way of the train was either kicked aside or climbed over. Some of the guys pulled the flowers out of the vases to throw the wet tangle at the unwary. I started out in the train, and a bit of shin-knocking got going as the guys on the sideline tried to trip up the train. Things got rapidly rougher and pretty soon a couple of tables collapsed with a crash, which triggered a crossfire of the contents of the drinks, followed as expected by the shattering of glasses. I hadn't been in their club since they had completed the interior decorating and it was rapidly being remodeled.

We visitors sort of faded to the sidelines as a melee like rugby developed. The finale was Hicockalorum, in which the smaller guys hop on the shoulders of the bigger ones and they attack similar teams. Each team was either charging, dodging, or crashing. I've done that before, but only in a pool or lake where you aren't so apt to get ruined. But those Aussies are tough and don't seem to care about broken bones or skulls. It looked like murder to me, but they call it sport.

Those fellows have the close outfit spirit and what-the-hell outlook that gets fighter pilots the evil eye in most of our Air Force. I don't mean that we have to go hog-wild as a regular thing; they don't either. I mean, their attitude is: We're in this together gang; this is *our* club and *our* sport and *we* like it, let's keep it that way— Yahoo!

The next day they are right out there in their Meteors giving the same business to the Commies. What a bunch of tigers. With the club a wreck and everybody pooped out, we made our way back to our area, thoroughly satisfied with Saturday night.

Sunday I joined the big bull session in Combat Ops with the gang when they returned from the mission where they put the strafe on Uiju. I wish I'd been on that deal. Ken Chandler and Rags Ragland peeled off from the squadron and went to the deck to make the attack. I guess Ken really shot the hell out of the MiGs parked on their alert pad. It's about time we kicked those buzzards off their privileged flying field on this side of the Yalu—what ridiculous rules. I'll bet that was a big surprise up there.[11]

It was my turn to schedule the squadron mission for today so I spent the evening in the room with my flight having a few brews while making out the lineup. As we had no big wheels flying, I figured I knew as much as anybody about a regular combat mission now, so I put myself in for squadron lead and it was approved. I can't remember when a lieutenant was scheduled to lead a squadron in this outfit, but I can sure remember the overflow of rank when I came to the 4th Group last summer: Majors and LCs were leading *flights*! As frustrating as that time was at Johnson Field, I realize now that I lucked out getting to Korea later, after all the rank had gone home.

After I hit the sack I got very little real sleep and then early in the morning I had a lot of running around between maintenance, armament, and operations to make sure everything was set up. The "nice" surprise at briefing was that I got tapped for the job of escorting the RF-80 photo ship to look into the dragon's mouth after yesterday's strafing of Uiju. On top of that, the B-29s bombed the place last night. I know the other two squadrons were only too glad we had the escort headache.

In the later, short squadron briefing, we figured we would be met by a hornet's nest of irate MiGs out for revenge—another adrenalin job. The RF-80 reccy pilot was quite understandably in a sweat and asked, "Please don't lose me, you guys."

Well, I got Red and White flights formed up and at 20,000 feet we rendezvoused with the RF, call sign Dignity Blue. In case the escort had to be terminated because of weather, a big dogfight, or some emergency, the break-off call was "Coca Cola." We all tooled up north and to stay with the slower RF we had to "S" continually over him, with the flights working into the old Thatch weave.

As we approached the Yalu, the sky became very cloudy with several layers and poor vis. It was literally all I could do to keep track of the RF-80, who was probing the weather and looking for holes for picture-taking. The poor guys in the squadron following me were working crack the whip, bending their planes around; the other squadrons were somewhere high up calling out bandits.

We got to see the mouth of the Yalu momentarily through a hole, and as bandits were called over Antung, I ordered our tanks dropped. The poking around showed the weather was just impossible for photographing the Yalu airfields, so Dignity Blue took his alternate target and we headed inland and southeast for the two airfields north of Sinanju—Namsi and Taechon.[12] I just hoped my squadron had eagle eyes as I was completely eyeball-locked onto the RF ahead and below. I only checked on a couple of calls and saw some high contrails and some drop tanks fluttering down through a thin overcase above us.

We let down for the photo runs over the airfields and picked up some interesting flak, but it wasn't very accurate and there was no real sweat. When the RF finished, he dove for Anju and the Chongchon River; we strung out behind and trailed him to the Yellow Sea. By that time we were bingo, so I climbed through the overcast, ran out a quick time estimate, and then we made a formation let-down on course as the gang was sort of low on fuel. As we broke out past the Han River, I noted that I had gotten a false ADF swing and wondered if it could have been a false enemy beacon that had been noted by others. The big sweat we'd had at briefing was all for nothing and I had had my fourth flight in an E model, which I'm finding less strange each time.

At the moment I'm taking on the all-night duty officer job; I relieved Kotok at 11 p.m. so he could go to sleep and get himself and my flight an extra slot on the schedule tomorrow. Glen Stalker left for K-2 this afternoon after a swell three-night visit. We both enjoyed comparing notes on fighter-bomber and fighter day work.

When you get into the procedures, there is quite a difference in concept and outlook between the two. I never participated in any air-to-ground work except strafing; I've always been in the air-to-air business since I started flying and I run my thought processes and combat experience together on that subject.

If I had known last night (while I was trying to sleep) that I was going to lead the squadron on that photo escort job, I probably wouldn't have gotten any sleep at all. And then this all-night duty tonight—one thing about a war: It really makes you appreciate sleep. The more sleep you miss (pre-dawn alerts, early missions, air raid alarms at two or three a.m.), the more you get keyed up. Then you are so intent on catching up you toss all night.

I see that it's 4 a.m. now. The sentries come in one in a while and a little conversation breaks the monotomy of standing by this crazy telephone switchboard. All we need is an air raid. Oh, yeah!

These damn peace talks—they're worse on the nerves than bullets. Ever since I've been overseas they have been beating their gums and rumors have been flying. We'd be a lot better off if we never heard anything about them.

It is far more practical for us to concern ourselves with overcoming the lowering temperature and challenge of winter. The nights are bitter now and the days rarely come up to what you care to endure for long in the open; you learn to appreciate simple things like long-handled underwear. We are anticipating snow any day and are only too aware of how *that* will compound our already serious flying and aircraft maintenance problems. I've been back for ten days from that ferry trip to Japan and have flown three missions; that's about average, and everybody is wondering how slow operations can get.

Squadron of F-86s of 4th Fighter Group during the full-power run-up just before brake release and takeoff for a mission. Kimpo, Korea, fall 1951. (photo from John P. Green collection)

When I was relieved from that all night duty officer job I really felt groggy and slept half the day. That night I got into a session with B Flight—Beck, Chris, Mossholder, and others; we really shot down some hooch discussing flying, how to win the war, and, of course, women. We got pretty snokkered and expounded solutions to everything, ha, ha. With our appetites fueled up we broke out C-rations—yum, yum, how I love 'em, especially those meat patties. I wish we could get more C-rations; sometimes the regular chow tells my stomach we are on a diet. I went on back to my flight and hit the sack about 2 a.m. My itch is about healed up from the former raw state, so to really cure things up I didn't bother to try to get on a mission. The weather is real lousy now and the mission didn't get off anyway—just a three ship weather reccy, ugh.

I sampled some more Korean social life by dropping in on A Flight to shoot the breeze. Mathews, Mitson, Mac, Rapp, and Dawson were there. Each guy was telling a bigger story than the other and I contributed my share. With so little else to occupy our free time, personal stories and viewpoints are our most dependable source of entertainment. As usual, we all had our say about what the Air Force ought to emphasize, such as a much stronger force of day fighters to ensure control of the sky, all-out realistic training, and the opportunity for the working fighter pilot to have a voice in recommendations.

I was on today's schedule, but as the briefing wasn't until after lunch some of us loafed on our sacks and read kind of late in the morning. We heard that some VIP was coming in—somebody biggern' Vandenberg. Yeah, man, the mess hall was really decked out for the occasion and we waded into a big Thanksgiving Day feed. While we were finishing, our Wing Commander, Col. Thyng, and General Everest, 5th Air Force Commander, entered in preparation for the other VIPs.

After eating we cleared out of the mess hall and saw a great line of shiny staff cars and Air Police vehicles with mounted guns splashing up the hill by the barracks to the mess hall. The word went out that *the Veep*—Vice President Barkley—was here!

We all went to our little homes and got suited up with our sidearms prominent—big war and all that stuff. Then we trooped to Combat Ops for the mission briefing. Heh, heh—in this weather even the birds were walking. The fighter pilots on the schedule (about 24) got properly situated, leaving the front benches open,

The Lockheed Constellation, personal aircraft of Gen. Matthew Ridgway, Commander-in-Chief of United Nations Command and Far East Command, on the ramp at K-14, Kimpo, October 1951.

and then Vice President and Mrs. Barkley entered, followed by General Ridgway, General Van Fleet, General Everest, and other dignitaries. In fact, a whole flock of VIPs attended the briefing.

Col. Thyng really gave us a great buildup to start things off. Man, it was tops. What an outfit—boy, I felt proud. Simmons gave the briefing—real sharp, the edge-of-the-chair sort—and I believe the visitors got a real feel for the proper atmosphere. We also showed some real good gun camera combat film—in fact, a clip we call our VIP roll. Mrs. Barkley had, I'm sure, the natural reaction to a sudden film exposure to death in flames at close range: some oh's and sharp intakes of breath. The boys in the rear rows gave suitable tiger growls for atmosphere, and some wag in the back commented in a whisper about Ridgway's trademark: "That's no handgrenade, that's a cigarette lighter."

At the end, Vice President Barkley got up to give us a few words. Now I guess there is no bunch of people so skeptical about old politicking stuff as those directly involved in the shooting war business, but his extemporaneous speech was really okay, and we heartily accepted it. After all the VIPs departed, we sweated out the weather, eventually cancelling the mission because of the apparent static, gluey conditions, and everyone went off to take care of their various ground jobs.

At the end of the day I moseyed through the various flight

A distinctive view of the F-84C at 30,000 feet. The pilot was author's Squadron Commander of 121st Fighter Squadron, the late Willard Millikan, then Lt. Col., later Maj. Gen. Millikan had been a member of the Eagle Squadrons of the RAF and the 336th Fighter Squadron, 4th Fighter Group in WWII. He was a triple ace of the ETO.

rooms on the way to my gang. I lucked out on the mail; a letter came from Tom, continuing our commentaries about flying, which I enjoyed reading. I also got a swell reply from my former C.O. in the Air National Guard, Col. Millikan. He wrote a fine letter with all the scoop about his operations and I appreciate his considerations of my review of the latest combat dope. He reminded me that he was in the 336th Squadron, formed out of the RAF Eagle Squadrons, in World War II. Nobody here from the 33rd Fighter Group at Otis Field, where he is now, can say enough about him. That still won't hold a candle to the respect *I* have for him. He's keen on our work here and I'm sure glad he has a fighter group.

I hope the weather breaks tomorrow, but it doesn't look like it will. Anyway, in case it hangs in we are all conniving . . . a small party, neh?

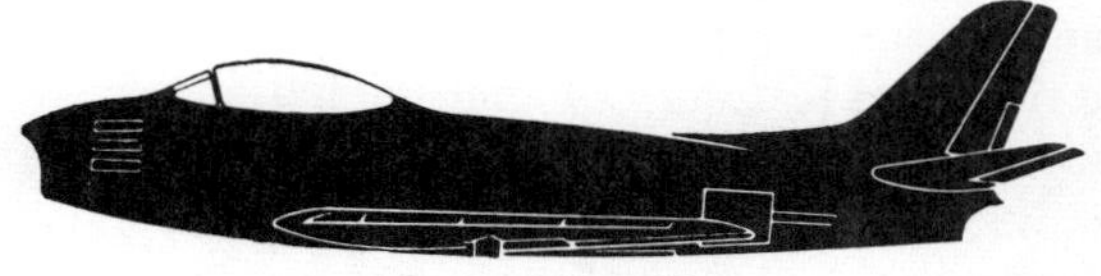

VII
Hot and Cold Winter

SUNDAY, NOVEMBER 25th

It's 9 a.m. right now and snowing. I have looked for it first thing each morning just as I did as a boy, and at 6:30 there it was on the ground and floating down. So far we have about two inches, but sleet is beginning to alternate, turning it into a sloppy mess. The cold was intense last night—that's actually what woke me up, so I got dressed and slogged over for breakfast. We don't have any mission today, so I'll go down to the squadron to take care of some paperwork and see what's going on with my airplane. The poor crew chiefs have only the crudest of working conditions and facilities. No wonder we're in such a bind.

The bunch of new pilots has arrived, more to come, and already four more Captains are assigned to my squadron Hmmm. Naturally that means I'll lose my flight. We need more pilots like I need an extra hole in my head. What good are more pilots with no airplanes? The weather and shortage of aircraft is so bad already that I've only gotten four missions in the last 21 days.

On Friday, the 23rd, we did get off on another mission, escort of an RF-80. We went right up to the Yalu and picked up occasional flak along with the opportunity to get a good look at the bomb craters in Uiju airfield. Then we made a sweep down the river from about Mizu to the mouth, our high altitude and the extreme clarity of the sky enabling us to see all the Commie airfields and far into Manchuria.

As we got opposite Antung at 30,000 feet I could see spurts and small clouds of dust all around the field as the MiGs fired up and moved out of their parking spots. The sun reflected in silvery sparkles and flashes off the planes on the taxiways and rolling down their runway for takeoff as they apparently scrambled a swarm of fighters. Some appeared very high on our side, but they didn't bother us. We cruised by the mouth of the Yalu and ran well out to sea along the coast of Manchuria before swinging around south and back east. I could see Ta-ku-shan and pick out the islands near the tip of the Kwantung Peninsula in the vicinity of Dairen and Port Arthur, the most spectacular view I've ever had of all that country up there.

That night we burst out of the monotony of recent days with a roughhouse party that took the roof off the group. After starting in our barracks, we went down to the wheel house where we gathered by our C.O.'s room for singing and yelling war whoops. The booze was really flowing. After we got really roaring, the whole squadron went through the wheel house like a cyclone, waking up the rest of the squadron C.O.s and finally the Group C.O.

Then the tide washed back to our own building where we proceeded to have the wildest wrestling matches this outfit has had so far—bodies flying through the air, guys overturned in their cots, cots broken and crazy pilots in bunches, struggling in the midst of the furniture. It was funny as all get-out, except we all got pretty well beat up. I got some gashes in my side and back that look like I'd fallen in barbed wire, bumps on the head, and assorted bruises. It's a wonder someone wasn't crunched. I believe the Aussie practice may be better: They accept their club as the natural arena and tear *that* up rather than their living quarters. Boy, we sure found out what happens when we really release the brakes around here. The expression "GCA" (gone completely ape) pretty well describes that "party." Something you wouldn't want to miss, but couldn't survive as a regular thing. No doubt about it—I sure am in a great squadron.

The package with the loafer socks arrived from home today. They have high ankles and soft leather soles and I know will come in real handy around our room with this winter temperature. Actually, I need very little in this place; items like that are just the thing. The package reminded me that the six month mark has passed since I left the Land of the Big PX.

We just got through listening to the news—more of the same. We don't have to worry like the home front about the question of whether the war will be fought another winter—we're in it *now*.

DECEMBER 1st

I just haven't felt like writing lately; I suppose there are a number of reasons. For one thing, the weather bugs us all, and then there are complaints from home, irritations that are thousands of miles removed from our world. The simplest way I've found is to live it like it is and not try to dream up solutions beyond my control. So I sit with my pen in my hand and a blank stare at the wall, occasionally taking part in the usual conversation and putting off writing until I get back in the mood.

We have again been involved in some terrific fights. The mission on the 27th put me back in the action. Creighton was Red Leader and I was leading White Flight. The squadron probed deep inside Long Point, northwest of Sonchon, and we found out where the action was all right when a MiG squadron appeared suddenly on our right. Without hesitation, as if a mutual challenge had been tossed between us, each outfit broke around right to engage. You could just sense the determination by the way we piled into each other. They were good and we really went at it.

My flight stuck with me while I was maneuvering the beginning situation, unable to cue up on any MiGs as both sides were going all-out and turning with all their might. Then another squadron of MiGs dove onto us and six of them fired in a head-on dive at my flight, but their aim wasn't too hot and it wasn't difficult throwing them off. I started a right turn on two MiGs with four more in front of them, all of us in a right turn, and checking back I saw six more boring up our tails. I told my flight, "White, haul it around." Those red MiG cannonballs were streaming at us, but in this odd predicament I didn't pull as hard as possible because those behind were not cutting inside for proper lead. If I had turned hard right, I would have cut out the MiGs in front and put them on our tails—sort of like a trapeze act.

We swirled around in a great big wheel and while doing so, two more MiGs from somewhere cut across the circle, took a squirt at us, and were gone in a flash. When we got clear of that tangle I spotted two more at twelve o'clock and took out after them. They saw us coming, cranked around in a right chandelle, and went up like elevators. I went hunting elsewhere. White Three came on the radio and advised, "Look out for that flight right on top of us."

There were four MiGs above, maneuvering to work a bounce on us. I ducked under them and we broke away. During a left turn, one of the flight called an urgent left break and I put everything into it. Four sneaky ones had tapped us and commenced firing. I saw an 86, belly up, flick under me and looked way back to see if it had been my element, Three, or Four. I couldn't see *any* 86s, then my number Two said he'd lost me in the break and did I have him? I pulled tighter while I rocked my ship over to check and told him no, I was alone. Those four MiGs were still on me and pumping out bright tracers, so I really put the business to my turn and threw them way outside. When my position looked just right, I rolled over inside, pulled through, and dove for Long Point, calling my number Two to meet me there.

I was flying an E model and really appreciated those hydraulic controls as I got that baby going over the Mach, gaining distance before the MiGs could get turned around and down. As they lined up well behind and fired, I did a few small jinks so I wouldn't be a steady target—no effort at all in the E—like waving goodbye. The MiGs gave me a parting burst and went off. I kept my Mach up heading for the coast.

As soon as I picked up White Two, we headed back inland and upstairs. My element leader, Dawson, got a MiG at this time. I could hear him call his wingman: "See that parachute, White Four?"

I just couldn't suppress a big grin and chuckle over that. It's too bad we got split up when we did because the MiGs were breaking their larger formations as we were and the fight had spread out. You could say we were sort of saturated initially. Well, the two of us snooped around, but our bit of sky was clear of jets, so we headed out low on fuel. We had really gobbled the JP in that lash-up. I think that was my record number of times to be shot at on one mission. Those MiG pilots were no slouches. Dick Creighton, our squadron commander, got his fifth MiG to become the fourth jet ace—a just cause for celebration.

The next day Ragland got shot down. Damn, I felt bad over that—I wasn't even on the mission. He was a swell egg and I hope he's alive and will make out okay.[13]

I listened on our ground radio in squadron Ops to a later mission. Such gasping and yelling—it really gives you the clanks to listen to a hairy mission so we don't indulge all the time. It's good, though, that our crew chiefs and other ground personnel (especially the office types) can listen to the real thing. Some of them shake their heads over that wild stuff. I'm sure it convinces them we're not a bunch of privileged, overpaid flyboys. The shot-up planes that come back make everyone thoughtful too.

I'm writing rather late and now I'll quit to listen to "China Nights" playing from Osaka-Nagoya Radio. I know I'll never forget that song.

DECEMBER 6th

On the morning of 30 November I had trouble with my headset, which gave me a long delay on takeoff. I went out with the throttle bent over the stop, but couldn't catch the squadron. On the way after the gang I noticed what shined suspiciously like aircraft parked at the old strip at Sariwon. I looked things over from altitude and reported this to Dentist and went on north to the Hey Rube area near Chongju. The radio talk sounded like sort of a fight going on, and though I put out a call for any singles I couldn't find other aircraft to join. I gave up early and went south, letting down to reconnoiter this Sariwon bit. Whatever metallic objects I had seen before were no longer there, so after a low-level look-see I continued home to Kimpo on an interesting low-altitude tour of the enemy countryside.

Before the afternoon mission there was another of those last-minute alterations in the scheduled lineup. Because of that reshuffle I was called on my field phone to suit up and bring Merrick with me to Combat Ops. During the briefing it was brought out that the Reds had tangled with ROK (Republic of Korea) forces holding some islands off the west coast. Not only had troops hit the islands, but Commie aircraft as well. While on our CAP (Combat Air Patrol), we were supposed to be on the alert for any chance of catching these guys at their dirty work.

We trailed squadrons on a fairly deep-in course, and when well up north made a westerly swing toward Hot Spot. Swarms of MiG contrails could be seen forming across the Yalu and several formations conned very high over us while we cut behind them, studying their moves. The increasing MiG traffic drew our attention in an even wider scan and our vigilance paid off—a formation of bogies appeared out of Manchuria heading south along the coast toward Long Point. They turned out to be prop aircraft well below our altitude—twelve Tu-2 bombers escorted by sixteen La-9 fighters, or so went the later count. At first, to me, they were just a big bunch. Col. Preston called the Tallyho and the whole outfit went noses down for a diving attack.

Our position at first sighting was an awkward 90 degrees abeam, so our initial run was such a high angle-off I went by behind them in a vertical bank as everybody bent around for another pass. We were all going at a terrific speed and I was mashed down by the Gs while trying to keep position in our formation. I noticed we were all at about 8,000 feet and curving around to the front of the bombers. And then it was pick your man—what a charge! Like the horse cavalry.

I had a rather unusual deal as the extra third element in Red Flight, and because of my position in our formation I picked a bomber on the side of the last box, going in on a quartering head-on pass. I spanned right on him and began firing while pulling like hell on the stick to keep the pip on as I raked him with a long burst. As I went right past his wing and tail I looked back and ha! Flame was bursting out of his right engine. I almost pulled my wings off straining to come around to make sure I finished him off in another pass and called out, "Red Five's got a flamer," to stake the claim to my kill. There was no need for sweat; the flames enveloped his engine, spread over the wing, and he fell out of formation going down like a bonfire. Another quick check, still turning, and there was a big splash in the Yellow Sea and no more bomber.

I was then around on the enemy course and out in front of me I saw an La-9. Closing at a terrific rate, I got the pip right on him and let go a big squirt. The results surprised me—the ammo went out like a long arm reaching for the La-9, and almost at the instant of contact he broke left and the bullet stream went right through the spot he vacated. Closest thing I ever saw, and *flash*—we passed him. That little tiger then racked back and squirted at Dave Freeland, who was flying my wing. At our speed we could have cared less. Those La-9s sure resembled Focke-Wulf 190s.

The fuel was really getting low (we had bingo at Tallyho), so I attempted a quick beam attack on the bombers, but was too close in to pull enough lead and about blacked out as I passed right by the tails of one formation. I was looking through the top of my canopy at them in a vertical bank and felt the thump of their propwash as I saw the gunners' heads following me. I didn't notice their guns (probably because I was looking down the barrels), but I distinctly heard guns firing.

Blast it, I wanted another pass. I saw the wings of one bomber just fold up and another hit the sea with a tremendous eruption of fire, smoke, and a column of water like a volcano. His bombs must have exploded. I couldn't resist giving out a "Woooeee!" Then an La-9 right above got blasted and disintegrated as it went along.

I remember saying to myself, "Look out for all that junk

raining down," and particularly eyed that big radial engine, separated and roaring down like a safe. I passed within a hundred feet of two tight-turning La-9s; every detail was distinct including the pilots—another of those odd slow-motion feelings. Then I had to dodge two guys in parachutes and watch out for other 'chutes going down all over into that frigid sea full of scattered ice—what a fate! It doesn't pay to be the loser in this business—*or* think about it.

I had to break off my next pass and hop over the gaggle as other 86s were firing into the formation with their noses aimed right into me. Everybody was going wild; planes were just missing each other and bullets were literally flying in all directions from both sides. The sky must have been chock-full of lead. Planes were smoking, there were splashes below, and radio fight talk was intense. It was the damndest violent action I ever saw—kill-or-be-killed destruction. I even heard someone who had momentarily clamped down on his mike button, breathing like a steam engine, interrupted by the roar of his guns. Holy smoke!

Col. Preston put out the order to withdraw. By that time most everybody was split up; Dave and I were separated and the group tore out for the open sea at low altitude in a great scattered pack under the darkening sky. The late sun reflecting off the sea silhouetted the speeding fighters to my right. Each man was getting his climb speed, planning his climb to our distant base, and sweating his fuel—which was so low you dreaded to look at the gauge. Way, way above us there were still streams of contrails of MiGs that somehow didn't get the coordination to involve themselves in our show—a real fortunate break. In the last calls from Dentist that I remember the train count was up to 14, the highest number I had ever heard. They must have launched every MiG.

I did a long idle descent and just made it home with 15 gallons showing—good thing I broke off when I did. Everyone was close, but every man in the outfit got in okay. You can't beat that for a good show.

Combat Ops was a regular madhouse. It seemed as if every pilot in the Wing poured in to hear the story. The resulting commotion was like the locker room of the winning team of the game of the year. After that, who needs games? The eager guys not on the mission felt like bashing us all in the mouth. There was back-slapping, hand-shaking, yelling and cheering. It was some job getting the debriefing accomplished. The Intelligence and PIO people were turning from one pilot to the other trying to straighten

Right after the bomber interception south of the mouth of the Yalu River. Major George Davis (left) had made ace and so had Major "Bones" Marshall (right). Colonel Ben Preston, 4th Fighter Group commander, is in center. (Air Force photo)

out the war stories. In those early moments of ground reunion, the pilots couldn't have cared less about the paperwork. We all had a great time unwinding after that one.[14]

Much later, when I found time to myself, I couldn't help but revive memories of 1940 when I was a teenager during the Battle of Britain. I had listened to the sound recordings of BBC through CBC with my head almost stuck in the radio in a fever of excitement, regretting that I wasn't able to get in on it. Little did I know.

It was cold as blue blazes during the early-morning preparation for the mission on 2 December. On the way back, Andy and I had enough fuel to avoid the traffic jam and have a good old-fashioned beat-up of the local area south of the field—rolls on the deck, buzzing the beach and rice paddies. What a change of pace; it hardly seemed like the same war.

The weather was lousy on the 3rd, but we went off anyway. We used only two flights and I led the second. Because of the heavy cloud buildup, we climbed as steep as possible right after takeoff and join-up to stay in the clear and get on top. The whole outfit got so slow I got right under the lead flight and began essing to hold my position. Just before we had to enter the clouds, my airspeed was way too low to suit me, so as we penetrated I went on my instruments and lowered my nose to pick up proper climb speed.

There was a long climb on the gauges before we broke out on top and after a quick visual it was apparent that there was just my flight and we were on our own. I started to patrol on top toward the northeast, scanning the endless rumpled cloud expanse. Surprisingly, it wasn't long before we found a single hole in all that stuff and through it saw, of all places, Pyongyang! Balls o' fire, what luck.

I told the flight to get into tight trail and down we went, lickety split, in a tight spiral. The flight was hanging right in there as if we were making a fast slide down a barber pole tunnel. It was an enjoyable bit of hot exercise and a whole lot easier and quicker than a groping formation descent on the gauges.

When we got down the hole and under the weather we scooted on the Sinanju, where I set up a patrol at 13—15,000 feet. The visibility was terrible and I went into a lazy S-pattern to look around better and keep the flak from plotting us against the cloud ceiling. I heard Preston's voice and through the murk saw his bunch from the 335th in the area. None of us encountered anything. Watching our return fuel, I got everybody to close up in diamond and then climbed south to on-top. I began a let-down on estimated time and we broke out okay just north of the field.

During the debriefing I gathered what I had figured out when my flight found itself alone on top: Red lead must not have been sure of his position. His flight troops (on the side) said they were sure they patrolled between Haeju and Chodo, which could have been confused in the weather with the Long Point area. What really surprised me was the report of MiGs patrolling towards Seoul. Just before our initial cloud penetration and flight separation, a fair-sized formation of contrails had been sighted east of us, going south. I saw those aircraft make no turns as they proceeded on a straight course south, which our F-84s usually do on the way home from missions. Also, I have never seen MiGs up in the kind of weather we had been probing. Red lead was adamant about their being MiGs and as I couldn't offer anything positive otherwise, the report went out that MiGs had been in the Seoul area.

I got my first chance to fly a T-33 in the afternoon. It handled different than I expected in a way, but was kind of fun. It seemed sort of squat and stiff-legged on landings, otherwise okay. What a checkout—we had no Dash One or checklist of any kind, nothing but a talk around the cockpit, get in and go. What a crazy fuel system—what's this cold weather stuff? Start in bypass? Oh well, the crew chief knows, and he stands by.

On the 4th of December, what with aborts, I ended up being Red Leader of four ships and saw 16 MiGs pass on our right—gulp. I turned in behind them but couldn't keep them in sight, so turned right (west) to the sun and climbed awhile, figuring to be on top of them and in the sun when they headed back toward the Yalu. I then turned 130 degrees left and Dawson, Red Three, called MiGs below. I couldn't spot them and asked for their clock position. Rather than waste valuable time looking myself and lose a bounce, I told Red Three to lead the way. Down we went and there they were under us—eight MiGs.

They were in an awkward position for us to get in a bounce— right up under our feet, so to speak. We dove from 32,000 to 30,000, but the MiGs got alert and poured on the coal—climbing like rockets, giving us a worse angle-off. Then one of the flight called, "MiGs coming in high at six o'clock!"

There on our backs were eight more MiGs, evidently the other half of the squadron we were initially trailing. The foxy guys had split high and low. We "diverted" from the eight in front—the eight behind and on top of us probably alerted those in front. They did a good job of messing up our bounce and it was round and round with the foxy eight and nobody ended up with any advantage.

As we had started into this hassle Nick Kotok, Red Two, called, "*Toksan* at one o'clock!"

I checked as were bending around and replied, "I'll say, *toksan!*"

Approaching us were two squadrons of four flights each—32 more MiGs, an unpleasant addition to say the least. We had only our original four 86s and naturally proceeded to "very carefully" dodge around and play cat-and-mouse with all this hungry company. Some of those MiGs would sit a little high, watching us, then—having evidently come to a decision—nose down and come in on a nice pursuit curve. All I could do was turn into them, and as we got close each one of their flights would pull back up to the main pack. With all the advantages of numbers and position on their side, they sure flubbed the dub. If the odds had been reversed, we would probably have collided with each other trying to get a piece of MiG. I have found in a number of actions that a well-knit flight of four can salvage a pretty bad situation and come out okay.

Yesterday I had to pull out of the formation up north with Andy Merrick, as he was having serious electrical problems. I escorted him to home base and then went back upstairs for a workout on my own. I dove the hell out of it, up to one-point-one Mach, and pulled max Gs using trim while trying to simulate that hairy bind I'd been in with McPherson. I never could accomplish what I had done while getting shot at; I felt I might break something. After that interesting experiment I ran through a series of acro, which I hadn't practiced in some time.

I missed a real hot one in the afternoon. I almost blew my top listening to the mission over the squadron radio—and, later, talking to the boys who were on it. They caught MiGs that were fumbling around down low, looking for our fighter-bombers, and really worked them over Maj. Davis, the C.O. of the 334th Squadron, has gone hog-wild and is shooting down MiGs like mad. He got two more on that hot one. Davis is a very mild-appearing guy, but when he straps on a fighter he's all tiger—a hell of a sharp pilot and gunner, and he must have the eyes of an eagle.

We got into a goody this afternoon, a real interesting mission. We started out with twelve ships; I had the *last* element, but with aborts and reshuffling the formations we ended up with four, and I became Red Leader. Talk about fast promotions! Soon the C.O., Creighton, came back in (he had had a hung tank but managed to

Major George Davis, commander of the 334th Fighter Squadron, gives the double victory sign after a mission. Before his death he scored 14 victories. Although by the end of the war he ranked fourth in the ace list, in the opinion of the author, he was the top F-86 pilot of the war. He got his kills during the toughest of all the air fighting. Davis carried WWII combat experience (where he got seven Japanese victories) to Korea, where he set a meteroric pace. He was one of only two Air Force pilots to receive the Medal of Honor in the Korean War—both were posthumous awards. (Air Force photo)

clear it off). He told me to keep the lead and became Red Five and Six with his element.

I set up our prearranged CAP northwest and southeast. It started out over the top of solid weather. By stretching our NW course, I was able to see that the Yalu and Antung were clear. On one of the northerly courses I saw MiGs coming on the right in the cons, so I turned south and paralleled them. Col. Thyng, Black Leader, crossed his squadron over us, so I turned with his formation and paralleled him while we climbed our squadrons into the contrail level together after these MiGs.

At about Ping Pong (on top), the MiGs must have realized our presence or their ground radar warned them, and they turned around hard. There were about two squadrons of them, somewhere between 24 and 32, and as we swung into each other it was contrails cutting into contrails.

It appeared that my formation was going to meet them first, but my position was such that if I took a cut at the leaders, I would put the rest of the pack on our tails. I let Col. Thyng cut his squadron over us and then I swung in, making the first contact in an angular head-on with eight MiGs.

That sure was an exciting scene and made a lasting impression: the MiGs precisely spaced with wings steeply banked, smooth and graceful as if coasting toward us on some invisible sheet of ice, their colorful noses and polished skins expanding in view in that odd slow-motion effect I sometimes sense when detached from reference to the ground. With our radios inactive, there was a vast silence about it all as if it were happening in outer space. Then as every detail of the MiGs stands out, the closure changes to a great slash as we pass each other. Wowee!

At times like that this combat really stirs me up; I wouldn't have missed this sort of experience for anything. My comment for those mighty hunters of big (or small) game is that there is plenty of contest for all in a place like MiG Alley—but this hunting is fair, and the game has an equal opportunity of blowing your head off if you flub your vigilance or goof a maneuver. These counter-moves of opposing planes trying to kill each other is the damndest game of chess; you hardly have time to realize how dangerous it is.

Neither side was in firing position as we met so each formation reversed to grab the advantage and it was round and round in another mad circus. What a sight—swirling contrails tangling and hanging in the bright blue at 32 and 33,000 feet, the signature of the fighter pilot. That kind of hard maneuvering lost all-important altitude, which each side was determined to hang on to, so everyone soon had to relax the Gs and try to get back up on top of things again. The extreme altitude made it tough for anybody to turn very well; there were some obviously awkward and frustrated passes made by both MiGs and 86s. I would plunge into the maze of thick cons to bounce a couple and discover 86s, so back to the grind of more climb. Two planes went right over me—one an 86, the other a MiG firing at him. All I could do was call for an 86 single to break—a real contrail lash-up.

Many of the MiGs soon chickened out and used their altitude performance to stay just out of our reach, where we were standing on our tails trying to get at them. Our 86s were pooped out as if we were in a rope-climbing contest with monkeys. Though most chose to run in higher circles, a few characters stayed to play a bit longer.

One MiG approached my nose so I figured I'd swing across and crank onto his tail, and on doing so discovered his pal was trailing and behind Kotok and myself. I called a hard left to Nick and almost cut back on this MiG, but he wasn't dumb and pulled around with us. No sweat really, but I couldn't get an advantage on him. While we were making a max rate turn I couldn't see him any more, so thought we were okay and called, "We're clear." A later look to the rear and there he still was, but in a poor position. It was pull around again, but he'd had enough and left the mix-up. Nick and I laughed about that when we got on the ground—do you suppose he's still there!?[15]

After considerable prodding from the outfit I'm going on R&R tomorrow, the 7th, with Dave Freeland. Everyone is supposed to get one every couple of months, whether they want it or not. Well, frankly, I don't want any R&R after all that previous time in Japan, even though that generally was a seven-day-a-week work schedule, but as I've been overseas over six months, I have no choice. I suppose after making out on that bomber mission, they feel I should get lost for a while—just when I was all hopped up and trying to get on the good missions. Now, with all the additional pilots and rank coming, I'm back to assistant Flight Commander, but I'm told my combat seniority will count in my favor.

DECEMBER 15th

Dave Freeland and I lucked out and made the trip to Johnson Field in a C-54—plush travel for us compared to a C-47 or 46. We spent some of the trip up front in the crew compartment—there are certain advantages in wearing wings and I'll gladly use them.

By the time we unloaded at Johnson I had one of those miserable headaches that won't let you do anything, so I had to admit I really needed some rest. After a long and wonderful shower, although early in the evening, I just went for that comfortable bed, crawled between those fresh laundered sheets, and the lights were out.

We didn't have any particular plans except slow ones for the following days. About the only thing definite had been brought about some time before the R&R. One of the CAT crews (Civil Air Transport of Formosa) had been to Kimpo with supplies for us, but because of the nighttime runway construction and air defense requirements the field was closed during darkness, which left them stuck for the night with their aircraft. Dave had done a fine job of arranging accomodations for their RON with us and they had invited him to call them anytime he was in Tokyo. When we made contact we had a swell visit with the pilots and their families. The Far East had been their home for a long time; they lived on the economy, and their kids, who went to Japanese schools, were fluent in the language. They took us as their guests to their own membership club, the CAT Club, where we had a Number One time meeting their friends.

My original D Flight in rear, which became E with additional pilots. Left to Right: Kotok, Merrick, Green, Mitson, author. In front: Keen, new D Flight Commander and later Operations Officer, unidentified pilot far right. November 1951, Kimpo, Korea.

During our free days we got up when we felt like it and tooled into Tokyo for sightseeing and shopping. On several nights we had a good time visiting the best American clubs in town; we usually ran into people we knew and sometimes joined for a spell. I particularly enjoyed that swell Japanese band at the University Club—you could swear you were listening to Glenn Miller. They are so good I believe they'd be a sensation on a tour of the States. The view of the city and expanse of lights at night from the roof garden terrace made a much more agreeable impression than the daytime street-level madhouse. I couldn't help but compare our particular routine with all this unrelated commotion. For us this is an intermission, and what a contrast. Yet in a way it seems to me the nervous pace of a big city grinds up people as relentlessly as any war. I feel more comfortable in the company of my outfit; at least we share something in common, unlike this restless sea of strangers. Even among other military this difference shows up in the expressions on the faces of nonflying folks produced by our *lingua flya* speech. When I realize I'm getting nowhere in such thoughts and wasting my time besides, I go back to living up the R&R.

On the night of the 13th, while in the Johnson Field O-Club, some of the guys came dashing up and said, "Doug, did you hear what happened over there today? Those lucky *#*&!!%*'s got 13 of them today! Davis got four himself!"

We all turned green with envy—what a ruination of an R&R. That news called for toasts all around and some extras to drown our regrets. To have all this comfortable living topped off by missing such a great show was too much to take. What really got me was that Dave and I had already been trying for two days without success to get back on MATS. The next day, yesterday, we finally managed to scrounge a hop on a courier down to Tsuiki on the Island of Kyushu, where we arrived in rain and real sorry weather. In fact, the weather was so bad one of our F-86s augered in trying to cut it on a ferry trip. After getting something to eat we made it into Kimpo late last evening.

I discovered the squadron had added an E Flight which was housed in another building separate from the other flights; I was the Flight Commander and the gang had already moved my stuff. I honestly felt like I'd been away for a month; I'm going to have to hustle to get back in swing. And think of those juicy missions I missed! I really winced when the fellows told me about *toksan* MiGs below them, and then catching a whole lock-step formation of dodos boring holes with their tanks still on. Davis had led his boys in a join-up on them and they cut loose all at once—what a shoot-em-up *that* was on film. Japan and R&Rs really showed me schmaltz then.

My gosh, a lot of the gang got kills on the missions of the big day of the 13th. Al Dymock and Pinky Pincoski each got another MiG. Ken Chandler got one and Charlie Mitson got another himself in the closest point-blank blast I've ever seen on any of our gunnery film. Talk about a windshield full of MiG—wow! George Davis got four in two missions—gadzooks! He gets them by the bag full. They say two of them just bailed out in fright as soon as he got hits on them. Al Simmons, who I'm happy to say is at last a Major, got one on the 11th and I was glad he was able to make up for that scramble we got into back in October.

Pat Green was kidding me about associating with the soft life and bright lights stuff while the tigers were getting the good action. Pat had also gotten a MiG in the big hassle. It seems this MiG boob had tried to scissor with Pat, who knows his stuff, and the MiG went into a spin. Pat had his speed brakes out and power back, trying to match the MiG's corkscrew and fill him full of lead, when the MiG pilot gave up and ejected in his face. I then kidded Pat that he was supposed to shoot these guys, not *scare* them to death. It's great to be back.

DECEMBER 21st

On the 16th I got back into the saddle in an E model. We had something new to work with—escort of an RF-86 (Sabre modified for reccy). As Al Simmons had aircraft trouble and couldn't get off, I got the Squadron lead, lined everybody up behind, and led the Group off. It turned into just another escort and routine patrol, but it sure was valuable experience. We saw a fair amount of flak while on photo runs over Namsi and Taechon, but no MiGs.

On the 17th I got on a deep-in, high patrol as Red element lead in 86Es. We were up east of Huichon in what we call the Race Track area. The MiGs came down way west of us, toward Sinanju. We had seen them earlier west of us in the con layer above and those guys must have been all of 50,000 feet up. Man, they were high.

We eventually went over in their direction and the squadron charged around, but couldn't find the MiGs, only a few 86s. I think we stayed up high too long and the MiGs sneaked home after dropping out of the cons.

I just remembered a little deal I went on with Walt Raby before that R&R. Walt had asked me to go with him as copilot in the base Gooney Bird to K-6, Pyongtaek, to pick up Bob Draney, who was returning from a tour as a Forward Air Controller with a ROK Division. I honked the C-47 around a bit feeling it out, and at K-6 I had a chance to look over the T-6 Mosquito fleet. They're operating off PSP on that strip. I noticed they are using belly tanks on some of the birds and have removed the main gear fairings. They all looked like they were getting a real workout.

Raby can sure handle that Gooney. Most people fly them like grandmothers in rocking chairs, but Walt could bend it around like a big old fighter. He showed me a great 360 traffic pattern—in idle, yet!

The 4th Fighter Group has now put in a year over here in the Far East and it sure has done a good job—in fact, such a good job with so few airplanes that I guess the home front thinks they have nothing to worry about.

Another wandering mission today. A good part of it involved a long climb-out and return let-down in lots of weather. There were lots of 86s dodging through the stuff to keep you alert, but no MiGs. We've been having lousy weather lately; I wish now that I hadn't gone on that R&R as I really missed some Number One missions.

In a few days it will be 1952—I can hardly believe it; where did '51 go? A lot of things have happened this year and yet it doesn't seem as if a whole year has passed. I'm sort of deadened to time; going out for the next mission is about the only thing that conveys any real passage of time. It's unfortunate how we must spend days like they were dollars from an endless bankroll.

I got tied up with another Mickey Spillane novel last night. That guy can really write a slam-bang story. The way everybody over here is buying and reading them, ol' Mickey must really be making the dough. It's kind of funny in a way to see combat pilots reading wild west, detective, and adventure stories for amusement or entertainment. I remember when I was a kid how those old aviation pulp magazines of the '30s used to fuel my dreams. Of course, it was my reading of years ago that made me want to find something exciting to do in life instead of the usual dumb-dumb existence. I always envied men who had led adventurous lives and my own years of flying have filled some of that desire to be a participant rather than a spectator.

I sent out a batch of our special 4th Fighter Group Christmas cards to a lot of people including relatives, friends of the family, and four of my World War II buddies. They are pretty nice cards showing F-86s taking off. I wrote a note in each, which may generate some correspondence.

Oh, these blasted shower facilities—they hardly ever operate properly and when they do we don't get the word in time to join the rush for a bath. The construction people are fixing one of our shot-up buildings into a sort of bathhouse/ latrine in the pilot area. In the meantime, I'll continue bathing with a washcloth out of our spare steel helmet plus the basin and washstand arrangement we have in our room. It's not much, but we have to try to keep somewhat clean.

DECEMBER 31st

On the 23rd I got another flight lead. Chandler was leading the squadron, Hammond had White Flight and I had Blue. After we had set up our patrol, the squadron turned right to the east and towards an approaching formation of aircraft, which put my flight in trail. The bogies were MiGs and Red and White Flights went through them head-on. I was in a position to cut across them and did so. They were all around us in a wink. I chandelled left after two and then saw two more right behind them so I slacked off to let them pass under my nose, but the pursuit curve was then pretty well fouled up.

I had had those first two perfect, but would have put the other two right on our tails. Dawson and I had the two souped-up jobs (the engines were adjusted to get redline tail pipe temperature at 96 percent and unknown things at 100 percent). We called them the short-fused time bombs, and easily left Blue Three and Four far behind in our chandelle. I tried to line up on MiG number 4 for shooting and found I had problems. The damn sight image kept floating around on my windshield and wouldn't erect; it reminded me of trying to stack one billiard ball on another. When I pulled Gs the reticle would drop down out of sight and then float up at the side. Was I steamed! I squirted a couple of bursts of tail light tracers in hopes. The MiGs reacted like they'd backed into a hot stove and really hauled out. They sure looked neat curving up steep into the bright sky. Another squirt going uphill, but as our speed was falling off, I broke off the climb chase and looked for other business. Two more MiGs then tapped us, but we broke away and hunted around to find only more 86s.

On the 24th I managed to get some more T-33 time and jumped Ken Chandler who was on *another* test hop in an 86. He was doing some loops so I got in trail for three of them and he never saw us. I then found three F-51s that seemed interested in some action, so I went round and round with them—what sport. Whenever I see a Mustang I want to fly that little beauty again. Charlie Mitson was riding in the back seat through all this and we then went back to Kimpo and shot three landings.

That Ken Chandler is the biggest flight time sniveler in the squadron. Of course we all mooch what we can, but being the Operations Officer gives him an advantage and he grabs darn near *every* test and training hop *every* day. He's absolutely whacky over building up his flight time and immune from protests, so I delight in advertising his obsession by performing the phantom "handwriting on the wall." When nobody is looking, I chalk on the blackboard in big letters: "Capt. Kenneth 'I can't stop till I get a million hours' Chandler." Then I busy myself where I can watch on the sly and enjoy his reaction. I don't know whether he is wise to me or not, but though I have done this several times, he still hasn't got the message.

Another blurb I have put on the board is a saying I remember reading of the French Air Force in World War I: "The pilot should not be overly familiar with the intricacies of his machine—it is apt to destroy his dash." A pilot today is expected to know all the complexities of every system in his bird: electric, hydraulic, fuel, oil pressurization, *ad infini-tum*. My feeling is, if the pilot can't solve it or affect it from the cockpit, why clutter his mind with all that junk? Like the French saying infers: He may learn so much about what *might* happen that he's just liable to get too smart to do this job—then what? Among ourselves we get by on the popular expression: "You don't have to be crazy to be a fighter pilot, but it helps."

In the evening we had a small egg nog party in the club lounge with a bunch of the RAAF people who had been invited over. It was a sort of reserved affair, but I enjoyed talking with them as I know a few of the pilots from my visits to their club. When that broke up, our fellows trooped back to the buildings to tap a little firewater. After we had settled in our room, Bob Draney dropped in for a few brews, and in the spirit of Christmas Eve our Armament crew came by and sang carols outside. They sounded real good and we invited them in. Other guys came by and we had some rounds of drinks and laughs together—just a bunch of songbirds.

On Christmas Day—rain! I was on the first mission and went down for briefing, but the weather got worse and it was called off.

E Flight, 336th Fighter Squadron. Left to Right: Spitzer, Mossholder, author (starting new mustache), Mitson, Borowski, Green. Korean houseboy, Johnny, in front. Combat mission and MiG tally board behind author's head. Overhead is a Japanese painting popular at the time; the two tigers symbolized the fighter element—leader and wingman. December 1951, Kimpo, Korea.

All that accomplished was to foul up the morning, but that was all forgotten when we got into the Christmas dinner—which was excellent. My flight went early and we pulled two tables together so we could all dine in style in an enjoyable gathering. It's a swell flight and as we are sort of separate from the rest of the squadron billets, we stick pretty close together. Pat Green is Assistant Flight Commander; Charlie Mitson is with us too, and Mossholder, plus Spitzer and Borowski who recently arrived. We call ourselves E-the-Eager Flight, and I'm proud to say that the pilots in my flight have more air victories than any other flight in the squadron.

After paying a Christmas social visit to the rest of the squadron pilots in their building, we set to work on our oil space heater. That became quite a project—disassembling the pipe chimney, knocking all the soot out, and cleaning the heater itself. I guess all that junk in it contributed to several minor explosions in the morning. In a way they were humorous, but didn't do our room a bit of good. The mess and clean-up resulted in raising our tempers while lowering the temperature as the room turned into a deep freeze without any heat, and we had to leave all the windows open to get rid of the smell which had penetrated everything.

By the time we got all *that* mess straightened out and back in working order, we resembled amateur chimney sweeps. All through this exercise we were anticipating the best present of all, a Christmas Day shower, after which we each felt like a new man. The long-awaited facilities had just opened for business in a nearby building. I realize it's rather unfair of us, but we are already wondering when these new bathing and toilet facilities will go out of commission. The toilet is a kind of trough flushing arrangement and there have already been comments on the great possibilities for the burning toilet paper prank.

I must add here that on the night of the 23rd we had a full squadron party in the Airmen's mess with plenty of steaks and beer. I joined with Frenchy Richard, my crew chief (who will return to the States in a few days) and everybody had a great time. Of course I'm happy to see Frenchy go home to Louisiana, but I sure hate to lose him. I'm never going to feel the same here without him to keep my plane in flying shape.

My flight doesn't have a radio and though we haven't listened to any good programs or music lately, I heard some news the day after Christmas—same old stuff on the peace talks; they're practically a joke. The way the Communist forces have been conveniently building up during the bad weather, I guess they'll go hog-wild when it breaks—after all their blab about negotiating. We wonder what the home front will do about it.

On the 27th we had a medium altitude escort to Uiju for a look-see at activities there. While we were patrolling, two lone MiGs appeared high on our right and a little behind—just sort of pacing the squadron and looking us over from their lofty perch, sparkling in the sunshine. It was unusual for one of our squadrons to be shadowed by two of these guys. As they hung up there we got careless, and in one of our squadron turns these two MiGs disappeared and then reappeared slightly below and right behind us, closing like the devil. I was sort of surprised and at the moment admired the nerve of the two of them charging into us.

As they got close, they spat out a string of cannon tracers; the radio filled with chatter and the squadron gyrated. I pulled left and they swished by outside, pumping those red balls at the squadron gaggle. They didn't attempt to latch onto anybody in particular, which made their bounce a wasted show, but I thought it was kind of funny the way they had screwed up our nice formation and then zoomed up and away. I wondered later if that might have been this rumored MiG leader, "Casey Jones," showing one of his wingmen how to taunt the Sabre pilots. We'll never know.

I had been having defrost trouble with my canopy so I let down taking Cheever with me. We patrolled with our separate element, but found no other activities.

On the 28th I really had lousy luck. I got completely frosted up and then my drops wouldn't feed—what a sick bird. I pulled out of formation and dropped down to tool around the Sinanju area; Col. Preston met me toward Pyongyang and took Spitzer. I heard Able and Black squadrons in a fight with more of the usual yak by Bones, and then there was a very ominous transmission by someone: "Better turn hard left, an 86 is getting strikes all over it." That ended up being a bad one and we lost both plane and pilot in a terrible crash right on the home field. Boy, I was real low on fuel when I got home.

In the afternoon I took up Bob Hotz, a correspondent for the *Bee Hive* (United Aircraft Corp.), for his first jet flight in a T-33 to follow the Sabre mission to the Chinnampo area and indicated points of interest in the scenery. We could hear the gang calling out MiGs north of us, but they didn't get involved in a fight. On the way home I did a few maneuvers and then demonstrated how a jet does a vertical dive with a high-G recovery. At the field we dodged among the cluttered pattern and I topped it off with a bounce on landing, doggone it.

On the 29th we had another of those deals where a twelve ship formation ended up in six ships—real swell. I'm getting a case of the jaws over some of these aborts. We hunted all over MiG Alley and still couldn't find any MiGs. We heard Bones yakking like mad about MiGs northeast, but no action developed.

When we were well on the way home I put my flight in trail (Evans, Spitzer, Green, and Mossholder). Whoopee—the slam-bang kind of stuff I like: sudden violent pull-up, at the peak a whip-over into a hard split-S, a hard roll straight down, high-G bottom out and back up, pulling like crazy. Sort of a weirdo vertical scissors; hard on the guts and somewhat disorienting with other variations thrown in.[16] Anyway, I lost everybody in the confusion, but picked up Spitz, and we all got into the gaggle at the field. The workout was good for us as the night before my whole illustrious E Flight had stopped in the club for "just a couple" and we ended up going ape in the place, yelling like the last roundup, and returning arm-in-arm to our little home singing and hollering for the benefit of the nonparticipants.

On the night of the 29th the whole fighter group had a club warming party in "Swig Alley"—boy, what a circus. A bunch of nurses from the Forward Evacuation Hospital at Yong Dong Po were invited and the drinks were free! Everybody cut loose—sort of a spontaneous celebration for just being alive and in good company, I guess. For the nurses particularly, the opportunity to get away from constant blood and death must have been a cause to celebrate. There wasn't a man there who didn't respect those gals for the gory job they have to perform here near the front. I don't see how they stand up day after day to all that misery and bloody emergencies. We'd be ruined if we dwelled on that every day.

But to hell with the gloomy stuff; the joy juice was really flowing and everybody was mixing everything. It's a wonder we didn't have one of those high-school chemistry lab explosions. I tried Tom Collins', rum Cokes, champagne, and whiskey—wow, a walking bomb. Some of the good songs were sung with laughs and cheers. Occasionally you could grab somebody and take a turn trying to dance in the midst of the churning press. All that body friction sure did things to the room temperature—the place was steaming.

Some of the nurses took their shoes off and it's a miracle they didn't get their toes crunched with all our clodhoppers happily stomping around. We had trays of little goodies set on some of the seats and one gal went through a tray of stuff barefoot crossing over to another group—what fun. Another gal who passed caught me unaware while practicing her New Year's smooch—I thought I'd been had by a stomach pump. The end door was open to let some oxygen mix with the other chemicals, and while I was outside near the bluff overlooking the airfield, one nurse stepped out into the night and I heard her voice: "Where's the latrine?" From the dark by the convenient slit trench came a gruff reply: "You're almost standing in it, baby."

Getting in or around the club was about like boarding a subway at rush hour. Everybody was talking at once, trying to get acquainted, and you had to stretch your voice hoarse to get a conversation understood in the happy din.

My throat was raw the next day after all that firewater and yippee. We were all in nifty shape to carry on the war, but the way I feel about it, it's *our* war, *we* fight it, and the way we live it is *our* business. I was fortunate and had a chance to rest up until the afternoon mission.

We were faced with a real mess of lousy weather; the sky was clobbered up in all directions. Col. Thyng was leading with Red Flight, while I had Blue Flight. As soon as everybody got joined up after takeoff, we plowed right into the mung and proceeded to climb through two layers and twenty some thousand feet of this junk. At first you could see enough in the soup to keep flights on flights, but as the soup got thicker, the job of cross checking my own instruments, keeping an ever-tightening position on the other flights, and doing it all smooth enough not to mess up my own gang got to be too much. I split off as did White Flight and we bored onward and upward in fours.

The faint glow of the sun above can sure be deceiving at such times; it seems to be close overhead and going right along in formation. When I'd look up, wondering when we were going to break out, I had to resist the tendency to pull up toward that tantalyzing ball of light that indicated clear skies so close above. More than one pilot has spun out of that sort of situation.

At 32,000 we broke out. All of a sudden the world wasn't all gloom and instruments anymore, but an endless expanse of pure

The F-86A in clean (no external load) configuration, depicting its birdlike, trim lines. (U.S. Air Force photo)

white, reflecting a new and painfully bright sun. What a startling sensation it is to pop out like that—from seemingly motionless in the murk to suddenly springing free with all the whiteness falling away. The planes around you appear freshly polished and you can sense the smiles behind all the oxygen masks.

The other flights popped out about the same time. First you're looking at nothing but an endless white ocean, and then suddenly like flying fish springing up from the depths appear those beautiful Sabres sparkling in the sunshine. Just like drawing a spoon out of whip cream, the vapor clings momentarily to the aircraft and a tiny plume or crest is plucked from the clouds to slowly round off and settle as the fighters rise into the blue.

Before we draw flights together again to continue the climb, the thought strikes me: Flying is so wonderful that you can't adequately explain what it does to you. In comparison with the motionless clouds so close beneath the other formations, the passage of the fighters conveys through the eyes the sensation of rocketing speed—a flock of shining birds skimming over the frozen ripple of this endless ocean.

We continued our climb to 37,000 feet and patrolled in the contrail level. I guess my mood wasn't very warlike as the long curving cons of the formations again reminded me of ski trails over this white world. The job of maintaining position at that high altitude with so many planes was a real workout and got my attention back to business instead of all the star-gazing.

After awhile at that altitude, this cold I have made me quite uncomfortable. We let down through again and found we could patrol around Sinanju a bit at 23,000, and then we headed out. On the way I looked over the MSRs above and below Pyongyang and with all the snow on the ground you could really see the bomb blast effects for miles along the roads—black craters and the drift of fallen debris printed in dark fan-shaped smudges upon the white carpet. The fighter-bombers had really beaten up the place on this mission, especially south, below Ping Pong.

As the interdiction guys below withdrew, we went all-out with flights in close trail—down and down, scraping under the ragged edges of the cloud ceiling, which slanted to low altitude—as enjoyable as a happy gang sledding down a steep slope. The visibility underneath got progressively worse the lower we went, until by the time we got to Kimpo it was sort of a group grope in the murk with everybody trying to keep oriented and get into the pattern—all rather low on fuel.

We had a fairly heavy snow last night, so at 5 a.m. I checked on the predawn alert requirement while the other pilots in my flight got up just in case. At 5:30 the orders were for standby only, so I told the crew chiefs to stay in their sacks and we pilots went back to bed ourselves, all very thankful to escape that miserable preparation in the dark with this snow and bitter cold. We all got up kind of late after making up the loss of sleep. I stayed off the mission schedule, but with this weather there is nothing much doing anyway.

We have been getting more weather time in our flying lately. It's really been crummy instrument work and prowling seas of clouds the last few missions. The dim winter light under this stuff projects a dismal, frosty grey tone to the enemy landscape—overall a rather sinister scene and a good setting for some Dracula movie. From what we can see, the fighter-bomber boys have been going great guns these days, but as the MiGs won't mess around in this stuff, we have been more or less boring holes. I sure hate these missions, especially when we get several in a row. My time over here is all downhill now, but I don't like to waste it that way.

I get as scared occasionally as anybody, I guess, but there is a challenge about aerial combat like a mountain or jungle that dares you to explore it, and I don't feel like cheering because I see the end in sight. I know that others far removed from this sort of life wouldn't understand or appreciate that philosophy. When I look back, I know this is the experience I've worked for over so many years and I get momentary feelings of awe that this has come true. I get those feelings sometimes in the middle of a conversation or in bed at night, and sometimes the thought occurs when the contrails approach and the real thing is probable.

I finally got paid and gave a bottle of V.O. to Frenchy so he could have some New Year's cheer with his pals.

This evening after supper a funny thing happened. We heard some sort of commotion and people calling out, so we went out and there down the hill near us at the Army antiaircraft compound a building was on fire with their guys running around in and out of the dark and the firelight. What a blaze in the night! At least I'll say it was funny to us fighter pilots—unusual entertainment between missions. Sort of like when the boiler to our old shower building blew up: "More hot water, papa-san!" They got it, too.

I'm sure the wheels couldn't see the humor of this particular fire, and there was some concern about ammunition, but we see a lot of that on missions, so continued right on as an attentive audience. The whole business burned up—I'll bet the Army really hit the fan over that.

Enough of this writing for awhile and time to join in the conversation. Charlie and others leave for Japan on R&R tomorrow. I guess we'll go see what's cooking at Swig Alley, but after that party on the 29th, everything has been very quiet around here—nobody needs any New Year's Eve celebration after *that* practice.

1 JANUARY 1952

Last evening Charlie and I got a couple of beers in the club and quietly drank them in front of the fireplace. Funny how you get to thinking when you watch a fire on the hearth: winters as a kid, skiing and thawing out, and popping corn over the coals. I went back and climbed into bed to read a book by Max Brand, my favorite western action writer. I remember when, as a youngster sick in bed, I was introduced to Max Brand by a present of one of his books, *Rustlers of Beacon Creek*,—still, to me, Number One in his line.

At about 3 a.m. the air raid siren went off and then all kinds of AAA guns began blazing away. My gosh, what a racket. We scrambled out of bed, pulling on boots and jackets in the dark, so we could watch the show. Amidst the roaring of the guns I could hear a plane and then—*blam, blam, blam!* Bombs. The 40mm really went at it, wicked looking stuff. Things eventually calmed down and as we were already back in bed I went right to sleep. The raid was just a deliberate attempt to start the new year off by shaking us up, but the fighter pilots merely took it as entertainment.

I made sure I got up in time for this blasted early mess schedule and then waited around until time to go off on the morning mission. I started out as a spare but picked up the 335th Squadron spare (Smith) on the runway. We started the patrol with the fighter-bombers hitting way up north from Sinanju to Long Point.

The cons began coming from three directions—MiGs. A fight developed in the cons west of us, so over we went with Creighton leading the squadron. There were MiGs chasing around all above us, but this time there were also Sabre formations all over the place. We had real strength for a change.

A bunch of MiGs came in suddenly at six o'clock and we all broke. I could see them firing at someone in the squadron. While I

was in the turn, four MiGs passed my nose in an overshoot so I
reversed and broke after them. Three of them went hard right in
perfect V formation, but their number four pulled up in a wild
chandelle. As they still had their initial bounce speed, I couldn't
catch any of them. Flights of MiGs would dive through at terrific
speed and pull back up without concentrating on anybody—their
usual idiot maneuver, which we could do nothing about. Like the
RAF expression: They must have the wind up something terrible.

I wasted time chasing what turned out to be 86s and avoiding
bounces by other 86s. We had some interesting moments pacing
MiGs right over our heads, but they were too cagey to let us get up
into them with their rate of climb. Things just sort of petered out
and I could see 86s and MiGs withdrawing in opposite directions,
everybody calculating their fuel as usual. It was a great break in
the routine, and I was hopping with excitement during the whole
thing.

I did some reading in the afternoon and then faced the fact that
I had to do some laundry, so I washed my underwear and socks (I no
longer send *that* stuff out).

Whew—I just got finished with tomorrow's mission schedules,
as it's my turn as Flight Commander. What a juggling act:
matching pilots with plane number preference, lead positions and
wingmen, fair share of missions, and trying to keep everybody
satisfied. Now to bed and tomorrow I'll tackle the revisions.

JANUARY 5th

On 2 Jan, when I was doing the mission scheduling, I planned
on E Flight flying together in the afternoon. But we've had more
snow and the weather was foul, so only the morning mission got off,
and then not until the afternoon—more revisions. We didn't miss a
thing; all that occurred was a sort of mass weather reccy or group
grope anyway.

In the morning, to be on top of any schedule changes, I hung
around Combat Ops and read a bunch of Intelligence on MiGs and
combat info. In the afternoon I edited combat film with Borowski
and located some of mine, making some notes about which reel, etc.
It was rather disappointing, though, as the positives seemed to be
worse than the negatives that are first shown to the pilots—and
they were bad enough. That seemed to be the case with most of the
film.

My curiosity has been stirred and for the last couple of days
I've spent the slack time in Intelligence. Some of the articles are

much more absorbing than this action fiction with which we usually pass the time. I saw the issue of *Air Intelligence Digest* that included that letter of mine, plus photos. I didn't plan it, but I think they fit it in well with the other stories. Everybody has been kidding me about it.

Bob Draney showed me a press release he got from home about the boys in the 121st Squadron at Andrews Field. I imagine the squadron has a get-together over the holidays and I hope Tom was able to spend time at home. The news about the old gang is always interesting to read. In a couple of days it will be eight months since I shipped out.

We have a ping-pong table in our squadron pilot's room and it's really getting worked over now. We all get impatient for our turns. It's been too calm around here; Bedcheck Charlie hasn't even been over since New Year's Eve, when he dropped those calling cards on us.

The lights in our building have been out until 10 p.m. The repair crew finally came around after numerous phone calls, so now we can read or write letters again. This GI field phone we have in the room for my flight is a real convenience as we are separate from the squadron and it saves a lot of running around.

Author's brother Tom on ladder by F-84C of 121st Fighter Squadron, filling out Form One and ready for flight with his WWII fleece-lined British flying boots. Andrews Field, MD.

An element of two F-86As of the 4th Fighter Group. The black and white stripes around fuselage and wings were adapted from the D-Day stripes of World War II. This paint scheme gave a differentiating identification from the painted noses of the MiG-15s, which were usually red. (U.S. Air Force photo)

One favorite subject of our discussions (like when the lights were out) has been the differences and similarities in air war between World War I, World War II, and here in Korea, with the different planes involved. Dogfighting hasn't changed, basically—it's still a matter of seeing first and trying to get on the other's tail or shaking him off yours.

On 3 January I went off on the afternoon mission and we saw some contrails and heard Able Squadron really mixing it with some tough tigers. We all started honking around to keep from being surprised while we searched for the scrap between the Yalu and Sinanju in the Roulette area. I was Red Three and kept my element tacked onto Red Lead, Chandler, while we bounced and were bounced by 86s—very frustrating, especially as I thought we had some good deals. We pulled a hell of a lot of Gs in some terrific turns sparring with these 86s and wasted most of our time in that fashion. I saw bogies, obviously MiGs, going north in cons high above us, but never really identified them.

In the evening we saw *Love Nest* with Marilyn Monroe—ay, yi, yi! That gal has everybody running up the walls, but we did notice the show was pretty funny.

Yesterday, the 4th, the weather was really lousy all day. We had three calls for missions, so I piled all my gear on three times and we were briefed twice, but we never got off the ground. All the buildup and letdown put everybody in a bad mood—*and* a sweaty condition as we were all dressed in heavy clothes and either sitting in hot Combat Ops or waiting in Squadron Ops. In the evening, after knocking out a letter, I got completely lost in some reading.

Today (5 Jan) as we were assembling for the morning mission briefing, the weather looked doubtful for action. En route north there was a high cloud layer, so with Col. Thyng leading, we climbed on top. My defrost wouldn't work properly and my canopy got worse and worse as we climbed. Anyway, as we couldn't top the con level and were streaming them behind us, Col. Thyng, Red Lead, decided to let down through the high stuff for a look. Down we went to 23—25,000 feet. We made a couple of patrol turns right near the Yalu and then Red Lead called for a 90 degree right and "Let's go up through."

We made the right turn and then bogies were called at one o'clock, traveling left in front of Blue Flight (I was Blue Three). Someone said they were 86s and I came right back and said, "No— MiGs!"

We cranked hard left to get after these and lost sight of them. More showed up slightly high at one o'clock and Blue Lead turned left on them as they passed. I said hard right as there were more right behind them, which would have gotten square on our tails. I turned into them and found myself making a quarter head-on with six MiGs. Some more quick turns and then I went for an element of two MiGs; they chandelled and so did I, firing at their number two. I saw no hits, but they were pretty far out before I could track. Though I tacked onto Blue One and Two again, I had to immediately tell them to break left as MiGs were behind. When I crossed the bounce on these MiGs, they pulled up and away and our formations split up.

Spitzer called that he'd lost me in that scramble as I went after two of those guys. I rocked from side to side; when I saw him below me, I told him to pull up and to the right quick and then I whipped back on those two MiGs and banged away at the number two again. As Spitz got back in position I called out two MiGs coming in ahead, noses on us, and we broke aside as the MiG leader blazed away. Two more MiGs came up right behind us and boy, did I break; left and around, and we were clear. Then two more MiGs in front. This time I beat them to the firing position and made a head-on, firing at number two as we zipped through each other. I didn't see any hits, but what a closure rate! Just too fast for a calm range estimation peering through a gun sight. Nothing like a head-on collision at that speed—what an aluminum shower that would make.

Right at the start of all this hassle I had pulled up real steep on two MiGs crossing over our noses, gave them a good squirt, and rolled back down. Spitz said later he couldn't figure out what I was doing as he never saw the MiGs.

We were hunting now between Antung and "Mizu" (Sui-ho Reservoir). I had noticed in the initial fighting that we could look right down on Mizu, so we were pretty deep inland—further than usual.

After that head-on in which I had fired, we cranked around to the left to try to cut them off and get on them. These guys were black-nosed MiGs for a change. I guess they didn't like the situation, as they chandelled high across our noses over Mizu and I lost them in the ragged underside of the overcast. We followed the Yalu down to Antung and then went home, letting down through the weather enroute. For real fast action, that mission was hard to beat.

JANUARY 6th

I guess I was sleepy or tired or both—anyway, I got up too late for breakfast so I just waited around until briefing time, when I piled on all my gear and went on down to Combat Ops.

We got the escort job with one of the 67th Group photo reccy RF-80s. After takeoff, we assembled en route to Chinnampo and there picked up the RF, but we couldn't establish any radio contact so I took my flight into close formation with the RF and signalled for him to go home. We all then firewalled our throttles and proceeded to get in on the fighter sweep.

North of Sinanju we began patrolling and watched contrails and specks of aircraft coming in our direction. Suddenly there were MiGs at eleven o'clock and we passed through them. They fired, but it was inaccurate as hell, just nervous hosing of ammo. There were more turns in formation (I had become Red element) and then a call for a left break, but Red Leader delayed for some reason and then we swung left as four MiGs came in at eight o'clock. I sort of cross-bounced as I cut across the turn and the noses of these four MiGs. I only managed a strained head-on, high-G firing burst at two more that were following. That was right after the first four had really pumped the lead at me. As I cut across them, they took turns, one right after the other, spraying me as I passed each of their noses. I was in a vertical bank and shrank

down in the cockpit, expecting one of those big red balls to hit me
right square on top of my dome.

Red Four called that he'd snapped out of that last turn and lost
me. Still pulling Gs, I guessed that it was him I saw way below me
going west toward the coast. I headed that way myself while trying
to answer his call. The whole outfit had scattered and the radio was
so boggled with fight chatter you couldn't maintain a sensible
transmission or understandable reception. I simply couldn't coordinate or communicate with my wingman, and this really
torqued my jaws.

A lone 86 came into view and I managed to get a call through
for him to join up with me. As he closed, I could tell from his buzz
numbers that he was from another squadron—the 334th. I made a
transmission in the blind for my original wingman, telling him to
head out if he couldn't find friendlies, and took my new element
back inland.

Plainly in view were the cons of old fights hanging all over the
sky, and fights in progress with contrails going in circles for all to
see—the familiar signature of the fighter pilot. As I headed for
distant bogies, I noticed there was a layer of what was more like
thick haze than real clouds between 23 and 28,000 feet. Besides the
haze there were several thin, scattered-to-broken cloud patches—
good for all sorts of surprises.

I picked out both F-86s and MiGs and aimed toward two red
noses that chandelled away. A flight of MiGs that I then went after
also pulled up and climbed out of the scrap; they must have really
been the clanked-up variety. In the distance two different planes
spun out of the haze. I'm certain one of them was a MiG—great!
Then another plane came spinning through; it looked like an 86 for
sure. At the same time I could see planes zooming up through this
stuff and others split-essing down through it—what a hassle!

As I completed a 360-degree clearing turn I found myself
right in the middle of a hell of a fight. There were 86s firing on
MiGs and MiGs firing on 86s—really wild. I went to latch on one in
this mess, but then I saw a MiG on a lone 86s tail and firing like
mad so I took him, got a quick bead on, and fired like mad myself. I
saw the flash of a hit on him and he wasted no time breaking off the
86, whipping left and inside tight as hell. In that moment of
banking to follow, I caught sight of six MiGs on my right side and
above, undoubtedly watching me. Something told me to check my
six o'clock. I swished my rudder and discovered no wingman—
damn, no 86s *anywhere.* Swinging a look through the top of my

canopy I saw two more MiGs crossing over me with two others on my left. It looked like they were all set up to converge on me. I knew I was in a real bad situation and the quickest move I could think of was a sudden right turn into the biggest bunch of six.

Just as I threw into the bank, another MiG appeared like a hand passing over my head, sliding left. Evidently my sudden turn had spoiled his pass. I watched him reverse on my left side to scissor me. As he was my most immediate threat, I scissored into him; he had a black nose, I noticed. He goofed his maneuver, so I reversed as he overshot me and was all worked up to shoot the buzzard. As I rolled my nose on him I ticked off a squirt, but in the next moment I was badly shaken by a very unnerving sound I only heard this one time: the distinct and hair-raising muzzle blast of heavy cannon fire. Judas, I was in the middle of a stream of red balls streaking over my canopy and right wing—20mm and 37mm tracer shells!

As I went into the most violent left break I ever made, I looked back to see this new MiG practically joining up with me. His nose intake was so close it looked like the Holland Tunnel with flame and red balls spitting out of it. The next thing I knew the world came unglued and tumbled and I found myself hanging in my safety belt, head jammed in the canopy with the misplaced world going slowly around *above* me. The sensation was that of being a stationary target hanging on a string in space and just waiting for the butcher's knife—what a hell of a feeling.

The survival impulse took over and I just sort of grabbed hold of that poor ol' 86 and hauled it into a rough split-S. Another look back over my tail and—no MiGs. But what was that white stuff coming out of my tailpipe, smoke? Have I been hit? No, my plane was conning in a vertical dive. I was so relieved I couldn't help laughing in the middle of all this.

I could hardly believe it—there were no MiGs in sight. They must have rushed home to claim me as a kill and get their "Hero" medals, or else tell about that "tricky" maneuver I pulled. Point blank and he missed—what lousy shooting. How lucky can you get?

I stuck around a little longer although by this time I knew for sure I was alone. I was hoping for another shot to even things— damn, I'm getting too eager again, I guess. The action had disappeared, so I cruised down to the river mouth and saw some 86s, but ended up going home alone.

My original wingman told me afterward he sure was ticked about snapping out and not being able to rendezvous to continue in

The MiG-15, produced and furnished by Russia, and flown by the Communist air forces encountered in MiG Alley. Though similar to the F-86 in swept wing and tail aspects, distinct differences were apparent for recognition purposes. (National Archives photo)

the action. I found out the 334th pilot I'd picked up had left me when I went after the flight of MiGs as we reentered the fight. He claims he thought they were 86s I was joining, so he went off looking for his outfit. What burns me is that he failed to notify me— I didn't know I was alone until too late and damn near bought the farm. I complained about this careless SOB wandering off, but apparently nothing will be done.

Further in the debriefing it turned out that Bob Draney had been in the 86 I saw spinning out of the haze, and when I told him about the result of my "tricky" maneuver we both had a whale of a laugh.

The afternoon mission, from what the boys tell me, was more of a mass weather reccy than anything. I'm hoping for tomorrow. We lost a pilot from the 334th in the fighting today. . . . I'm wondering if he was left alone?

In the evening we had a bull session about the mission that developed into quite a tactics discussion, after which I climbed into my sack for some more reading.

JANUARY 8th

We had a regular sightseeing run yesterday morning. We patrolled up and down the Chongchon River on top of the con level. Our CAP extended from the river mouth all the way past Kunuri and Huichon, where the river gets quite crooked as it winds through some rugged country. I could see the fighter-bomber boys sending up columns of smoke along the MSR by Kunuri. Contrails were visible far off to the north on top of the hazy undercast. We heard that the 51st Group had had a fight up there at the Yalu; they got two and lost one of their guys.

Our gang went home with a decent fuel load, so while the traffic pattern was congested, Mossy and I went southwest of K-14 and zipped along the desolate beach, some dykes and rice paddies. I did some low rolls on the treetops and generally hedge-hopped around the boondocks. It was a relief to have a little sport for a change.

I didn't do much for the rest of the day, but I tried to snivel two birds and get off with Borowski for a local tactics hop. No dice; not enough planes in commission.

The movie last night was *The Desert Fox*, and I enjoyed seeing it again. The story of Rommel is not only interesting, but I think the movie is very well done. Later, after the show, Mossy, Boris, and I got into a heck of a discussion about the subject of a World War III and world prospects. You better believe we think about such things.

I had the scheduling to make out for today and put myself on the morning mission. After we got assembled, we drove straight to the Yalu directly south of Antung. As we approached the river we could see cons on the other side coming in our direction. We were at 30,000 feet and in cons ourselves, so all the fighter pilots on both sides could see what was coming off.

You might say we were "reluctant" to turn our formation and give these MiGs a position advantage on us, but we had no choice and turned at the last moment to keep from crossing the damn river. I'm sure there was a general sweat about turning away while expecting them to dive right on our backs. Our turn was left and to the southwest (to parallel the river) and we watched intently for the MiGs' next move. Still on the north side of the river, they turned left and to the *northeast!* They must have been the real chicken variety. We made an immediate 180 and proceeded to patrol on opposite sides of the Yalu with these MiGs, who were practically on top of their home bases. Most of the MiG cons disappeared as they climbed above the con layer, but they didn't come across to challenge us. I wonder what their ground troops thought of that little air show?

We finally withdrew when the fighter-bombers finished beating things up down below. When we got near home I took my

Blue Flight through another of those rip-roaring rat races. I think there's no better way to keep in shape—and besides, I like it!

I had to run around the squadron area and take care of some fast changes in aircraft on the schedule for the afternoon mission. After the gang got off okay, I went into Squadron Ops and listened to the mission on our radio. What a fight those guys got into; it sure sounded hairy over the radio. Our clerks, crew chiefs, and other support people sure got an earful of the action. Nick Kotok got hit and *heard* the MiG guns shooting at him. He and I have a sympathetic understanding between us now.

I got into the gunnery film again and tried to cut my combat film, but no luck; the stuff is too mixed up right now.

Some of us are planning to take in a movie tonight if the projector can just manage to avoid breaking down for a change.

JANUARY 19th

On the 9th of January we had what turned out to be a rather dull mission over the top of a bunch of weather. I flew on Col. Thyng's wing in an E model. I don't know why, but I just couldn't get to feeling comfortable in the cockpit of that particular airplane.

On 11 Jan Chandler led Red Flight on his 100th mission and I was Red Three.[17] We watched cons approaching and were in the con level off and on ourselves. There was a chase after some cons and in the process we found 86s and got bounced by other 86s. Finally a lot of cons were seen heading north; we never did positively identify them as MiGs. We slogged along on our patrol where we were supposed to, but from the radio talk, the MiG action was apparently all east of us. There were a lot of false alarms and it was frustrating in general.

On the 12th there was a pretty hot mission. As we came near Antung we saw a few cons approaching from the north, and then a tremendous swarm of them appeared on the other side of Mizu—a regular cloud of cons. It was the biggest single mass of MiGs I ever saw. My pulse increased; there was that feeling of jungle fever again. They proceeded like an overcast over the river and then evidently ducked below the con level as we lost visual contact. We patrolled east in their direction parallel to the Yalu and over the con level at 37,000 feet. Then Col. Thyng, who was leading the show, called a head-on attack and we were among 'em as if in a cavalry charge.

The flights split off in the sudden meeting and in the process of looking and maneuvering I had quite a separation with my element. Thompson was White Lead and I was White Three, trailing with Mossy on my wing. We were conning and there were MiGs passing above and on either side of us with everybody twisting around and calling them out.

Then a flight of 86s passed above our side in the same direction, while two MiGs passed right over me, closing on them. I called the 86 flight to look out at six o'clock, told White Lead I was leaving, and pulled up in a zoom behind the MiGs. I made a quick check and Mossholder said we were clear so I lined up in good range and banged away. It seemed to me that the sight was off my flight path as my zoom was straight and I was in trail to the MiGs. I had no tracer to check my pip alignment and damn, I didn't get any hits. Anyway, the MiGs broke off the 86s and chandelled right as my zoom speed pooped out. I lowered my nose and turned after them, but I was too slow by then and they left us.

Mossy and I chased all over after various bogies and formations, but couldn't get closure on any MiGs for reasonable shooting. We chased two MiGs that were way out in front; after several minutes of this without seeming to gain a bit, I gave up rather than run out of fuel in a useless cross-country race.

After bingo fuel we started to withdraw when a radio call came from Maj. Martin (of the 334th) that he was alone and tangled up with a MiG, which he had smoking. Hearing that, we swung back and dropped lower to try to locate him. I strained my eyes until I thought they'd pop out, but we couldn't see a blasted thing and were getting low on fuel. Other flights were on the radio doing an intensive search of the sky when Martin said four more had jumped him and he was in a terrible hassle, grunting and gasping in his efforts. This really raised everyone's anxiety level, but with so many others searching north of us, I was told to pull out my element because of our low fuel state.

We were climbing just north of Pyongyang when Bones Marshall called that he had Martin and he was clear. Then, all of a sudden, Bones and his flight were grunting and gasping in turn and evidently found more than they expected. Everybody managed to maneuver out and all got home safely, but there were some hairy binds for a few of the guys. After the mission we all said it sounded like a chorus singing "The Grunt Song." Man, this teamwork and lookout sure is important.

I wrote up my gunsight in the Form One and complained so it would get immediate attention. When the armament crew checked it out, what did they find? The sight head had been removed and not reboresighted, so that at 1,000 feet range, the pipper was off left *86 feet*—gadzooks!

On the 15th I got off on a mission with one drop tank as the Wing had nearly run out of our supply of tanks. We found no MiGs, so there wasn't any sweat about the fuel problem. Spitzer and I pulled out of the formation when we got low on fuel and headed home. As we approached the Han River, I shoved the nose down and we went for the deck like a couple of bombs, on the weeds from the river to Kimpo damn near on the Mach. It's interesting what you can do at that speed and low altitude with just a flex of the hand and wrist.

We managed to work up a training flight in the latter part of the afternoon, after the final mission for the day. Al Simmons was leader with Lawyer, myself and Borowski in the flight. What a G-rat race that got into. Al was really going at it and we all got a good tactics workout. Gosh, that's great stuff. We ought to have a flight of four up every day with different pilots doing serious tactics. That way each pilot could get a turn each week. Couldn't you keep a sharp edge that way, and what a morale-builder!

On the 16th we went in high over the Chongju MSR that runs from Sinuiju, Namsi-Dong, Sonchon, Chongju, Sinanju and on south—a busy target area. Some of us were in this one-tank configuration again, which we had to keep in mind. Contrails could be seen swarming across the Yalu and then they disappeared.

Maj. George Davis with his separate squadron called that the MiGs were turning at Pyongyang and were out of the conlayer. We moved out of our patrol area of Chongju-Sonchon on a course east and south toward Pyongyang. Planes could be seen turning ahead and slightly low and cons were swirling about. I was tensed up for a bounce by our "gang" of six on this swarm. Suddenly MiGs materialized all around us. It was some job trying to maintain my element in formation, call possible bounces, plus check our tails and it seemed like a general mill with everybody dodging around at full bore. There wasn't any sweat, but our one-tank, low-fuel endurance messed us up because before we could properly maneuver and position ourselves, we were forced by fuel to pull out. I guess the MiGs had their fuel problems too, as both sides broke it off—otherwise they might have had us in a bind.

I lucked out and got in on another training flight in the

afternoon. Simmons and Borowski had aircraft problems and aborted, so I took up Lawyer and we pulled our guts out. I was flying an A model and really thumbing trim and bending things trying to give him a proper workout in his E model. I say again, there is nothing like a local rat race and tactics hop. A hop like that really gets your tiger blood to circulating and I always feel a lot sharper when I've had the chance to work on some particular maneuvers.

There was no flying for me on the 17th, so three of us who were free took off for Seoul in a jeep taxi. It sure was good to get off the base for a change and explore the city again, even though it is badly damaged. I wish I'd had a movie camera to record the street scenes—the war wreckage and the people busy through it all keeping things going. The Koreans have really been through the mill.

We made our way to 5th Air Force HQ before the end of normal duty hours. For once, we were in uniform and much more presentable than in the few fast visits of the past. This gave us the opportunity to look over some of the HQ facilities while we were there. I felt like splurging for a change, so when we got around to chow I ate *two* steaks and afterward enjoyed guzzling some Tom Collins. Even though brief, the trip was a relaxing change from our usual crowded hobo life with the daily charge-up-north stuff.

The next day I was scheduled on the afternoon mission for another of those one-tank apiece jobs. The takeoff lineup was as usual with my wingman on the right—and fortunately, my single drop tank was on my left wing. Just as we broke ground, I followed normal routine of retracting the landing gear. As the gear started up there was a loud explosion, my joystick momentarily jammed, my left wing dropped sharply, and the whole plane lurched left and down—directly in the turbulence of all the smoke and jet wash of the formations ahead.

It all happened so fast that I reacted by gripping both hands on the stick to raise the left wing. I thought sure I'd had it and was going to plow right into the ground. Luckily, there was a dropoff at the end of the runway into a series of rice paddies stretching beyond. I jammed in right rudder and thumbed the trim button for full right aileron along with my adrenalin effort on the stick. The plane dished pretty damn low and as the end of the runway flashed past, I managed enough control to commence a staggering left climbing turn away from the field and the rest of the formation. My wingman thought I'd bought the farm for sure, and it's a damn good thing my tank was on my left wing; otherwise I would have dipped right square into him and we would have clobbered together on the spot quicker than you could yell "Look out!"

Once I got some altitude under me I felt my first relief and relaxed my choking grip on the stick. If things got any worse, I could just eject and get rid of the thing. With a chance to reach the mike button I declared an emergency, aborting the mission, and wrestled the plane for more altitude. I don't know why, but I felt bad about aborting. When I could afford to look around, I watched the formations and smoke trails climbing and twisting into the distance.

I decided to burn off some fuel before attempting a landing and circled wide around the base until my single drop tank was empty. As we were short of tanks, I figured it would be okay to hang on to this one, so I pulled the landing gear emergency extension lanyard, selected nose gear, and slid out the hydraulic hand pump extension. While wobbling around flying left-handed, I worked the nose gear down. No hydraulics meant no flaps or speed brakes, so I set up a nose-high, flat approach and put her down.

On touchdown I also remembered that I had no nosewheel steering or boost for the wheel brakes. I held the nose off as long as I could, then caught one hairy swerve with just enough brake pedal remaining to keep on the runway and get the bird to the taxiway. I stuck around to find out what had gone wrong and it was discovered that a replacement hydraulic line had been twisted when tightened up. That had caused it to rupture and blow the system. Then I was glad it was an A model I was flying instead of an E, but I sure missed my old crew chief, Frenchy, who had recently rotated home. I just haven't felt as good about my airplane since he left, and then this incident. That took care of the day and the missions.

Last night I went around visiting other flights in the squadron. That staves off that feeling of cabin fever you're apt to get from being holed up in your own place so much. They, like our flight, usually have a beer to offer callers, plus the latest flying news about other fighter outfits that we get in our mail. I like to drop in like that during our leisure time. If one flight is wrapped up in letter writing or reading, I just mosey on to the next.

There is no flying for our squadron today due to the shortage of tanks, so we all got a chance to goof off. Everybody who could made up by getting some extra sack time. I took advantage of the interval to get my teeth cleaned at our dental unit.

JANUARY 25th

One of the crew chiefs who recently shipped in from the 121st Squadron at Andrews Field showed me a clipping out of a D.C. paper about the outfit, and Tom was in one of the pictures. I appreciated seeing that and reading about the squadron. Although I've written Tom about some of our hotter missions, I can hardly wait until we can sit down together and compare some war stories.

The other day when my flight got off predawn alert we stayed down in operations for some roaring games of ping pong. They are always good for a laugh and we work up quite a sweat in these crazy contests. The singles are funny enough, but some of the doubles are downright hysterical.

On the 21st we plowed through and around lots of weather on our patrol, but the Yalu River area was clear enough. Due to some aborts I ended up leading a flight, which allowed me to play my lookout position. We beat back and forth along the Yalu with a close watch on the cloud formations, but no MiGs. The squadron curved over the mouth of the river and once again I had the opportunity to see deep into Manchuria and clearly observe the other inland MiG airfields. Antung, its big airfield, and the surrounding countryside in particular appeared to have gotten quite a snowfall.

The view was tremendous and during such periods of calm, when there is time to think about it, I often wonder what goes on down there while they watch us patrolling around. What do the MiG jocks think or talk about? You feel detached in your plane, but you know the fellows suspended out there in space near you—and probably hundreds of others on the ground—are also looking and thinking their own thoughts—a funny business. With all the careful lookout we still saw no MiGs flying.

In the evening of the 22nd we saw the movie *Capt. Hornblower*. The action part of those old naval battles was pretty interesting, but all that hot lovin' doesn't do us a bit of good. We get a movie every other night or so—good, bad, and indifferent. Even though it's a way to pass the time, I don't go to all of them any more than I did on the troopship. We'll all appreciate seeing the latest show in a theater with good sound and focusing. I understand we've missed some good movies over the months, but as the family recently got a television set, I'll have to see how that is on a regular basis. When we're discussing such subjects, we also wonder how the prices are back in the States; even the cost of a meal over here has gone up.

Gad, our daily ritual is getting boring. We sleep, we eat, we perform routine duties while the winter cold has driven everyone to cave-like confinement. Endless conversations and reading are the big time fillers.

But then, for the pilots there are reserved the really great events of the day that make the war worthwhile and very personal. The combat missions require complete concentration; almost without realizing it, we have escaped into another world that for a time totally absorbs us. Because of the significance of efforts, risks, and events, the time occupied on a mission seems to span a greater share of the day than all the other hours of routine. Those shared experiences are the great sources of our conversations—the fuels that keep our engines running between flights.

This change from the humdrum to acute alert (a sensation "outsiders" can never share) is experienced only by the pilots in our outfit, and then only in the planning and flying of a mission. I have felt that difference when joining with the audience by the radio in Squadron Ops with a mission in progress. The calls we hear seem produced by detached, almost ghostly voices out there "some-

Author's brother Tom standing by F-84 on 121st Fighter Squadron ramp at Andrews Field, MD. Photo taken by author from cockpit of another F-84.

where." We pilots, from experience, can imagine a picture of events, but still we are not there, just listening to that other world.

When airborne, each of us alone in our cockpits rely on eyesight and the habit of constant scan to relate our maneuvers with other planes in the surrounding sky, whether floating alongside or drifting in the distance. The F-86s with us, no matter how recognizable, hold pilots likewise isolated, cut off from the normal identity so that the fighters themselves almost assume a personality. The radio thus becomes an important link between us as it confirms the presence and strength of our friends in these remote actions. Even though this void, the sky, is for us a special and familiar region, the voice of a friend can be a great comfort.

I've gotten into some serious discussions about this life and what makes a fighter pilot. I can't even explain it myself, but I'm hooked, and look on any other kind of occupation as downright sickening.

On the 23rd the weather was fairly clear and we got way up at high altitude—40,000 feet and a little above. The squadron had split into separate flights for patrolling, which was a rare but welcome change in tactics. I was Red Three and had the element in Red Flight. In our patrol we had turned to a northeasterly heading to follow up the course of the Yalu. Looking back in our turns, I could see that we were trailing nothing—which meant we were way above the con level. I noticed my canopy was beginning to frost up and then at one o'clock some specks and cons showed up approaching opposite to our heading. I remember thinking, "If these guys are MiGs, they must have crossed the river a hell of a long ways east of Mizu."

MiGs sometimes did just that to come down southwest and catch us in the flank. I just couldn't believe my eyes—a whole squadron of MiGs two or three thousand feet below our level and driving along into a perfect bounce position abeam of us. Evidently, without telltale contrails, they didn't see us in the high deep blue. They were pulling short cons; as they got closer and closer, the whole setup made me sort of hold my breath in anticipation— like getting all tensed up to spring on the prey.

To cover the Yalu country north of us I had positioned my element on the right, which unhandily was the same side as the MiGs, but I didn't shift as I was afraid the movement and sun reflection might give us away. When what I figured was the right moment arrived, how I wanted to whip over and get in shooting position—I could taste it. I had better sense, though, than to cut one of the big wheels out of the pattern, so I waited for Red Lead to make his move. He peeled down across me; I swung to the side to let him pass and then followed him down.

The pursuit path puzzled me. Instead of aiming ahead of them with an initial high angle-off and flattening the angle when assured of intercept and at close range, our curve was so gradual it was like an arc keeping us at the same distance all the way down as the MiGs moved along. I got a sinking feeling—here we were trailing them in the cons at the same range as the height we'd had above them. At least we had some overtake speed remaining, so we crawled up behind them, and I mean *crawled*. I thought, "I've got to get something out of this." I centered one of the trail MiGs in my windshield. All my nerves urged me to hurry; I was straining at the shoulder straps, sort of like using body English when shooting pool.

Just as the range was getting good, Red Lead moved in front of me, evidently deciding on my MiG. If my helmet hadn't been on I would have pulled out some hair. Anyway, I slid off and just as I picked another MiG and was anticipating the roar of my guns, two new 86s suddenly appeared diving at the MiGs' flank. They were in vertical banks, bellies to us, and at 90 degrees to the MiGs. Theirs was a wild and acute pass that did nothing but completely panic the MiGs and blow the whole works for everybody.

The MiGs broke like a school of fish in all directions and maximum climb. I tried to stay on my MiG, but Red One and Two crossed again in the zoom and all chance was lost. Red One got only a steep parting burst of tracer as the MiGs went for the moon. The two other 86s had fallen out below and disappeared. That was that for the day.

I was steaming in frustrated rage all the way home. If I ever saw a dream bounce that one was it; oh, to have it flubbed like that. When we got into Combat Ops I was so browned off I could just sputter out a debriefing report.

Yesterday evening at the end of the day, all the fighter pilots got together for lectures and briefings by test pilot George Welch and his engineering team from North American Aviation Corp. We got quite a discussion going about the MiG vs. the 86, high tails vs. low tails, and went into the subject of the hydraulic flying tail, a special feature of the F-86E. Some of our experiences and MiG-15 capabilities didn't quite jibe with the conclusions of the aeronautical engineers. They believed that the high horizontal stabilizer and elevator could not be as effective or efficient in turning capability as the low tail, particularly the flying tail. We could all relate instances where there had been pretty hair-raising even-steven turning contests with MiGs. Of course we admitted these had been with obviously highly capable MiG pilots who could produce that extra something beyond the majority of MiGs. But isn't the pilot the really decisive factor anyway?

The engineers may have something, but we feel that, as they explained it, in our present equipment (i.e., wing loading, angle of

Beginning of surprise promotion party for the author; sign and photos overhead. In rear, left to right: Cheever, Merrick, author, Mathews, A Flight Commander, Liles, C Flight Commander, Dews. Foreground: Lawyer. January 1952.

wing sweep, speed range, etc.), the tail position isn't as critical as it may be in future developments. We let it be known we are dissatisfied with our lack of thrust, which makes us deficient in climb and altitude contests with the MiG.

The flying tail concept in use in the 86E model is certainly convenient and gives a more rapid response in sudden turns, breaks, and reversals, and although the factory people see it as the coming thing, we are still leery of the total hydraulic control system. When one fighter nails another he's usually boresighted right up the butt, and at such low angle-off shoots up the tail first, which in the case of the 86E zaps all the hydraulics that join together there. Then your stick is in cement and you either bail out or buy the farm. We've already had unpleasant and fatal experiences with that, and I, for one, prefer my 86A where I may at least have a chance of manhandling the bird home if badly shot up, with loss of boost.[18]

We all found the talks real interesting and satisfying; that sure is the way to get the honest word back and forth for developing fighters. I remember the first time I heard George Welch speak on the F-86 in 1949, just before my initial check flights. A bunch of us had never flown *any* jet and the lingo going around was like Buck Rogers and completely over our heads. Now I feel like I'm in the saddle of the jet business. We've sure learned a lot in that span of time.

After the meeting with the North American Aviation Corp. people we went off to our billets, where there was a real surprise in store for me. In the morning I had found out that my spot Captaincy had come through, so I had gone to Wing Headquarters and picked the orders up myself. They were ten days late coming in, so I had actually been a spot Captain since Jan. 14th—yahoo! By a conincidence, I had also just received a bunch of photos from our Public Information Office—the sort of photos sent to the home front.

Well, when I entered our flight room it was all decked out with the photos on the walls; hanging from the ceiling was a big sign lettered, "Eager Flight's Secret Weapon," with a photo in the middle. Gosh, that looked great—we are E Flight and we say E stands in our case for Eager. There were also big cardboard Captain's tracks hanging from the ceiling. The fellows in my flight had really worked up the decorations, and for me it was a wonderful feeling and surprise.

Man, what a party got going. Most of the pilots in the squadron

Pilot gathering for author's promotion party. In rear, left to right: Cheever, Neubert, author, Mitson, Green (with hand raised), Mathews, A Flight Commander, Liles, C Flight Commander, Dews, Spitzer. Mid-photo: Rapp, Akin, unidentified pilot. Foreground: Keen, Operations Officer. January 1952.

came into our flight room to get in on it. I brought out my hidden reserve, a fifth of C.C., and we had lots of beer and other whiskey available. There were photo flashes going off as lots of pictures were taken.

We all proceeded to go able sugar, and with so many tigers full of firewater, we really wrecked the room. There were beer shampoos, singing bouts, and rebel yelling at the tops of our lungs. Two of the guys put on a strip dance, waving bottles—they peeled everything off while we all yelled, "More, more!" Geez, it was hilarious. There was kick the can (empty beers), and somebody put a boot through our trash box, which shattered. More kicking scattered *that* stuff—some kind of soccer game. The stove got hit and the chimney fell down—oh, wonderful. Someone threw up out the window (an activity referred to as "laughing at the ground"); another barely made the door before "laughing," which made a rather slippery entrance. One of the boys spun in so we parked his carcass on a mattress in the corner. Young Borowski had the Combat Ops Duty so he missed the entire affair—too bad; that will probably stunt his growth. Everybody was saying it was our *best* party. Just think of our standing in the Social Register!

All the pilots think we have a hell of a good flight and we sure get along well. It's mighty nice wearing Captain's tracks; I wish I could wear them home, but this is only a "spot" promotion so I lose them when I leave combat. But what the hell, this is the place where they count.

Whew, what a hangover I had today. Charlie thankfully took the tower duty for the morning mission. As the afternoon mission got ready I took the tower, expecting the usual routine. The Fighter Group got off okay in normal fashion and through the binoculars I watched them snaking off in the climb until they disappeared. A short time later we got a call from one of the boys that his engine was running rough and losing power; he was returning and said he would hold some altitude until over the field. With that word I was straining my eyeballs looking up in a northerly direction, trying to spot him.

About that time a B-26 taxied out for a test hop or something and requested takeoff. I hold the tower boys to hold him in number one position until we got the emergency down. The 86 pilot called again that his engine had failed and he was in a deadstick pattern. I was still looking up, wondering why I couldn't see him, when suddenly the tower operators and I spotted him on a *low* entry for a 360 deadstick. With his gear down and rate of sink in the turn I felt positive he couldn't make it; that damned rocky slope off the south end of the runway was sure to get him. I knew it was going to be a bad one and wanted to turn and look the other way, but kept watching to see how he'd make out.

The 86 went into the slope and the overrun with a terrific crash and was practically obscured in a cloud of dust and smoke and flying parts at the end of the runway. One landing gear strut and wheel whirled toward the waiting B-26. From where we were in

Damaged F-86 comes to rest after gear-up belly landing; crash recovery vehicle standing by. Kimpo, Korea, fall 1951. Pat Green's caption: One of the guys coming back from a mission the hard way. (photo from John P. Green collection)

the tower it looked like it nearly parted the hair of the B-26 crew—
a hairy scene, all right. Then, like a miracle, out of that dusty,
smoky shambles appeared the 86 pilot making speedy tracks away
from the crash. What a sight! What can you say to something like
that? Do you laugh or what? We all gasped with relief.

I told the tower troops to clear the 26 for takeoff. The 26
replied, "Negative, we're returning to the ramp." After witnessing
that smashup practically in their laps, they probably found a
reason to forget the whole thing. I sure didn't blame them. The rest
of the mission went off okay and I left the tower after all the gang
got in.

The day before yesterday I saw Keith Meggs of No. 77
Squadron, RAAF, and we shot the breeze for quite awhile. Boy, he
sure had some trip after he left here. I knew he was going to the
U.S. and gave him the phone numbers and addresses of Lu and the
folks. It still seems strange that in such a short time he could have
been in England, toured over the U.S., visited the family, and then
returned to Korea—what a deal. He also handed me a letter from
Lu—quite a way to get mail. I haven't been over to visit the Aussies
in some time, so I don't know how many of their old gang are still
here in Korea. Ray Trebilco, who really got me acquainted with
their outfit, has gone home to Australia.

I saw some 84 pilots from the 49th Group in here today and
they said Smithson has finished his missions and is in Japan now.
Those guys fly more often than we do, plus we've hit another slow
spell for awhile, which has meant only four missions in ten days for
me. That's about average—the old bit of too few planes and a lack of
parts to keep them in commission, though I may fly again
tomorrow.

Today the mail really came through for me, so with a nice easy
evening to read it over and think about some answers, I'd better get
on the stick and write some letters myself.

FEBRUARY 4th

The night after that crash, the lucky pilot and the boys in his
squadron's flight next door to mine got a real rip-snorting
celebration going they were so glad their ol' pal had made it. It was
a typical whoopee free-for-all that we let them have all to
themselves—each gang to their own turn.

But the next morning—what noises of agony from next door.
The Docs came and the poor jock had to be carried off in a stretcher
to the hospital. It turned out that he had broken his back in the

crash, but what with the state he must have been in immediately after and then the welcome nerve medicine of the celebration, the effects took a long time catching up. It's a wonder the free-for-all didn't ruin the poor guy.

On 28 Jan. Charlie and I were in Combat Ops, ready to cut some gun camera film, when Al Simmons asked us how quick we could go on a mission. Well, 25 minutes later we were heading north. I was leading a four-ship special flight to cover the withdrawal of Able Squadron and Black Squadron. Evidently interference with this withdrawal was anticipated, and our Red Flight would arrive on the scene with a fresh fuel load to counter any end runs by the MiGs on the return route of the squadrons. Fortunately (because of what was to follow) I had three very sharp pilots with me. Fred McPherson was Red Two on my wing; my old buddy Charlie Mitson was leading the element as Red Three, and Kenny Rapp was on his wing as Red Four.

On the way north I kept a steady climb for lots of altitude. We overflew the Group and got on top of the con level, arriving in the Mizu area at 41,000 feet where we found MiGs. I watched two of them on our right a little above that were pacing us. Then two more showed up on the right and crossed under to our left in the con level just below. I guess it was a sucker deal, but I turned over them to make an attack. At that moment my flight called they'd lost sight of the two high MiGs. Planes sometimes seem to vanish or dissolve in the blinding blue depths of very high altitude. Then, in a twinkle, those high MiGs had tapped us and Rapp, Red Four, called for a left break.

Well, you sure don't do a real break at that altitude or you will fall right out of the sky and maybe go out of control. It's more like max effort instrument flying, to allow your wings to keep some kind of a grip on the thin air. Another reason I had to be as careful and precise in turns as possible was to prevent spinning out anybody else in the flight. You get the feeling of exploring for footing while trying to win a footrace on thin ice. The MiGs did worse in this turn and we cleared our tails.

Some more MiGs arrived over us; the turns were really getting serious now. Any of us that might fall out had a good chance of becoming meat on the table. We couldn't help it, but with the maneuvering we had lost some altitude and now we were all in the cons. The MiGs kept attacking us in elements, one after the other, and we were real busy outmaneuvering them. I warned my gang to stick together in a four-ship flight—if they had split us, we would have been goners.

Then I saw a quick chance for a shot and in one hairy go-around I outpositioned two, but those characters pulled up and I couldn't match them out of the turn with any climb ability left. I had to continue hard around, but did manage to meet the next two head-on. What a weird scrap—Sabres and MiGs in turn were swallowed and then popping in and out of these solid, heavy contrails, and we were laying more in an ever-increasing tangle. I kept pulling around in this web with McPherson hanging right in there and strained to keep track of two more planes I could vaguely make out in front.

Then an urgent call: "Hey, don't shoot, it's me, Red Four."

Damned if I wasn't behind Charlie and Ken, Red Three and Four of our flight, groping in these thick contrails—what confusion. I nearly laughed over the radio, "Okay Red Flight, Lead will go inside of you. Let's close together." We reassembled and clawed out of the tangle of cons like swimmers surfacing for air.

Three elements of MiGs were ready for us and a very interesting duel began. One MiG element came in from three o'clock and another from nine o'clock at the same time. I waited till the last moment, then had Charlie and myself split, with one of our elements into each of theirs. As they went outside our breaks we reversed into them, but before we could press an advantage, they pulled up and over, so we rejoined and they repeated their attacks the same way two more times. The third element of MiGs criss-crossed over our heads and were either calling the play or waiting for us to mess up so they could nail us. It was all very tricky. I never felt worried, just completely absorbed in the maneuvering—it was fascinating.

We could see other, more distant, MiGs that were going for the Yalu and these guys pulled away and left us too. As we were almost on the Yalu anyway, I thought I'd make one last sweep southwest downriver to the mouth.

I had been concentrating so hard on the hassling that I hadn't paid attention to radio calls other than our own. One of the fellows said it sounded like Home Plate was calling us. I gathered that everyone else was home; we were alone up there and were to return. Right about then, low on our right, we saw a formation of 14 MiGs climbing hard for us in the low con levels. They had a real steep climb angle and looked like rockets coming up with the short cons streaming behind them. More cons appeared following those, and Red Four made an outstanding transmission (too bad I can't quote it). I'll bet the Russians had the veins bulging out in their necks.

The ground radio calls, the fresh MiG gaggle, and our fuel state added up to an appropriate moment to get the hell out, so we swung south and had a relaxing cruise home. We left the sign of our work behind: From miles away I could still see the spider web of contrails remaining from our duel suspended in the void. Though the weather down low at home was pretty lousy, we cut it okay. You know, by golly, Mizu is 200 nautical miles from Kimpo.[19]

On 30 Jan. we went up very high again. Col. Thyng led the squadron; I was in the flight led by Creighton. We chased some cons only to discover they were other F-86s. Then I was sent off with my element to check on two other cons, so I took Jersey and went on up to the Yalu to sit right in front of Antung. We cruised east and west at 42,000 feet above the cons. I saw a lot of reflective flashes from MiGs on the field at Antung, but no business showed up, and there we were in a perfect position perched on their porch roof, so to speak—very frustrating. I pulled my element out last as the others left and returned well east of Kaesong, letting down over the front lines. There was some artillery firing going on as we swung west; then we dove to a tremendous speed for a bit of aerobatics on the way home. The tower wondered where we had been as we landed late. Actually, by patrolling at high altitude most of the mission, we had plus fuel and then some when we landed—a lot better than the usual sweat.

Late last Tuesday night I was awakened and told I would go over in the transport to Tsuiki, Japan, with three other pilots to bring back four F-86s from maintenance. I wasn't at all in the mood for a ferry trip and when I woke up the next morning thought maybe I had been dreaming, but it was true.

As usual, the courier gooney bird was late in getting off so while we waited I managed to collect my pay, then Mitson, Neubert, Beck, and I got on board for our trip. The courier stopped at K-13, Suwon, and from the air I could barely recognize the place. When we taxied into Base Ops we were all surprised at the building progress of the base. Besides the new runway, the whole field had been pretty well changed—a lot different than when we were there last summer.

Those gooneys are cold without heat of any kind, and for the two-and-a-half hour trip across we all nearly froze in the passenger-cargo area. We were continuously stomping our feet and beating our hands and sides to keep up the circulation.

At Tsuiki the four 86s were about ready for us, so after a late lunch we figured out our flight plan and I filed the clearance, as I was leading. When we got on the runway Charlie had to abort, so I pulled out with him as we must ferry with at least two airplanes. Ernie and Beck, together in the element, went on with their two birds. Charlie's plane required more work than a quick fix, so he and

I were stuck for the night. As we had not planned on an RON, none of us had taken along a thing but our flying gear. Oh well . . . In the evening we got with Raby and Hefley and had a few laughs together.

The next day we explored around the base and took advantage of the chance to get a decent haircut. It was wonderful just walking around, seeing a new place, and enjoying the mild weather that gave off a feeling of the coming spring. It all brought on those sensations and thoughts that creep up on you in the drag of a rough winter. We were getting a sort of sneak preview of winter's end by visiting the southern island of Kyushu. All of our M&S Group people are out of Johnson and now at Tsuiki, so we won't be making any more trips to Johnny. It must be kind of nice in Tsuiki in the summer in sight of the sea, even though it is a tent city. Of course, my feelings may be caused by the winter conditions in Korea. By that afternoon Charlie's plane was finally fixed, but as the weather at Kimpo was down with snow, we got another RON in our flying suits.

We managed to get back to Kimpo in the afternoon of Feb. 2nd. On arrival I discovered Simmons had a training flight up, so we immediately bounced them and we all had a wonderful thrash throwing ourselves around. We saw Borowski after we got down and had a laugh over his combat experience that day. The 4th Group now has 127 MiGs destroyed, eight bombers destroyed, and about 170 probables and damaged—not bad.

Last night we got a good gang together for a party for Maj. Al Simmons, our Squadron Exec, who is leaving. We all had a good time and frequently sang our version of the "Old Soldier" tune: "Old Majors never die, they just smell that way . . ." We also sang our updated version of an old song: "Beside his shattered Sabre the young pursuiter lay . . ." We all like a songfest and it's better than saying goodby, so we cranked up a lot of our favorites: "When the Ice Is on the Rice in Tachikawa," "Bosom Buddies While Boozin'," and many others. I'm sorry to see Simmons leave; he's one guy who understands and has said how lucky we are to have gotten this air-to-air combat assignment. I realize it—I guess that's why I make the most of it.

It sure is cold today; you feel like you're going to turn to solid ice just by stepping away from the heater. Last night when we hit the sack the heater was roaring and as the room had gotten quite hot I turned it down, but it still put out too much heat for me. Later I got up and cracked open the sliding window over my sack, and then this morning *something* woke me up like a shot about 6 a.m.—rigor mortis was setting in. The heat had gone down all right—I was nearly frozen and that sure played hell with this cold and cough I've had for the last couple of weeks. Wonderful combination with this frigid weather *and* flying. In this business it seems like we're either too hot or too cold, and I've gotten so used to sleeping on these canvas cots that my back will probably kill me whenever I get back again to permanent use of an inner-spring mattress.

On today's mission we were up over 40,000 east of Mizu; there were *toksan* MiGs above and all of us were pulling cons. Gaggles of over 50 MiGs approached us from three directions and they were set up in ideal attack positioning. I don't understand why they didn't give us hell. Later, on the way out, Mathews (Red Lead) and I both saw a bunch of planes on our right heading north. We wheeled the flight around and went for those guys neck and neck, throttles at the firewall. As we closed up their tails I saw the tip tanks and called them out, so we quickly broke away in a diving 180. They were F-84s and I'm glad we didn't startle them or cause them to jettison their loads as they often mistake 86s for MiGs. We didn't have to get close to identify them so they probably never saw us, and for a few moments I thought for sure we had some MiGs cold.

Another mission tomorrow and also a little flying in the T-33. I hope to take up Walt Raby—heh, heh.

FEBRUARY 6th

Yesterday I was up at 5 a.m. to get set up for runway control. While the mission got ready for takeoff, I ended up dashing into the tower as the mobile control unit went out of commission. By 8 a.m. the temperature had gotten up to four degrees above zero. The wind hadn't picked up too strong though; man, when it blows it's like being doused with ice water. When preflighting for a mission the water wells up in your eyes and runs our of your nose, and you're shaking like you had the clanks. During the missions the cockpit heat is turned up so your canopy won't frost over; this all works up a great sweat, so when you get out again and this frigid air hits you you've *really* got a cold—nasty break if you already have one. I guess it's 50° or so below zero at the altitudes we fly, and when you think about it on a mission and look down at frozen white North Korea, you know it would be bad news to be forced down into that—much better to shoot down the enemy and let *him* find out about it. We just face the fact that we can't possibly wear enough clothes for outside conditions and still get in the cockpit.

After tower duty I got hold of Raby and took him up in the T-Bird. I put the go-handle to the stop and roared around the area to give Walt the proper speed impression, and for a while let him take the controls to get an idea of handling jets. When I found some 86s I wasted no time in getting tangled with them. I was calling out clock positions on these guys as we thrashed around, and Walt kept trying to figure out the action with all the sudden Gs and horizon flips of rapid maneuvering—I was laughing to beat the band. Then we found Neubert and White, and followed them around in trail acro. After that we went off for some acro by ourselves and a bit of old-fashioned beat-up on the deck. Quite a sudden introduction to jets, but I felt I'd had a good opportunity to show Walt the fighter pilot's side of this flying business. I ended up shooting a couple of landings to keep my hand in.

As soon as we parked I had to rush to eat and then head off on the afternoon mission. Maj. Creighton was leading the squadron and Col. Thyng led White Flight. On the way up north, we turned with two high cons that we found were 86s. Then further up and MiGs came high over us, between forty and fifty of them. We turned and turned, working for position, and finally Col. Thyng pulled up into twelve MiGs which reacted by scattering all over the place. Some even dove away and went head-on right smack over our heads, rocking their wings and looking us over as they made knots leaving. We got a real close-up view of those guys for a change, but couldn't get very near any others after that, so Spitzer and I churned around together and then went home east of Kaesong. I kind of like the change of scenery that way and we dove down for a speed run a few thousand feet over the front lines back to base.

In the evening I went to see Bob Hope and Hedy Lamar in *My Favorite Spy*, after which I had a long bull session with Raby, who just got his spot Captaincy, and we had a few beers to his health. We compared flying techniques and Walt realizes that a dogfight requires reaction and maneuvering that he really hadn't considered before. He was impressed at the way things happen at such high speed.[20]

I had a chance to sleep in this morning, and with my blasted cold I didn't feel at all guilty. The weather was rather sorry today; the missions got off but weren't too good—just sort of prowled around, I guess. The free time gave me a chance to get some paperwork accomplished in the orderly room and make sure my records were squared away with a new fogey for pay. As a spot Captain, for a short time until I leave, I'll make $594.00 per month; as a First Lieutenant I'll make $526.63 per month—not bad at all. I did some more on those cursed income tax forms—what a pain in the neck, *and* I've got to hurry on that!

I find I am to lead the squadron tomorrow so I sure will fly, though I feel like hell with this persistent cold. Pat Green is to be White Leader and it will be his 100th mission.

A swell letter arrived from Gordon Ellison; apparently he's really happy in his flying job with Capitol Airlines. He's doing a lot of flying now and gets all over the eastern U.S., including Florida. He gets into D.C. once in a while, but is based at his home in Detroit. Sounds like he's got a good deal; I'm sure glad for him. He and I are darn near the only ones out of our bunch in World War II that really craved this flying life so much we stayed with it.

Well, the schedule for 7 Feb. got completely changed, both pilots and planes, and I ended up with an element lead. When we fired up I found I had radio troubles, couldn't channelize properly, and my receiver seemed to be cutting in and out. With this problem I shifted to spare position and taxied out late after the squadron, hoping the trouble might clear enough after getting airborne to fill in on the mission.

The squadron roared off in the usual cloud of smoke and I followed at full bore, trying to catch up. My radio was messed up on the channel change, but I finally picked up the flights checking in. Then I heard Pat Green calling that he was having some kind of trouble. This was followed by excited calls of very bad news: "You're on fire, bail out!"

I was too far behind to see any of this and was really flogging my ol' 86 in hopes of joining them. Pat's voice came back quite calmly: "I've pulled the handles, but the seat won't fire. Anybody got any special suggestions?"

Oh yeah, lots of helpful hints, now in the shouting stage: "You're on fire!"

"Hurry up and get out!"

At this critical moment my receiver went out again. I felt like smashing the console with my fist. I kept switching the set off and on, tried some different channels, and finally picked up the emergency channel to hear the plane had crashed, Air Rescue had been alerted, and the squadron was continuing on the mission. By this time I was at the Han River and, with instructions from Dentist Charlie, started looking for the crash site. It wasn't long before a T-6 Mosquito showed up and we both buzzed back and forth in the front line area on the deck. I put down flaps so I could fly slower and still maneuver around. It's a wonder I didn't get my butt shot off sailing around low on both sides of the river, because I had no idea what the front line situation was.

The Mosquito pilot located the crash site and said some Koreans were there *with the pilot*. His parachute was spread out to mark the place. Was I relieved to hear *that*. I went in the direction indicated and the first thing I saw was a smoking hole in the ground with some metal scattered about—all that remained of the F-86. As I dipped a wing I saw the chute, but never did see Pat. The Mosquito pilot said he had moved and was laying down away from the site. A helicopter came up on the radio and the T-6 gave him instructions to the scene. I'd found out all I could and felt I'd be in the way hanging around longer, so, knowing Pat was going to be picked up okay, I headed back to Kimpo. I didn't have to take credit for a mission on that flight, so I could save it for another day.

As soon as I could, I got a ride to the Forward Evac Hospital in Yong Dong Po to see Pat Green. There weren't many emergency cases in evidence, but I noticed some spatterings of blood where some had just been finished. There were a couple of bad-looking, heavily bandaged casualties moaning and groaning. When you're in a combat job you can't afford to hang around that environment long—it does things to you.

I located Pat. They had him strapped down to one of those wheeled tables and he was still in his flying suit. I asked the Docs what kind of shape he was in, and they said his back was broken. Poor old Pat—he was still kind of in shock and sort of incoherent. All he wanted to talk about was finishing that 100th mission and insisted that I promise to put him on the schedule tomorrow. I promised of course, and that seemed to pacify him. When the Docs were ready to work on him I left the hospital in a cheerless mood.

I got to redo that mission on the 9th. The whole outfit has practically run out of drop tanks so most of us got slick planes with no tanks to go hunting in the Sinanju area. Can you imagine going 150 or more miles—and then patrol—all on internal fuel? It's ridiculous. If you get cornered in a bad jam you'll run out of fuel, and if you get over-eager chasing MiGs around you'll end up sucking wind too. It makes you wonder what's going on in the supply system and what kind of priorities we have. Suppose we had *dozens* of groups going at it as in World War II—what would we do *then*? If tanks are necessary for the mission, then they are like ammunition: You've got to have them, and expect them to be used. Why the hell haven't we devised a cheap, one-way, expendable tank? We don't need these high-speed deluxe tanks which are a permanent fixture for range and reserve back in the States. Every time we punch off a set of these we all say, "There goes another Chevy (or Ford, whatever your preference) into North Korea."

The 10th of February was a pretty busy day. I got two more missions, but only because of a tough loss for the Fighter Group. On the first mission, after the Group had gone off on the regular patrol, I took up a flight of four to cover the withdrawal as I had done before. This time due to the shortage we went without tanks, but considering the characteristic of the mission, endurance wasn't a requirement, while speed and maneuverability were.

After we got on our way my number four had to abort and as we don't use three-ship formations, I sent the element back together. That left just Beck and me to continue on. We climbed to a pretty good altitude without pulling any cons. The con layer must really have been high, but I didn't need to find out and headed up the center of North Korea toward Huichon while listening to Able Squadron patrolling somewhere up the Yalu.

Maj. Davis, who was Baker Lead, apparently had split off from his squadron for separate hunting and from his transmissions to his wingman had evidently sighted something up in the northwest corner. The patrolling squadrons weren't reporting any sightings, so I stayed on a northerly course. Then I heard Davis' familiar call: "Look now, Baker Two."

When we heard this call, it meant he was lined up ready to blast somebody and he wanted his wingman to look sharp and confirm what he was shooting. This sure got me excited. After a pause, Davis repeated the transmission; another pause, and then there was a call of alarm from his wingman: "Look out Baker Lead! Oh, no!"

He kept calling Baker Lead, but there was no reply. Other voices now came on the air wanting to know what was going on and the location of Baker Two. Baker Two, in a very agitated voice, said Baker Lead had been hit behind the canopy where there was an explosion and he was going down, apparently out of control.

I was looking toward the northwest at this time and saw two plumes of smoke going down in the distant direction of Long Point. I supposed one was a MiG and one was Davis.

Baker Two called out that Baker Lead had his landing gear down and was descending in a sort of falling leaf pattern. *Gear down?* I wondered what was going on. I told Beck to go 100 percent and headed directly to where the two smokers were seen going down. We got up to max speed but all evidence of aircraft ahead disappeared. Baker Two said Baker Lead had crashed; in reply to questions he said he saw no parachute.

Then Beck and I both saw flashes from what was probably a formation of aircraft moving south from where we had seen the smokers. Since they were practically on our path anyway, I decided to check the identity of this bunch. The flashes disappeared—now what? I guessed they had made a turn which changed the sun's reflection.

All of a sudden, right in our faces was a squadron of MiGs head-on. This was the bunch that had turned; we'd found 'em, all right. Their flights were staggered and ragged and we were on a level with the middle, as in a sandwich. It was a close, fast passage. I remarked, "Look at 'em right on top of us."

Beck replied, "Look at 'em right under us."

We dodged through the middle and I pulled right into a chandelle to get into position for whatever was coming next. A quick eye sweep of this gaggle talleyed about a dozen MiGs. While I was turning for position, I watched the MiG formation scatter like a covey of flushed quail, zooming for altitude north and northeast.

I was completing my 180 back at them when I saw one of the zoomers curving right at me. This sure got my attention, so I concentrated on him. We crossed in a scissor, still turning, and the MiG fired a burst of cannon shells that was wasted as neither of us had attained a firing position. We reversed back at each other. Ha, I liked this—I was already getting the best position, while he wasted another blast of shells and we reversed again. Man, I was hopping with anticipation now; another scissor and I'd be right in position to nail this guy. He let go another burst and I thought, "Now's the time to do it just right and I'll have a bead on him." If you foul up when you're committed like that, it's all she wrote, bub.

Beck broke in on my concentration: "There's four coming up right on us, hard left."

The F-86A, most widely used model of the Sabre during the period of this narrative. Attached under the wings are the auxiliary 120 gallon fuel tanks, jettisoned for aerial combat. (National Archives photo)

Oh *damn*. But I didn't hesitate; I switched the stick around to check this new problem.

A new voice said, "What's going on here?"

I recognized it and saw the newcomers were F-86s. What a time to be spooked by your pals. I reversed my attention and controls to the original MiG and that foxy little tiger was climbing out as only a MiG can. He must have recognized the 86s just as I did and decided to haul it. My double reverse had given him the time for good separation and as he climbed steeply away he was rocking his wings. I took that to mean he was thumbing his nose at us and that sure made me grit my teeth. One thing I had noticed during our little duel was that this MiG had a different paint job on his nose—narrow bands of red, white, red.

The only MiGs that any of the other 86 formations had sighted were the ones that Beck and I had run into. Everyone did a great deal of churning around the northwest area east of Long Point until their fuel was low, but there were no more sightings and we had to return to base.

What a hullaballoo there was at debriefing. The wheels in Wing, 5th Air Force, and up the line wanted to know what happened to Davis, our top ace. His poor wingman got a regular siege of debriefings.

The way I figured it was that Davis had stalked and bounced that formation I met minutes later. The MiGs in turn had been intent on hunting for our fighter-bombers and no one was pulling any telltale contrails. Davis had charged into them so quick the majority of them didn't know what hit them. With the flights staggered, he mixed with the pack and while shooting one MiG, another got a shot at him that sent him down. He must have fallen forward over the controls so that his head struck the gear handle and dropped his landing gear. He was flying a late-model E and the gear handle was a simple up-and-down switch—why else would the gear have dropped in mid-flight?

I think the MiGs were trying to unravel what had happened when Beck and I suddenly popped into their middle head-on. Then there was that rather peculiar action by the single MiG who wanted to scissor. The more I think about it, the more convinced I am that that MiG must have been the guy who shot down Davis, and he was so excited about it that he wanted to get another. But, of course, we'll never know for sure.

A max effort got cooked up after the debriefing and that's how I got on the schedule again for the day. The whole outfit went roaring up north looking for blood. Lots of cons were sighted up toward the Yalu and I had the fidgets—like I suppose everybody else did after the briefing we'd had about giving the MiG buzzards the business and wondering how things were going to go. Just at this gripping phase of buildup, my wingman called that he couldn't keep up the power setting as he was exceeding the redline in tailpipe temperature.

I felt I'd been stabbed when I heard that because I knew what was coming. In the next moment I was told to take my wingman back home, so I swung out of formation with him and told him to set the best power for his engine and I'd escort him. I was ready to froth at the mouth over this early return just when it looked like good action was coming.

How long had it taken this guy to notice the overtemp? If he had aborted sooner I might have been able to fill in somewhere and continue on the mission. I was fuming all the way home. After my wingman got down okay I kept listening for action on the radio and proceeded to get in a good workout in some local acro before landing. My fuming was for nothing as nobody got near any MiGs. The Antung crowd must have figured they'd accomplished something unusual and played it safe for a while.

Author's father at controls of Curtiss AH-3 (early designation: Aeroplane Hydro). This was at the early seaplane ramp at Pensacola, FL. Note flying attire - a decidedly drafty and probably very *damp* way to fly, but that was 1915. Another rare photo from collection of author's late father.

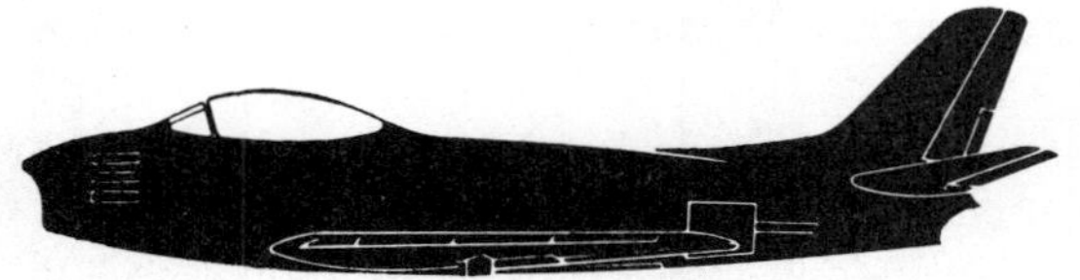

VIII

Last of the Way

FEBRUARY 14th

I'm beginning to make preparations to leave here; yesterday Charlie and I got all our shot records up to date. Same old story: You get all the needles or you don't ship out. Gad, my arms are sore. I changed my mind about taking an R&R before I finish; to hell with it. It's so much trouble to get transportation back and forth to Japan that it puts me in a bad mood just thinking about it. What really gripes me about R&Rs is the difficulty a combat man has in obtaining a reservation to stay in the choice resorts or hotels.

There sure will be a lot of changes in this outfit soon. A lot of us are finishing and lots of new pilots have arrived again. Many of us have been talking about getting new cars, but to make it easier financially, I think I'll wait a while—at least until after the big move and we're all settled down at the new base. I figure a new Chevy Bel Aire with automatic drive would cost about $2,500 or a new Chevy like our standard model about $2,225—just a rough guess.

I'm beginning to feel lousy. Evidently those immunization shots have given me a fever. I had to get up at 5 a.m. this morning and take my flight out on pre-dawn alert. The cold was pure agony and with shots and fever I felt weak in all my joints and muscles. At such times I can sure relate with Tom, remembering how he described stirring up the fellows in his P-47 flight during the weather of the Battle of the Bulge in France. These wars sure can give you the miseries. I ought to start some packing after lunch, but I really feel like merely piling into my sack.

On Feb. 16th I got on a fairly interesting mission. Actually, it was kind of funny. I got to lead the squadron, but that sure wasn't the funny part. I don't know whether I can explain how I feel about squadron lead. It's certainly the job I've been working for and hoping for. There just couldn't be a better job, but man, does it put a different slant to things—at least for me. You're not just gambling yourself or a couple of more guys right with you; you've got the whole outfit. In fact, you've got the *mission*. When that sinks in, you realize the whole problem of patrol position, direction, or attack is yours. To me it means: Don't mess up; everybody's expecting success.

We have an RAF exchange pilot, Roy Lelong, who has just joined us; he was flying my wing. Lew Powers, from 5th Air Force, who is with us for a few missions, was flying Red Three. He sure has an interesting job: Standardization with 5th AF HQ. He visits each of the fighter outfits and flies missions with them: 51s, 80s, 84s, and also our 86s. That must be great; he has a chance to get a taste of everybody's action. I'd sure like to be able to fly all the different fighters over here and try some of that fighter-bomber stuff.

Author's brother with members of his Flight in the 405th Fighter Squadron, 371st Fighter Group, ETO, in front of one of their P-47 Thunderbolts. Author's brother second from right. Galyon third from right. (photo from collection of H.E. "Ed" Galyon)

Mossholder was flying Powers' wing and Thompson was leading White Flight with Lilley on his wing; Charlie Mitson was White Three with Andy Merrick on his wing. Everybody knew the score, so when we left Combat Ops there was no need for me to make some elaborate squadron briefing; after a few words, it was merely *go*.

I took the center of Korea as a course, figuring to bend northwest after Huichon and set up a CAP over the fighter-bomber target area. We usually went up nearer the west coast, but I thought I'd be different and run sort of a curve. Cruising well up into the north, we began getting a lot of sightings of high MiGs. They were not in big gaggles; they seemed to have spread out or scattered more into flights. As far as I was concerned this meant more altitude, so I kept the gang climbing. You can brief all day about what you propose to do, but when the other side didn't attend your planning and doesn't cooperate, you improvise damn quick.

MiGs now appeared in range for some action; I saw some to our right passing left and cranked left after them. Boy, did they scatter. There was a bit of comment over this and about some more that came in sight trailing below them at right angles to our course. That sure wasn't ideal, but I tipped over after them anyway. Those MiGs didn't like that a bit and they immediately honked up into one of the damndest climbs I'd ever seen—like monkeys straight up a wall in front of our faces. My gosh, it was startling. And then, if that wasn't enough, a whole slew of them (just as we yanked back on the stick) shot down in front of us and tore off to the north with their dive speed.

All I could say was, "Red Squadron—get 'em!"

Boy, was that a dazzler. We broke up into flights then. All of us had been presented with a plan view of the low MiGs climbing for all they were worth, like *zip*, and then others diving across, like *zap*. It was just like blinking your eyes fast; you sure don't have time to set up some smooth operation. By that time I was way back on the stick (I thought), but the *zip-zap* had occurred so fast that we were off to the old chase up north.

Back on the ground again, the reconstruction brought out the funny part of the mission. I was particularly interested in getting the impressions of Powers and Lelong. They are both believers now in what we brief here—things really happen fast. When the other side is fully alert, the action can turn wild. Like Powers discovered: When the MiGs are at full throttle, they sure can perform. Lew sure is a character and had us all laughing with his remarks about trying to calculate the gyrations of those MiGs. With all his fighter experience, he feels like the rest of us here: *This* is the real fighter flying. He says he can't rest now until he can come back with us permanently.

FEBRUARY 21st

Not too much action to write about these days. We've sure been having a lot of happy gatherings in the evenings. Other people might call them parties, I suppose, but we just like the company of fighter pilots. With all the sidearms, boots, heavy jackets, and fur headgear we look more like a backwoods hunters reunion—a rough, noisy, good-natured bunch. There are a lot of fellows getting close to finishing and so there are plenty of excuses to celebrate. I think a lot of us are secretly sorry to see it end—the excitement of combat and the special kind of friendships we'll never find again. The separation from families makes our relationship especially close and valuable.

We've had a stretch of weather that's been holding us down. In fact, we just had more snow. At least that's given me the chance to get ahead on some required paperwork and fill in the dead time we're having in our daily routine.

I got a letter from Al Feldkirchner, my old flying school pal and fellow Flight Officer (F/O) of the last war. In those days of blue bar rank we jokingly referred to ourselves as "Bluetenants." Al is settled at home in Illinois and was sort of surprised to hear from me in Korea, but he figured I would be sent over when I told him about my Guard outfit getting recalled to active duty.

Uh-oh, I've just been notified of a "mandatory" party, and to rustle up my boys for attendance. Sounds like more of a challenge—we can't let any other squadron outdo the 336th.

FEBRUARY 25th

It's been snowing all day again, and I went down to two briefings that of course didn't materialize into missions. We thought for a while they were going to send us off on the first mission. Brother, that would have been lovely. Everybody wiped their brows with relief when it was scrubbed as we were slogging out through the snow to our planes.

I sure wanted to became an ace, but the prospects have faded now, so I guess I'll have to settle with what I logged—and my neck. At least I know I've helped more than one guy out of a jam and haven't gotten so carried away that I'd swap another man's hide for some personal glory. I've been able to find some good fights, and without anyone along with me getting shot down. You can take your share and more of chances, but combat can be very frustrating as far as really nailing an enemy plane. You might get on a mission with a hell of a fight, with even ability or agility on both sides where no one gets anything, or a boring mission. Then, on the mission you miss, they find a bunch of half-baked MiG pilots and pot a half dozen as easy as pie. It's enough to make a guy pull his hair out, determined to try again knowing that each mission must be a surprise package to be opened only after takeoff.

A lot of stuff has been running through my mind lately. Reflections of that sort, though they probably wouldn't interest or make sense to outsiders, are, for any keen fighter pilot, mighty important considerations.

After Pat Green broke his back and ankle on his 100th mission I went almost every day to see him in our base hospital, where they put him before transfer to Japan. The way he escaped that burning plane is some story.

When his ejection seat wouldn't fire and he got all that shouted advice, his aircraft commenced nosing over. There had been an internal explosion and his flight controls and throttle were jammed. As the formation was just initiating climbout, they hadn't gained much altitude while building up speed. When he saw the ground through his windshield, Pat knew his time was now or never. He unbuckled his safety belt and shoulder harness to try to go over the side, but he was simply plastered to the seat with his head jammed back against the headrest by the terrific wind blast when his cockpit canopy came off.

By this time, the plane was in a vertical dive with airspeed nearly 500 knots and Pat did the only thing he could: He pulled the D-ring on his parachute. The slipstream evidently sucked out the pilot 'chute, which pulled the main canopy! The details of what happened after that were lost to him in the great shock of getting yanked out, beat up, and slammed on the ground.

The other members of the flight noted that his fuselage had twisted from the explosion (this would have caused the control jam) and instead of the rudder being directly behind, there was a V-passage between the vertical and horizontal stabilizers. On the yank-out he must have passed through the V, missing the tail, but the high speed tore up his 'chute and he struck the ground with such force it broke his back.

It's nothing less than a miracle that he made it. I had never thought of trying anything like that. It was a hell of a gamble, but it paid off as he had only seconds before the plane crashed straight in. My God, what a hairy one![21]

These hospitals here really make you think, especially the evacuation hospitals where casualties first arrive from the front. When you visit one, you feel almost like a criminal because you're whole. They don't get many fighter pilots; most of *them* become hamburger if anything happens. After all, if you're so shot-up you can't fly or bail out, there is no one there to help, and you just auger in. In our base hospital there is one other pilot in the ward with Pat, a fighter jock—84s I hear. He got shot up and though he made it in, they had to remove his foot. He has spent some time under an oxygen tent and looks like wax.

The hospital has added a B-29 crewman—a radioman, I believe. The particular B-29 is temporarily on our field. They were on a night mission and got a direct hit with a large caliber flak shell. It failed to explode (very fortunately) and passed right through the 29, making a departure hole in the top like a metal flower. In its passage, the shell severed the right leg of this crewman—he's a real sick-looking kid. The hospital sure had been using the oxygen besides lots of blood and plasma. Those blood drives in the States are no joke. A lot of blood comes from the fellows over here—they know its value.

I felt bad about Pat, but he was taking it in good spirits and as I've spent some uncomfortable months in hospitals myself, I could certainly relate with him.

Whenever I go up on a mission now I look around and think about how strange it will seem when I no longer have this view. I've become as familiar with the look of Korea as any of my old flying areas of past years, and probably *more* so. It's really incredible in a way to think of the great distances we travel in our relatively short-duration missions. Although you get used to jets, they are still amazing machines.

There is an article on the bulletin board in Combat Operations that compares planes and pilots and dogfights of War I, War II, and Korea. Now I can read some writers' opinions and know what's what from my own experience. That is a great satisfaction and I wouldn't trade my combat for any amount of money. I suppose being alive and in one piece brings thoughts other than what they might have been.

Word trickles in about changes being made in many fighter

units at home and I wonder how they will affect the Andrews Field gang or our assignments after Korea. I'll have to find out what plans Tom has concerning the service. Since no one knows our national policies from one day to the next, we all wonder what we'll be doing in the future. If it isn't an election, it's something else. I get tired of thinking and trying to sort these things out and hope I don't blow my top about such subjects when I get home.

The few missions I've had lately haven't really been worth writing about. We see the faraway contrails of MiGs and with our eyes follow their distant progress, tracks which seem traced across the sky by the steady strokes of some invisible paint brushes. They have been very shy about letting us get near them. We've even gone right up on the Yalu and patrolled up and down like a parade without getting any takers. A good part of the time the weather has been lousy, which hasn't helped the situation. Our aircraft in-commission rate is terrible and runs about 50 percent because we lack vital parts; the drop tank shortage is still with us, making it impossible to send out as many sorties as we did in the past. To compound the problem, we keep getting more pilots so everybody is going stir-crazy from the limited mission opportunities.

MARCH 2nd

On the 29th I got another squadron lead job. It turned into another one of those spooky cloud-dodging affairs—probing a-round, wondering what you might meet. We didn't see any MiGs; those guys up there just can't hack weather flying, evidently. The score for the whole Group for January and February was only about half a dozen MiGs each month. Gee, after all this time I'm really getting out front, where I can lead the squadron, and the old action has fizzled out. And all this is coming to an end, doggone it.

One more mission today: It seems there was a reccy needed of MiG numbers and activity in the Antung complex. I tried to talk my way out of it as I wanted to save these last missions for Combat Air Patrols, but nothing doing; I had to go anyway. I guess there are a few people who have been lapping up these reccy jobs—and they can have them *all*, for my money. I gather that Headquarters is trying to find out if the MiGs are moving back to Mukden for the night and then deploying to their Yalu bases as needed for particular daytime operations. This requires a tally of aircraft on the ground at various times and our Group performs some of the visual count.

After I put together a flight of four, a big set of binoculars was offered to me. I couldn't see how I would fit that clumsy affair in the cockpit and, anyway, I told the Intelligence people that as long as I *had* to do this job, from where I'd be flying I sure wouldn't need any binoculars. They must be running their reccy from the stratosphere.

As there was no mission laid on during our flight time we'd be way up there on our own, and since there was no weather info available, we were asked to get *that* detail, too. This was going to be a play-it-by-ear job, so I briefed it that way.

Charlie was leading the element and we'd hardly got underway when his wingman had to abort. We don't operate in three-ship, but since this was a special mission I elected to go on with three. We each had only one tank, so as soon as they were empty I called for the drop. This helped our speed and we needed it because the way I calculated our ground speed, we were fighting a 200-knot head wind and must have been in the middle of a jet stream—we were crawling along. Upon arrival at Sinanju, we crossed over thick clouds which went on down to low altitude and extended north as far as we could see.

This posed several questions: What was the weather on the Yalu, ceiling and visibility? Could we get down and break out? Would I be able to see anything and do any good? Blast this mission anyway, but as long as I was that far, I was going to do the whole thing.

While I was running a time estimate on top, I saw a cloud opening that might give me a path down. I told Charlie to close up so we could stay together and nosed over. The opening became a rather erratic tunnel and in the maneuvering descent before Charlie got tacked on, we lost each other and I was forced to go on instruments the rest of the way with number two.

We broke out in the gloom under a dense 1500-foot ceiling right alongside of Sinuiju on the Yalu. After that . . . well, I got the info they wanted, and then some—mighty interesting. That low flak was the wildest I ever waded or wallowed through, wow! The surrounding ground surface lit up, sparkling and flickering with muzzle flashes from a hornet's nest of flak guns firing streams of stuff at us. A storm of exploding shells expanded to each side and behind, snapping at our tails without quite catching up. It wasn't too smart sailing around in that stuff, but I damn well finished what I wanted and told Charlie to meet us on top. Even at the start of our departure our fuel was low, *real* low for the 200-plus mile trip home, but I was depending on that tremendous wind at altitude to be our free ride south and plowed into the soup.

Charlie and I couldn't pick each other up on top so I said, "Just keep climbing until we pull cons." That got us together—and what a ground speed we ginned up. We were all sweating our fuel state, so I called for idle power and the rest was a downhill glide all the way.

We wasted no time getting into the debriefing. I gave Ops and Intell the weather for Hot Spot and all those other interesting sightings. The Intell boys took all that down and went right in and briefed the dope to the regular mission that was already in the briefing room. Some of the weather data and other details caused a few exclamations and there were laughs when I stuck my head in with a big grin.

MARCH 4th

We've had our heaviest snows lately and real flying snowball fights. Geez, they're fun—like being a kid again. Some of them become fast and furious barrages. We really work up a sweat in these exchanges, with a lot of laughs and shouting. At least in that respect the snow furnishes a benefit: a free and healthy outdoor sport. But when the pretty stuff melts, this place converts into a marmalade mess with ankle-deep slush and mud. It's a wonder we make it through the goo to our rooms in the black of night after a happy session in the club. We manage by helping each other as we slip and slide and pour one another in the sack. My fingers are all brown from handling so many cigarettes. With all the happy hooch in hand, it's a wonder we don't blow up everytime we light up.

Man, have we been having some knock-down *Sayonara* parties lately in our little club. The Group C.O., Preston, and our Squadron C.O., Creighton, are finishing, as are the few of us remaining who have now been the route. Creighton, Charlie and I will probably return to the States together.

One of the fellows received a large package of clothes sent from home as a gift to Korean families. A few items were temporarily retained, and in our party for Creighton several of the gang showed up dressed as girls. What a sensation that caused—a hilarious start for a hell of a good bash. We really tuned up all the good fighter pilot songs. For Dick Creighton there were numerous repeats of "*Sayonara* Dickie Lou, you're the best of all the aces . . ." My favorite and the ever-popular "Springtime on the Yalu," was chorused by all. To the tune of "Take Me out to the Ball Game," we let go with "Parties, Banquets and Balls, Boys . . . ," and yelled out "Sally in the Alley," with much pounding on the bar and tables.

Along with all the uproar of conversations there were outbursts of the Korea version of, "Cigarettes and Whiskey," which goes:

Kunuri and Antung, and wild, wild Pyongyang,
They'll drive you apes______, they'll drive you insane . . .

After some of the wild ones there is an occasional stanza of:

So stand by your glasses steady,
This world is a world of lies.
Here's a toast to the dead already,
And Hurrah for the next man to die.

In such a gathering of fighter pilots, it doesn't take much to get a roaring rendition of "Bosom Buddies," especially the chorus:

We are the boys who fly high in the sky,
Bosom buddies while boozin'.
We are the lads that they send out to die,
Bosom buddies while boozin'.

Down in the hangar they sing and they shout,
Talking of things they know nothing about.
We are the boys who fly high in the sky,
Bosom buddies while boozin'.

Lately the big sport is for everyone to stand on top of the tables and get with it as if we require more altitude to raise the roof. That's tough on furniture—and in case of an auger, you have to watch out for splinters. We've had the Aussie pilots over and I think we're finally showing them something with these parties. After all the singing, swigging, yelling, and crashing of the last four *Sayonara* parties in five days, I sound like a foghorn and feel like I've been run over by a very large tank.

With all the fun, I'm nagged by the realization that this is almost over. Even so, these happy gatherings are good for all, especially the new arrivals beginning their missions. They get the best initiation and proper attitude in looking forward to this terrific flying with such a great outfit. When they hear of the excitement of those roaring dogfights of last year and catch our enthusiasm for the action, it's bound to generate eagerness for their own tours.

You get so associated with fellows of your own time in the outfit that, as they disappear, leaving you among the oldest few, you have moments when you feel like a lonesome graduate of a *very* exclusive school in which the newest faces are taking their entrance exams. That brings to mind the difference I felt as a new arrival; now it is the opposite and a tremendous improvement over the beginning. Wonder, practice, and imagination have been replaced by the real thing—*and* confidence. You find yourself in the rewarding position of being able to put out the straight scoop when you pass on the benefit of your experience. I have to admit it's a great feeling to be looked upon as a knowledgeable "old head"— one of the guys who's been there and knows the score.

As much as I dislike a tour of a set number of missions, and hate to give up all I've worked for, we have no choice. I was reminded three weeks ago to forget trying to guess the good missions and get cracking to make my forecast date.

I'm convinced that an important factor and a benefit to the outfit is the name that the 4th Fighter Group has among fighter pilots. It's great to know you're going to such a name outfit and greater still to be a part of it and belong to it. Once experienced, it's always a valued compensation for choosing this kind of life.

Yesterday was mission 99. I had the Squadron lead; as that also meant leading the Group off, I got the opportunity to give the briefing. I thought rather than have the squadrons just trail up into the fighter-bomber target area to set up the standard CAP, I'd try a little variation. I would take my squadron up parallel to the coast but well inland; the second squadron would follow along the coast, while the third squadron would go furthest east and up the middle of the peninsula. If I didn't meet anything until the Yalu I would then turn west toward the river mouth. The second squadron would arrive at the mouth and then turn east toward me, while the third squadron would turn west last and sweep down the river toward both of our squadrons. I figured with that plan if the MiGs came across, at least one of the squadrons should be in a good position—or maybe our deep turns could get the Group behind a bunch and we could all assemble on them. If that didn't produce immediate action, each squadron would take its assigned patrol area. This plan was agreeable to each of the other squadron leaders, so we hustled off to our respective briefing rooms for the more detailed stuff.

There followed the tedious chore of putting on all the personal equipment and slogging out with this burden to the planes. Each month of this Siberian weather seemed to require more layers of resistance and we all waddled out like mummies. I had been wearing long johns for some time; over them went Army OD wool shirt and trousers, the G-suit, an OD knit sweater, and then my wool flying suit over all. On my feet I wore cotton socks under a heavy wool pair and the Army combat boots I'd bought at Camp Drake.

Before going out to the planes I tucked in a cashmere scarf, slipped on my Navy leather flying jacket and pulled latch galoshes over my boots (you won't hike far with a pair of frozen wet feet to depend on). Then on went the Mae West followed by the parachute. Most of us wore an ear flap hat to and from the plane and carried our crash helmet (brain bucket), oxygen mask, and map in one hand, heavy survival kit in the other. To retain some dexterity in my fingers I wore a pair of light leather gloves while flying and kept a pair of heavy leather, wool insert gloves stuffed in my flysuit pockets. We felt like pack mules by this time and it was a relief to get settled down in the cockpit, but that's when the sweat generated by all the packing and hauling begins to chill and you get very impatient for start engine time. All that routine is enough to give a man combat fatigue before the mission even gets under way.

We got off in order and as the squadron closed up I loosened up my straps and signalled full throttle for the climb. As we got to cruise altitude heading into the area, I put White Flight high on my right and discovered in a cockpit check that I was using internal fuel, which meant my single drop tank was feeding too slow—bad news.

At the Chongchon River, before I expected to see any planes, bogies were sighted heading at us slightly low from the north. There wasn't a compact formation—more of a loose collection of elements. I wondered if the planes could be the 51st Group F-86s returning and told While Flight to keep their altitude and nosed down Red Flight to investigate. MiGs! Man, that high tail was distinctive at the angle we were closing. I gave a hurried call to the squadron to drop tanks as it was going to be fast shooting; lining up one of the MiG leaders, I squeezed out a burst of tail-light tracer.

The head-on pass was such a flash that I had the impression I went by the MiGs faster than the stream of bullets. Back on the stick and I asked White Flight if they could bend around on them. White turned, but the MiGs did not vary off their course and went right on past the whole squadron.

I quickly advised Able and Black Squadrons to gain some altitude and told them the direction of the MiGs so they could get prepared. Both squadron leaders acknowledged and shortly each commenced rapid-fire fight talk as they engaged. Our squadron was now in elements searching for the MiGs and I proceeded into a wide S.

That damned slow-feeding drop tank had really messed up my fuel state. I was much lower on internal than I should have been. From the sound of the radio, the other squadrons were really getting in their licks with some good shooting going on. That, and my fuel state, had me squirming with frustration.

While curving to the right toward the east, I spotted two swept-wing aircraft way below, diving across the Chongchon in a northerly direction. As MiGs rarely, if ever, dived away from these hassles, I gave a quick call on the radio and asked if any 86s had dropped down to cross the river in the Anju area. There was no reply, so I rolled over and down and saw Red Two was with me as we went into a hell of a steep dive. If they were MiGs, I wanted plenty of overtake speed to counter their acceleration advantage.

On the way down I could recognize them—they were MiGs, all right. As they were in a slight dive, I wanted to come down on their backs in a steep cutoff, then match their flight path at close range. In those last tense moments, my nice attack plan came unglued. The two MiGs stopped their dive and went into a slight climb right under me, just short of where I had intended to flatten my dive. This presented me with a full plan view of these guys enlarging in my face while I was still diving like a bomb. I was at a terrible angle, so I called for speed brakes, reefed back on the stick, and thumbed the trim all at once. My poor old 86 reacted to this treatment with a real neat high-speed stall, slamming buffets and alternate popping of the wings. It's a wonder the slats didn't jump off. What it amounted to was a hopeless effort to salvage the pass. Still fighting the controls to reverse the dive, we went *zap* behind the tails of the MiGs and sank well below before I could get my nose back up.

Talk about rage in the cockpit—now I had lost my advantage and would have to trail the MiGs and try to close. My number two was back a ways but still with me—pretty good work considering that hairy pull out. I had the throttle jammed against the stop but it was obvious the range was too far to even think about a shot. Into this picture from the right appeared two 86s that swung in on the MiGs. That was all right with me, as we weren't gaining, and I called, "Go get 'em, you guys."

They got positioned between us and the MiGs, but their turn had been too wide and they ended up in trail also. I was concerned about my fuel state by this time and a bit overanxious about those MiGs: "Can you get a shot at them and try to make them turn?" I figured that if they would turn, we could all close better—and there would be four of us on them.

The 86 element leader then gave an exasperated call: "I'm trying, but my damn guns won't fire!"

What a mess. The poor guy tried twice to fire, finally telling his wingman to go ahead. His wingman came on the air: "My blasted sight isn't working. It won't come on at all!"

What *else* could go wrong? I really groaned over that, but suggested centering the MiGs in the windshield and shooting anyway. He did and got a strike or two, but the MiGs were smart enough not to turn and none of us could improve our positions.

That was all she wrote. My fuel was in a bad way, and I had no choice but to break off the chase and begin worrying about getting home. We had worked ourselves way up north by this time, so I climbed at full bore and then went into our old idle descent (we call it the "ballistic curve") to make my glide to Kimpo. My wingman had a good fuel state, so at least I didn't have to worry about him. He was right along while I worked on my glide stretcher.

When we had parked our planes I found that my wingman had rippled one of his ailerons—it had a corrugated appearance. That had happened in that violent pullout and would require changing. Well, that's combat flying and there is certainly nothing wrong with that. He was a new pilot just over from the States and I congratulated him for being able to stay with me. The swept-wing 86 had occasionally given some rough rides in extreme maneuvers with pitch-ups and violent snaps. Tails had been twisted, flaps had buckled, and some weeks ago one pilot flying my airplane in a dogfight had not only rippled an aileron, but split it all along the trailing edge.

We found out about the problems of that other element of 86s that tried to get those MiGs. The leader had turned everything on for gun firing okay, but had forgotten to push in the circuit breaker back by his elbow in an awkward place. Naturally, he was furious at that oversight, but I felt it was an example of having too many switches and safety procedures. The gun circuit breakers are to be pulled by the armament crews as an added *ground* safety feature, but for flying I felt it was one step too many. As in this case, there's nothing like being so safe you can't hurt anybody, including the enemy, who just may shoot you for being so ineffective.

At the Group debriefing we found that the other squadrons had gotten several damaged MiGs and they were grateful for my call alerting them so they could anticipate the situation.

I felt damned discouraged the way that dive attack had ended up, then the fuel tank shortage cutting our mission time, and my single tank not feeding right. What really stabbed me was that that was my 99th mission—I had lost an opportunity and time had run out. Only one more to go.

I thought I had been sorting and arranging my things at a reasonable rate lately, but I suddenly find myself in the midst of furious packing. I've collected so much junk I'm going crazy deciding what to keep and what to discard. Our houseboy, Kim, is very glad to get all the extra clothes and knicknacks we're handing over to him. I've made out several passes for him so he can carry stuff by the ROK Security Police okay; we don't want him to be locked up as a thief. He also has to have written permission to wear items we've given him and I've taken care of that. Kim has shown us all a lot by his diligent efforts with his schoolbooks in his spare time. That kid wants to get someplace when he grows up after this war is over.

Sometimes when I'd watch him studying, I'd think about some American kids, how they take their comforts for granted and barely try in school. Here is this Korean kid with no home, his country torn up by war, taking care of himself, studying his books and full of ambition and hope. I feel that his attitude is probably the best reward we'll get for being over here.

MARCH 6th

Well, yesterday was the big day with a ration of the unusual, to say the least. The way events turned out sure makes me wonder about fate.

I was scheduled in the morning for my 100th mission and so was Charlie Mitson. I felt proud to be leading the squadron for this one and Charlie was to lead White Flight, and we both felt great about doing our last mission together. My plan was to run this one

Outside of E Flight's building on "Nob Hill," Kimpo. Left to right: Kim, the Korean houseboy, author, Mitson, Borowski.

curving up the center of Korea for a hook to the northwest corner, perhaps latching onto MiGs before establishing our patrol route.

The plane I was to fly was brand-new, the latest E model with the new flat windshield, and after some extra moments to get oriented and satisfy my cockpit check, I taxied the squadron out for the lineup on the runway. When all were in position behind me, I gave the run-up signal and moved the throttle up the quadrant. As the rpm got to 95% I felt a lurching, shuddering motion in the plane. My first thought was of some contact from outside to my plane and I quickly looked up and out. What caught my eye was a trace of smoke coming *out* of my nose intake. At this instant the radio came to excited life: "Red Lead, you're on fire!"

"Red Lead, your aircraft's coming apart!"

"Get out of it, you're on fire!"

What a shock! My stomach knotted and I'll bet the expresson on my face was a sight. I could only think, "What the hell is happening?" Both fire warning lights flashed at me like two glaring eyes. They indicated a possible explosion at any moment. I yanked the throttle back into idle cutoff, held the canopy open switch, and before I cut the battery and generator switch I heard some more frantic calls while my wingman was pointing to my tail and waving to me in an outward motion. The calls were so alarming it's a wonder I didn't forget I was still on the ground and eject myself right onto the runway, especially as more smoke poured from the intake and around me in the cockpit.

It seemed that two hands just weren't enough to unbuckle all the confounded straps to let me out. With my parachute and survival seat pack still on, I stood up only to have my head jerked down. *Damn*, my oxygen mask hose was still hooked up. I grabbed that apart, swung one leg at a time over the side and dropped to the ground. Carrying the weight of all that heavy equipment I landed awkwardly on my feet with such force sharp pains shot through my legs. For a moment I thought I'd sprained both ankles so that I set off on a clumsy retreat, the survival pack banging my legs while I hobbled as fast as I could away from the plane to the edge of the runway.

It was not until I reached that position that I turned for the first look at my plane. There it sat with smoke pouring out of both ends, gaping holes in the rear of the fuselage, and about four feet of crumpled, drooping tailpipe projecting from the aft section. It resembled some sorry smoking dragon with a serious case of constipation.

All the engines of the squadron planes were roaring while my sick bird (or dragon) sat there in such apparent discomfort, taking up one side of the runway. I waved at them to go on, pointed at Charlie, and slapped the top of my helmet. He nodded and the planes filed by mine, moving down the runway in a deafening blast of exhaust. Charlie had the squadron lead and they were on their way. I remained off to the side of my plane waiting for the crash equipment and other vehicles that came racing across the field toward me. Major Creighton and a bunch of wheels from Wing and Group were there in no time to find out what happened.

I explained what occurred up to evacuating the cockpit and then we looked the plane over. The gaping holes turned out to be absent access panels that had blown off, exposing hydraulic lines and quick disconnects protruding and dangling like severed intestines. If this had happened seconds later, when I would have been airborne, the hydraulic flight controls would have locked and I would have augered in on fire, exploding like napalm at the end of the runway. Creighton and I looked at each other and we both wiped our brows—*whew*!

A short time later I strapped on another 86 to make up for that fiasco on a very enjoyable training flight high up in the local area.

It was a last lucky opportunity for a fun dogfight—tilting and revolving the horizon, zooming up and leaving it behind, rolling over to chase each other hurtling at the ground while the horizon rises up and closes in once more. I really appreciated that chance to just kick up my heels and thrust in a pet trick or two, demonstrating to newcomers that max performance is different over here and we can prove it.

The maintenance people and aircraft engine Tech Rep wanted a statement from me on the run-up mishap. I wrote down what had occurred and waited for their findings of the unusual explosion. An inspection revealed that the bolts for the clamp holding the tailpipe to the engine tail cone had not been safetied. The bolts had worked loose so that just at the time of my run-up, the tailpipe separated from the engine and crumpled, deflecting the full thrust power out the sides of the fuselage with enough backup to force some out the nose intake. The plane had flown eight times since its rush receipt from the factory and shipment over here. The bolt safety omission was a small but unfortunate oversight and made me think of the adage: "For want of a nail a shoe was lost . . . "

In the afternoon I was rescheduled for my 100th mission and accompanied Creighton, who was leading our squadron for the last time on *his* 100th. My final position was leader of White Flight.

The farther we proceeded up north, the more cloudy the sky became. It was fairly thick broken stuff with openings and breaks here and there, but from our level on top of it all the visibility appeared poor down below. We patrolled up near the Yalu but did not see any contrails or other aircraft. I felt disappointed, but perhaps it was just as well the mission was uneventful; my head was full of wandering thoughts about all the months over here. I wished that the visibility was clear so that I could somehow capture the whole scene and take it away to keep with me.

When our patrol ended, I wanted to prolong that flight path that brought us back to the familiar plunge to base. Each flight must end, but this one had a particular finality. Then there was the curve on base, the final flare, the touchdown, and it was all over.

So—we were committed—I don't quite know how to take it. All that Mickey Mouse of processing, arranging transportation, and signing out makes me feel like a stranger, an outsider all over again. After all that's happened, it's a hell of a note to have pieces of paper bluntly tell you that it's really ended.

Before our time to leave the air was filled with the throbbing whine of jet engines cranking up for a mission. There was no way I could have avoided watching those Sabres, those 86s, one more time.

The fighter squadrons began taking off. Two at a time the planes raced down the runway and lifted off for the sky; like a stream of polished swallows they climbed away, while the roar of their engines softened into a rumble of distant thunder. I couldn't move; I just stood there watching the smoke trails of their exhaust snake and twist into the blue distance until even the sparkle of their wings was gone and there was a vast silence.

They were going without us; they were on their way north again, only this time they were on the hunt without us. We who were departing were no longer a part of it all. I felt a terrible pang of regret. It just didn't seem right to be cut off like that.

We are not going home by troopship. This time it will be by air, but the disance is the same—a long trip.

> *O dimming trails of other days,*
> *Your lure, your glamour, and your ways*
> *Will last while those who knew you live.*
> *And, fading, to the past will give,*
> *To guard and to forever hold,*
> *A wealth of stories never told.*[22]

Author's late father in front of JN-4 "Jenny" in 1917 at the Philadelphia, PA, Navy Yard. This was during the program to increase pilots after U.S. entry in WWI. Author's father was in charge of training before going overseas to fly antisubmarine patrol duty.

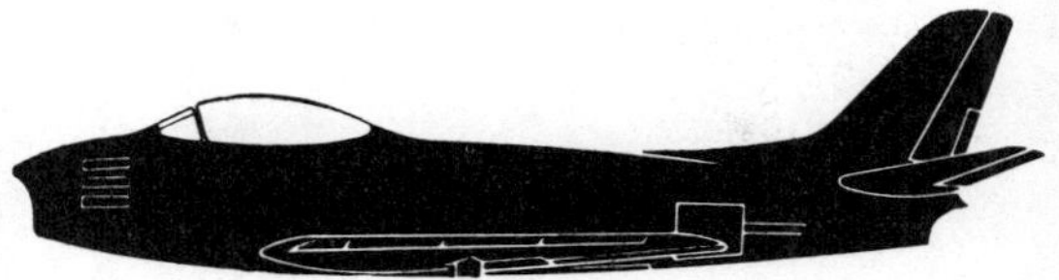

Postscript

The early period of 1952, which was so frustrating to the hunting patrols of the F-86 pilots, was actually the aftermath of an apparent Communist Command decision to give up the mass formation offensive for aerial victory. From that dissuasion they evidently preferred through succeeding operational practices to use the air war as a finishing school for large numbers of MiG pilots and units apparently rotated on short graduation tours with little regard for the support of their ground armies.

Thus what seemed to us an anticlimax after the wild fighting of 1951 was really a change of pace past the checkered flag for air superiority, a lead that the Sabre pilots tenaciously maintained. While the MiG-15 may have irritated us with certain points of performance, after the feathers flew, the F-86 was still able to rule the roost. Actually, after that peak period of MiG assault, with more Sabres available, employed with the emphasis on more and smaller formations initiating the hunt, the majority of MiGs were destroyed and 33 of the 39 aces of the war made their scores. The lessons of combat, the formation of the additional Sabre Wing, and the later introduction of the F model put the F-86 definitely on top of the situation.

It is unfortunate that our front line troops were unable to witness the contrail swarms and huge swirling aerial struggles of the contest. From a view of those engagements they might have gained some sort of an understanding of the efforts exerted in securing air superiority, which so benefited their own operations. The enemy on the ground below the remote battles certainly

A view of the F-86A that particularly portrays the exceptionally graceful appearance and the visibility advantages enjoyed by the pilots. (U.S. Air Force photo)

observed the "fallout" from those impressive spectacles, which influenced a more conciliatory ending of that war.

Thinking back, I don't suppose there was ever a fighter that was such a pure delight to escape with into the wild blue as the F-86 Sabre. We looked upon the graceful Sabre as the Spitfire of the new Jet Age, with all the fondness the Spitfire engendered in its happy pilots. This is said with mixed feelings, not meaning to diminish my first love with the F-51 Mustang that we flew with such enthusiasm and pride before we got our hands on jets. But the pilots who knew the old free-sky operational flying in any of those three particular fighters were indeed fortunate.

In its time, the 86 was *the* plane to fly, creating a stir wherever it appeared. Immediately apparent to the jet initiate was the elimination of prop oil from the windshield and removal of the engined nose from forward view. The Sabre retained the Spartan gunfighter cockpit; situated so well clear of all previous obstructions, the sphere of visibility from the canopy bubble was nothing less than fantastic, and produced a feeling of almost naked exposure on the early transition flights. Gazing back along those first swept-wings, one could imagine all sorts of exciting possibilities.

It was the first fighter we could gleefully plunge in the wildest prolonged dives without compressibility or structural worries. Sensitive, it would still freeze in place, wing to wing, through

234

formation aerobatics. The handling qualities were such a pleasure that an intense feeling of confident superiority was rapidly experienced by the pilot—the vital trait of a true fighter aircraft without which it is merely another flying machine.

When a fighter—any fighter—can literally fire up a furnace of loyalty, it's bound to be a winner. The rest will be flown by frustrated losers. Fighter pilots have always been eager to discuss this loyalty and keen in their ability to demonstrate the proof. In years of that challenging environment, our "sport" was a constant honing of the edge—analyzing style, refining, polishing, dueling, *always* dueling—separating the pros from the amateurs. We were so enthusiastic when we went up to "play," even the swallows, the happiest of all fliers, must have felt a twinge of jealousy.

My last rousing affair in the free-for-all fighter life was with the U.S. Marines' F8U Crusader. That sleek bird of prey was the master of any in its advanced class beyond the deep blue into the thin purple. If one of its contemporaries was a missile with a man in it (the F-104), the "U-Bird" was all that with wings—to turn all

The F9F Cougar, the type flown by the author on duty with the Navy after Korea—a fine little fighter with the trim look of a swallow and a delight to fly. (National Archives photo)

Flight of four F9F Cougars of VF-21 during the author's exchange duty with that squadron at NAS Oceana, VA. Author believed to be in third aircraft, 109. Author was also at sea with VF-21 flying off both the aircraft carriers *USS Hornet* and *USS Bennington*. (US Navy Photo)

others inside out. Roving on this side, or piercing far beyond the speed of sound, its performance was tremendous.

Perhaps it really is not fair to favor one love among a succession of exciting trim charmers that made the time aloft so complete—from the first tingling glow fanned at fine pitch into full song to the courting of supersonic sirens. But as you are by now aware, there was a very special affair with the Sabre and that spicy allure will remain.

The airways conformed to the inheritance of the jetliners, and with some nostalgia (for the old rovers anyway) we all became

236

Flight of four F8U Crusaders of VMF-312 during the author's tour of duty with that squadron at MCAS Beaufort, SC, and aerial gunnery at Guantanamo Bay, Cuba. This was the champion air-to-air fighter until the F-14 and F-15 came along. (US Marine Corps photo)

immersed in the sandwiched and spiderwebbed regulated maze. In their beginnings, though, what a curtain-raiser those early jets were.

For the follower of the growth of the Age of Flight, I would submit the belief that the Korean War was as influential a thrust as World War I, which brought the dramatic breakout of flight from holiday exhibition to imagination-stirring permanence; as World War II, which gave it a global affect and acceptance. In like manner, the Korean War truly opened the sweep of the Jet Age.

The competitive urgency of each of those wars accelerated the evolution of man's miracle of transportation: *flight*. The harsh proving grounds of conflict have ultimately gifted the everyday traveler with the magic-carpet opportunity to compress time and distance in an exhilarating vault of the horizon, while seeing this world as it was only dreamed of in ages past.

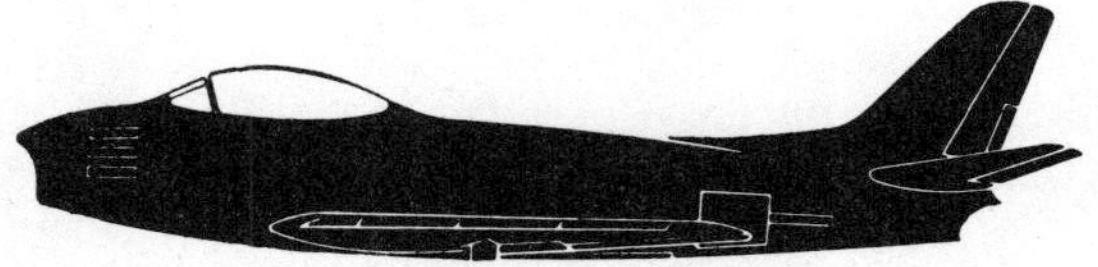

Notes

1. After Korea, Bill McAllister and I were together in the same squadron, one of the originals in the U.S. Air Force, the famous 94th "Hat-in-the-Ring" of Eddie Rickenbacker and World War I. While we were in the 94th, about a year and a half after this particular Korean mission, a sheaf of papers came in for Mac. It seems a captured North Korean soldier disclosed that he had been in the locality where he observed this encounter of Mac in his F-80 with the MiG and saw the MiG crash. Mac got a confirmed kill those many months later! Did we ever have a celebration on that amazing news.

Years later, when action was really hot in the Vietnam War, McAllister went on a combat tour as a Forward Air Controller. His exploits were so outstanding he became the legendary "Mac the FAC," and was one of the first men to earn the Air Force Cross. This had to be a posthumous award as he was killed on his last day of combat—a sad loss of a great tiger.

2. After Korea, "Ollie" Arquilla went on into years of Flight Test. While in the Fighter Test business at Wright-Patterson AFB he got interested in midget air racing as a side hobby and was killed when his racer experienced tail flutter and control failure.

3. Dentist or Dentist Charlie was the call sign of our radar site from which we sometimes got general information about MiG activity in North Korea. Our extreme ranges from friendly territory were evidently beyond the radar capability for regular or detailed advisories. Such as the case, at least, at this time in the war.

MiG formations were referred to as "trains," but we did not know the numbers of MiGs included in each train, whether flights of four, sections of eight, or squadrons. "Trains leaving the station" meant formations taking off or climbing up from the Antung airfield complex. Dentist or Control would on occasion issue orders, but as a regular practice, only advisories.

4. That now-old C-3 camera has been faithfully recording the scenes of all the years since. There were missions in Vietnam, and then the rewarding—and continuing—adventures in civilian flying.

5. After Ken Rapp returned to the squadron from a convalescent R&R he was raring to go and gave us a thoughtful and humorous comment: "If I ever get another hole in my head it will be between the eyes, because I'm going to be checking my six!" Ken got his revenge later and shot down a MiG.

6. Years later, in different circumstances, I acquired some of that experience on a tour of duty in Vietnam where I served as a combat FAC, but that's another story.

7. If this incident had occurred in the present era of missles I probably would have been shot down—as a mistake. In all our air wars, "mistakes" have been shot down at machine gun ranges, but

A somewhat different perspective than flying all those flashy fighters of the years before. The author went from the F-100 to these L-19s for Forward Air Control (FAC) duty in Vietnam, flying with a Vietnamese squadron. The two VNAF planes are flying the author's wing and crossing a winding branch of the Mekong River. The little prop planes over the column of smoke bring back scences of a much older war . . . shades of the Western Front!

On the parking ramp of the VNAF 2nd Liaison Squadron at Tan Son Nhut AB, Saigon, during 1962. The author checking with a VNAF crew before going to another L-19 to fly on a mission. Besides a shoulder-holstered pistol, author always carried the M2 carbine with banana clips. The carbine was hung very handily on the back of the seat for use in case of forced landing or while on the ground at remote and isolated airstrips. (US Air Force photo)

While not very speedy compared to swept-wing jets, these little L-19 (O-1) Bird Dogs did their job . . . an interesting change from flying the F-100 Super Sabre. Here the author and VNAF wingman are en route to a rendezvous point (to meet helicopters), not at all easy to find in the vastness of the Mekong Delta. In 1962 the VNAF 2nd Liaison L-19s were olive drab with broad white bands on top of the wings for easier sighting by the fighter CAP or strike force.

that unpleasant fact was overlooked in the stampede for missles and the long reach. Missles aren't particular who they strike after launch, and their long-range capabilities make the old problem of identification of friend or foe even more critical. With that in mind, consider that in an air *battle*—not a cut-and-dried controlled intercept—a loosed missle is a potential hazard to all. A similar problem was faced by the North Atlantic convoys of World War II with a torpedo speeding through their midst.

8. This was the first time I had had any opportunity to fire the guns of my F-86 into any kind of target. I was anything but the storybook example of "cool, calm, and collected"—a rather abrupt way to accomplish gunnery training.

An old friend of mine overshot in his P-51 on a "perfect pass" at a Focke-Wulf 190 and got turned into a sieve, but luckily made it home okay. Unfortunately, some people think "war stories" are baloney between pilots who are goofing off from "important" paper shuffling. I personally am grateful for combat stories, as I have profited from the experience of others.

9. My close pal Dick Panter went on home. I was never to see him again. About three years later, while on a firepower demonstration at Eglin Field, I ran into one of the 4th Group boys and mentioned that I sure wanted to get up to O'Hare Field and see Panter. It was then I received the bad news that Dick had been killed in a crash in very tough night weather. Another friend gone.

10. October was one of the hairiest months of all. We had tangled with a total of over 2,000 MiGs, our 86s knocking down 24 of them. We had lost seven F-86s, several B-29s, F-84s and F-80s.

11. We all eagerly awaited the gun camera film from that Uiju strafing mission. Fortunately, it came out very clear. Ken Chandler made a beautiful smooth pass that, as the film ran, looked like a high-speed approach and level-off for a landing on the strip. The runway sped by and the dozen or so MiGs on the parking apron loomed rapidly in the viewer's attention. As the guns started working, you could see the crashing results in the flashes of fire and puffs of smoke erupting among the parked MiGs. Men were scrambling off and around the MiGs in the midst of the lead storm as the whole scene zoomed to a smashing close-up and then dropped off the screen as the pull-up and long haul for altitude began. We replayed it several times and could witness the obvious commotion from what was a near-perfect strafing pass. Chandler got credit for four MiGs destroyed and I believe most of the others were damaged.

12. These Communist airfields were getting a considerable amount of attention—observation and bombs. In September and October, reconnaissance had discovered that three jet-capable airfields were under construction at Namsi, Taechon, and Saamcham. The towns were fairly close together and below the Yalu near the Chongchon River, where so much of our fighting was taking place.

The United Nations Forces were, naturally, seriously concerned with these enemy efforts because of their potential threat to our struggle for air superiority. Evidently, the Communist Air Forces intended to press their operations further south in Korea, and the airfields would expand their capabilities in the contested airspace. Besides the obvious advantage for MiG fighters using these fields to extend their radius of action, there was another threat: Enemy bombers would be better disposed to carry out attacks against our front lines and rear areas with fighter cover. Such efforts, if successful, would only have led to more advanced enemy airfields and further erosion of our campaign to thwart Communist operations.

The regular reconnaissance of these fields kept HQ aware of construction progress and before any of the projected schemes got to the tape-cutting ceremony, our bombers and fighter-bombers would "drop in" with all kinds of hardware and the airfields would be converted to a rock quarry appearance. It must have been very frustrating—to say nothing of *noisy*. Well-placed flak defenses put up strong objections to our visits.

The same systematic bashing was rationed out to airfield construction at the North Korean capitol of Pyongyang—"Ping Pong," as we often called it. Some of the bitterest aerial fighting was probably generated by the contest over these airfields.

13. Dayton Ragland was the first—and for quite awhile the only—black fighter pilot to come in the 4th Fighter Group He was among us, just what he wanted to be—one of the guys. He was captured and went through the terrible Korea P.O.W. experience. I finally saw him years later and we fought the war over again. Some time after that reunion, I read his name among the missing in the Vietnam War.

14. On that big shoot the other two squadron commanders became the fifth and sixth jet aces: George Davis really cleaned up with *three* Tu-2s *and* a MiG; "Bones" Marshall got a Tu-2 and a La-9. One of those La-9 tigers whipped around on Bones, nailing him in the canopy, which shattered. He had a very cold and drafty flight home. The Group Commander, Ben Preston, got an La-9 and so did John Honaker. Bob Akin, Ray Barton, John Burke, and myself each got a Tu-2 bomber.

One interesting feature of the mission was seeing those different airplanes. That was the only time I mixed it up with aircraft other than MiG-15s.

15. Nick Kotok and I last saw each other briefly three years after our combat tour. I finally managed to again establish contact when working up this book and obtained the loan of his movie film plus voice tape recordings of several missions of those days. Reviewing those was like taking a trip in a time machine. I was happy to discover that he is an airline captain in a well-established flying career. In the interval, he had changed his name to Nick Kendall.

16. Shortly after I left Korea I got a letter from Herschel Spitzer, in which he said that particular rat race was a good experience. Spitz had remembered it when he got behind a MiG

that tried some of that roller coaster stuff and by anticipating had nailed him at the top of a zoom, shooting him down. I sure felt pleased to get that good word.

17. When Ken Chandler got his MiG in that December 13th shoot, his F-86 also swallowed some flying parts which knocked out his engine. He bailed out by Chodo Island and was recovered so rapidly he didn't even catch a cold from the dunking. Some years later, Ken went on to win the jet division of the Bendix cross-country air race in an F-102. After that, while I was leading a group of F-84Fs on a "High Flight" across the Atlantic for delivery to NATO, I read where he had been killed in a crash while making a weather penetration in mountain country.

18. The North American Aviation Corporation was certainly right about the tail position and really thinking ahead. Later supersonic fighters with high wing loadings and high tails had some disastrous experiences with accelerated turns and high angles of attack. The airflow from the wings and fuselage blanked out the T-tails, which resulted in the flight becoming seriously unglued. North American's F-100, the world's first level-flight supersonic fighter, had the low horizontal "slab," as we called it. All the world's fighters of today have followed this principle.

Though necessary for high-speed flight maneuvering, over the years the complexity of the total hydraulic flight control systems incorporated in the fighters of all manufacturers resulted in the unfortunate loss of many aircraft and pilots. Only a year and a half after these talks, the death of my brother was caused by this problem, which brought the hazards of flight home in the toughest blow of all.

19. After Korea, Ken Rapp was also a member with me of the 94th "Hat-in-the-Ring" Squadron. He lost his life in an unfortunate midair collision.

Many years after this I had a get-together with Fred McPherson, where we relived the old missions. Fred was on his way to combat in Vietnam, where he was killed while dive bombing in an A-1 Skyraider.

Charlie Mitson also was with me in the 94th. We went on to serve simultaneous but separate tours with the U.S. Navy, flying off aircraft carriers in that frisky little jewel, the F9F Cougar, the first swept-wing fighter to go to sea with the fleet. My last reunion with Charlie, who is still going strong, was at Clark Field, P.I., where I ended up in the hospital from my tour in the Vietnam conflict.

20. During my tour of duty in the early Vietnam War years I had a surprising reunion with Walt Raby at the Tan Son Nhut Airfield at Saigon. We spent a lot of hours together recounting Korea and getting each other up to date on the years between wars by swapping the customary "top this" stories. I passed on a few about white-knuckle controlled crashes on flattops with the Navy, in-flight refueling, and supersonic stuff. In the interval, Walt had added another million hours of multi-engine time in the C-124,

penetrating the wildest weather in countless airlift trips across the Atlantic to Europe and all sorts of faraway places. No doubt about it, those airlift crews really get to see the world. Walt had even been behind the wheel of the C-99 (cargo version of the enormous Convair B-36) in his world travels. I told him I had intercepted the C-99 a couple of times over the Salton Sea and that it left the optical impression of a motel propelled by barber shop ceiling fans. Some of our conversations were difficult to carry on over the din of Tudo Street.

21. Pat Green eventually recovered from his injuries to go on for many more years of hot fighter flying. I gave him a real surprise when I contacted him by phone during the beginnings of this book. We compared notes on his spectacular bailout and other incidents and old friends. He also told me of a great tour of duty flying in South America. I was glad to hear how well Pat had made up for that hospital time. In our subsequent correspondence and reminiscenses, Pat has been a great help with details for this story.

22. The poem "Old Trails" (from *Bunch-Grass and Blue-Joint* published by Scribners) is out of the writings of Frank Bird Linderman, one of the great historians of the adventurous times of the Old West. I was struck by the similarity of dimming trails and the stirring sight of contrails threading the skies only to slowly dissipate, just as do memories of the men who were there.

The Vought 02U was the first plane to carry the name "Corsair". Author's father on left, buckling chin strap of his helmet for flight. Camera on rear gun mount for photo mission in 1930 at Port-au-Prince, Haiti. Author's father was Commanding Officer of VO-9M (old Marine Corps designation), Marine Observation Squadron Nine. Aircraft #909 was his personal plane.

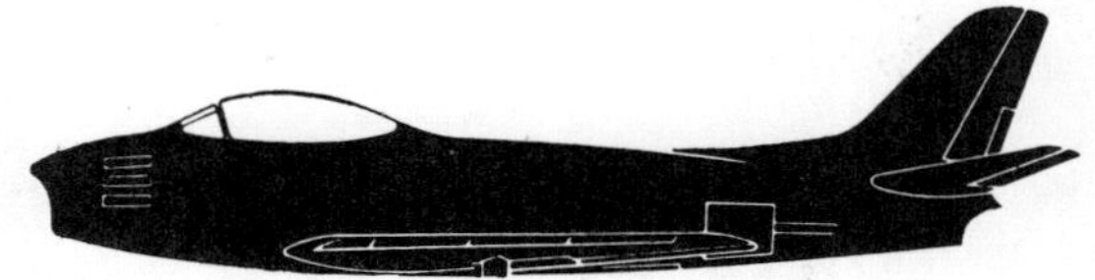

Glossary of Military Terms and Fighter Pilot Jargon

able sugar: Ape, as in "to go ape;" hog-wild. Also known as *alpha sierra.*

abort: To stop a takeoff roll, or cancel a mission, or to turn back before reaching the target or completing a mission because of aircraft mechanical trouble.

ADF: Automatic Direction Finder.

alert pad: The ramp space or special aircraft parking area set up for fighters, usually a flight of four, on air defense standby alert.

APU: Auxiliary Power Unit.

bandit: Aircraft identified as enemy.

Bedcheck Charlie: The night raiders whose favorite sport was ruining a good night's sleep. Sometimes their raids were far more serious than sporty; more than once they destroyed and damaged more of our aircraft on the ground than did the MiGs or enemy flak while on missions in North Korea. The aircraft generally used was the Russian PO-2, a biplane trainer similar to the Stearman.

bingo fuel: The minimum amount of fuel (the F-86A indi cated gallons, the F-86E indicated pounds) needed to return home with a small margin of safety. Bingo at the Yalu River was supposed to be 250 gallons or 1500 pounds, but with good hunting prospects, frequent altitude changes, or a red-hot action mission, those numbers were often stretched so low they produced very white knuckles seeking friendly territory while exuding gallons of sweat to match the fuel gallons dropping toward empty.

bogie: Aircraft that are not identified as either enemy or friendly.

BOQ: Bachelor Officers Quarters. Living quarters for single officers or officers unaccompanied by family. Such facilities can be buildings, huts, or tents, and in combat are "home" for all officers.

bounce: To attack other aircraft or to be attacked.

chandelle: A sudden rapid climbing turn; a curving zoom to change direction and gain altitude.

clock position: When calling out other aircraft, a target or terrain feature, or anything significant, the direction to look is in relation to the calling aircraft or team formation, the nose of which is 12 o'clock, the tail 6 o'clock, while 9 o'clock is left abeam and 3 o'clock is right abeam. This will be called as level, high, or low, or far out or close in.

con level: The altitude level or zone where contrails form or materialize. Usually between 30,000 and 35,000 feet. Below or above the con level, the white trails will not form and aircraft are difficult to sight at long distance.

contrails: Condensation trails, sometimes called *vapor trails*. The visible white streams trailed behind aircraft flying at high altitude. Then the aircraft are said to be "pulling cons."

echelon: A formation stepped back from the leader to one side, right or left, of the plane ahead. This formation is usually used to enter the traffic pattern and each plane peels off after the other to turn into the runway and land.

eject: Use of ejection seat for emergency escape from an aircraft. In US Air Force aircraft, this is accomplished by the use of handles on the armrests of the seat; on US Navy/Marine and RAF/RAAF aircraft by pulling a face curtain from the top of the headrest—*not* by punching or pushing a button. To "punch out" is pilot slang meaning to eject.

element: A formation of two fighters, normally the smallest tactical formation team used in aerial combat. The leader is the hunter and shooter, the wingman provides cover and lookout. In the US Navy/Marines, two planes are a *section*.

ETO: The European Theater of Operations in World War II.

FAC: Forward Air Controller, a fighter pilot who directs from the ground or from another aircraft the attacks of friendly aircraft on enemy ground targets.

FEAMCOM: Far East Air Material Command.

FIGMO: Politely, "Finally I Got My Orders." A short-timer.

flak: Anti-aircraft fire directed by ground weapons against air craft. Usually refers to visual sighting of tracers and exploding shells.

flight: A formation of four fighters, the basic tactical fighting team. The flight leader is responsible for all tactical direction: maneuvering, positioning, attacking, or defending to carry out the mission. Number two in the flight is the leader's wingman; number three is the leader of the second element and maneuvers to support the leader or coordinate his attacks as directed. Number four is his wingman. In the US Navy/Marines, four planes are called a *division*.

FNG: Politely, "Funny New Guy," a new man in an outfit who hasn't gotten squared away or learned the routine yet. Not to be confused with FANG, a rude term that refers—sometimes affectionately, sometimes disparagingly, depending on speaker and use—to the Air National Guard.

F/O: Flight Officer. A WWII rank of the US Army Air Forces (forerunner of the present US Air Force) given to pilots when they got their wings. The rank replaced Sgt. Pilot and was similar to Warrant Officer, but special and only for wartime so there would be fewer teenaged pilots with commissions. We called ourselves "Bluetenants" and our blue rank insignia the "purple shaft," while the cap device was referred to as the "stalled-out pigeon."
The rank meant that F/Os usually remained one step in rank behind their contemporaries who started as 2nd Lts.

gaggle: An assembly of airplanes that does not have a well-defined or orderly formation.

gauges: "on the gauges" means flying on instruments, instrument flight, or IFR. Also, occasionally refers to the fuel gauge, almost always a source of worry for jet pilots in combat.

GCA: Ground Controlled Approach, a system of radar-guided instrument flight approach for landing in bad weather. Jargon use is "gone completely ape" (see able sugar).

GCI: Ground Controlled Intercept. Flight operations directed or assisted by ground based radar to vector or steer fighters to target aircraft, or rendezvous of friendly aircraft. Also to recover or return aircraft on a descent through bad weather to visual contact with the ground or home base, or handoff to GCA.

Gooney Bird: The C-47, military version of the DC-3 airliner.

green dragon: The 4th had a few F-86s painted in experimental olive drab camouflage, in contrast to the Sabre's usual unpainted finish. The camouflage was abandoned when it was discovered that the rough paint lowered the aircraft's speed by 20 mph or so. A photo of one can be found in Larry Davis' book *Air War over Korea* (Squadron/Signal 1983).

Gs: Refers to multiples of gravity in centrifugal forces exerted on the body while in tight turns, strenuous aerobatics, or violent maneuvers in a dogfight, one G being normal weight and normal—or one—gravity. Multiple Gs may cause sufficient blood to drain from the head as to cause "blackout" or loss of vision. Normal vision returns when G forces are reduced. This physical problem is much more pronounced in jets than in prop fighters; the higher speeds when deflected into turns induce much faster buildup of Gs because of much higher centrifugal forces.

G-suit: An arrangement of air bladders for the lower legs, the thighs, and the abdomen that can be zippered up over the flying suit. There is a hose on the left hip that is plugged into the cockpit so that as G forces are added to the body air flows through the hose, inflating the bladders, which squeeze the lower body like a tightening corset. This pressure holds blood in the torso and head so the pilot can function properly and perform better in high-G maneuver missions.

Home Plate: Kimpo or Suwon airbases.

Jato: Jet Assisted Takeoff. Actually, attached rockets that are jettisoned after the aircraft becomes airborne.

JP: Jet fuel.

Lufbery: A circling or wheeling pattern of turning fighters, named after Raoul Lufbery, the leading ace of the Lafayette Escadrille of WWI.

Mach or **Mach number:** The relation of speed of aircraft to the speed of sound; 0.75 to 0.85 is the general cruise speed range of virtually all jets. Numbers like Mach 1.1 and higher indicate supersonic speed. "On the Mach" means riding right on the edge of the speed of sound, or, for subsonic jets, right on the limiting redline Mach number for that particular aircraft. Named after Ernst Mach, the Austrian physicist who devised the system.

Mobile Control: Sometimes called **Runway Control** and manned by an experienced fighter pilot. The unit could be a radio-equipped trailer with a glassed-in top, or weapons carrier or jeep with special radios for communicating with aircraft. The regular control tower handled all routine air traffic while the mobile unit was there to monitor and assist the tactical or mission aircraft for emergencies, special instructions, safety procedures, etc.

M&S: Maintenance and Supply Group.

MSR: Main Supply Route. The vital roads and railways of the supply network used by the Communist forces in North Korea. Routes were coded such as Red 7, Green 1, Purple 11.

O-Club: Officers Club, the facility where officers and their families may gather to partake of the social life of the service. Sergeants have their Non-Commissioned Officers' Club (NCO Club) and those below the rank of Sgt. have their Airmens' Club.

panic button: A single button to press for jettisoning all external fuel tanks and/or external munitions in an emergency. A situation requiring this can be a last resort or "panic," thus the nickname for the button. It has nothing to do with the ejection seat.

PSP: Pierced Steel Planking, interlocking perforated plates of steel laid on the ground in long rows to form airfield runways and taxiways and permit aircraft operations from terrain otherwise unable to support the weight or wheel pressure.

pulling streamers: During tight maneuver turns, such as in a tight traffic pattern, a streak of white vapor may at times be seen to stream from each wingtip of a fighter. Pulling streamers in the traffic pattern meant a "hot" pilot was at the controls. This term was adopted for parties where the whoopee bar action got fast and noisy.

reccy: Slang for reconnaissance, also known as *recon*, which can be visual or photographic or both. The reccy missions escorted in Korea were for photographic reconnaissance. The 67th Reccy Grp. at Kimpo was the 67th Tactical Reconnaissance Group and was equipped with RF-51s, RF-80s, and RB-26s. The RF-80s of this group were the usual escort charge for the Sabres of the 4th Fighter Group.

rolling horses: Bar game similar to Yat or Yahtzee; it's something like playing poker with five dice.

RON: Remain overnight.

R&R: Rest and rehabilitation.

sayonara: A Japanese word meaning goodbye. American often substituted it for "so long." In slang, to "speak sayonara" meant time to leave or let's go.

scissor maneuver: Two opposing fighters or formations simultaneously attack each other and after passing they each reverse and re-attack, criss-crossing in a scissor fashion, the trick being to time the reversals and tighten the turns just right to end up behind the opponent and in shooting position.

scramble: Getting fighters airborne in minimum time, usually for air defense interceptions from standby alert readiness status.

section: Two flights consisting of eight fighters when they are part or half of a sixteen-plane squadron formation. If eight fighters go alone, that would be a squadron mission and referred to as a squadron.

skoshi: A Japanese word adopted by Americans serving in the Far East signifying small, little, or few.

split-S: To roll an aircraft on its back and pull through, diving and recovering level in a reverse direction.

Stove Pipe mission: If enough aircraft were available and the mission important enough, two spare F-86s, call sign "Stove Pipe," would be detailed to orbit between Chodo Island and Chinnampo and monitor the primary fighterbomber radio frequency. If MiGs interferred with the ground attack interdiction mission, Stove Pipe relayed the details to the patrolling Sabres, who in turn went after the MiGs.

TBF: Grumman Avenger torpedo bomber; General Motors built versions were referred to as TBMs. In Korea, some were fitted with radar and used to intercept Bedcheck Charlies.

T-Bird: The T-33 jet, a two-seat version of the F-80.

TDY: Temporary Duty.

toksan: A Japanese word adopted by Americans serving in the Far East signifying large, big, or many.

T.O.T.: Time on Target. Usually set by the bomber or fighter-bomber strike time on their main or primary ground target. The 4th Fighter Group adjusted the Sabre patrol times to overlap the TOT.

trim: To fine-adjust the balance of the aircraft and eliminate or enhance the control pressures needed for a desired flight path or attitude.

trombone: Heater control in the cockpit of the F-86. It worked somewhat like the slide of a trombone, hence the name.

wheels: The higher-ranking officers, sometimes any field grade officer on up into general officer ranks. Usually the term "big wheels" meant Lt. Colonels and full Colonels. My research indicates the term originated in WWI while many Americans were flying with French squadrons. The American pilots called high-rankers *big guns*, while the French pilots in their own language jargon called them *grosses huiles*, which translated is *big oilers*, but oilers is pronounced in French just like wheels, so the Americans apparently copied the word that matched the sound.

won: The Korean monetary unit, just as the Yen is the Japanese unit.

yo-yo: To attack by diving on the target aircraft and, if unable to finish the job on one pass, to use the excess speed to zoom above the slower target and repeat the diving attack from the position of advantage.

100 Percent: Indicates full throttle or maximum power. Jet tachometers indicate percentage of power, 80 to 85 percent being cruise setting, rather than rpm as in propeller-driven aircraft.